D1072757

THE THEOLOGY OF THE GOSPEL ACCORDING TO THOMAS

THE THEOLOGY OF THE GOSPEL ACCORDING TO THOMAS

By BERTIL GÄRTNER

Translated by Eric J. Sharpe

HARPER & BROTHERS
PUBLISHERS · NEW YORK

This book was originally written in Swedish
and translated at the request of the author

THE THEOLOGY OF THE GOSPEL ACCORDING TO THOMAS

Printed in the United States of America

This book is published in Great Britain
under the title of *The Theology of the Gospel of Thomas*

Library of Congress catalog card number: 61-5261

CONTENTS

FOREWORD

APPROXIMATELY a hundred miles south of Cairo lies a town which during the Greek and Roman periods was one of Egypt's cultural centres, and which after the introduction of Christianity to Egypt became a focal point of the Christian Church. The name of that town, Oxyrhynchus (now Behnesa), is to-day linked with one of the most extensive and valuable discoveries of papyri ever made in Egypt. Among all the excellent texts of Greek and early Christian literature discovered by the English scholars G. P. Grenfell and A. S. Hunt during the course of their first excavations in 1897 there was, however, one solitary leaf of papyrus which stole the interest from all the others. This leaf had evidently formed part of a papyrus book written about A.D. 200, and after the usual careful cleaning, the excavators were amazed to find that on it were written seven hitherto unknown sayings of Jesus, all introduced by the words "Jesus said" and arranged consecutively. What had been found was evidently a trace of some collection of sayings of Jesus, but this was not at all easy to understand. Those scholars who at that time occupied themselves with Biblical questions had certainly been given something to think about!

Six years later, in 1903, the same scholars were once more excavating at Oxyrhynchus when they found in a heap of rubbish two more leaves of papyrus similar to the one discovered earlier. One contained six sayings of Jesus; the other probably two, though comprising only twenty-two letters in all. Once more there had been found traces of an unknown gospel. Once more the sayings were consecutive. Some were variants of known sayings, but others were quite unknown, and bewildering in their content. Since the leaves of papyrus were very badly damaged the reconstruction of the gaps in the text demanded much hard work and a great deal of learned discussion, which naturally also ranged over the meaning of the discoveries. But despite the many scholarly attempts at editing these gospel fragments, which had been given the name *Logia Jesou*, no solution of the riddle was forthcoming.

It is unfortunately often the case that many of the problems which scholars of the past racked their brains to solve by all possible—and many impossible—means are never answered definitively. It is all the more cheering, therefore, that in this case the gospel in question has been found—complete and in good condition; not, it is true, in Greek, but in a Coptic translation. This is the by now well-known *Gospel of Thomas*. It is quite certain that some of the scholars in the early years of this century must have dreamed of the day when more of the unknown gospel would be found, and the air of mystery surrounding the little pieces of papyrus from Oxyrhynchus would be dissipated. And now in our days we have been granted the privilege of seeing this gospel turn up in reality—and not only this document, but many others belonging to the Gnostic religious groups who lived in the area around the south-west corner of the Mediterranean, documents which we knew to have once existed, but which we presumed we should never see.[1] These writings, and particularly the *Gospel of Thomas*, belong to those discoveries over which we may genuinely rejoice, for they enable us to make a much closer acquaintance with an epoch of great importance for the early Church, an epoch the details of which were extremely obscure.

The Egyptian fellahin who in 1945 or 1946 were searching for fertiliser among the ruins of an ancient cemetery had no idea what

[1] For the circumstances surrounding the discovery, see J. Doresse, Les livres secrets des gnostiques d'Egypte (1958); H.-Ch.Puech, The Jung Codex and the Other Gnostic Documents from Nag Hamadi, in The Jung Codex (1955).

an astounding discovery they had made when they came across twelve volumes of Coptic Gnostic scriptures.[1] The village of Nag-Hamadi, where the discovery was made, is a little village on the Nile in Upper Egypt, forty-five to fifty miles downstream from Luxor; it is now a village with a world-famous name, thanks to the world press and thanks to its connection with the *Gospel of Thomas.* Just as the fragments of unknown sayings of Jesus had caused such a stir—far more so than the other discoveries—a half-century earlier, so now this complete logia-collection has suffered the same fate, and has far outshone the other documents. It has even been called " the Fifth Gospel " as a sign of the great value placed upon it. This is, however, quite unjustified; its character is so far removed from the four canonical Gospels that it cannot possibly be placed on a par with them.

There is a great deal to be said about the *Gospel of Thomas*, and a large number of essays and articles have already been published, dealing mainly with its outward structure, the appearance of the individual sayings and their relation to the textual traditions of the New Testament.[2] What we shall first attempt to do in this book is to determine the purely literary principles on which the gospel has been compiled and arranged. Then we shall give an interpretation of the sayings, and combine them on a basis of their theological content into an overall picture. It will be necessary in the process to place the gospel in the context of the currents and tendencies to which it is most closely related, and we hope as a result of this to come to some understanding of its distinctive milieu. Such an interpretation is, however, both difficult and risky, since we shall be working for the most part with Gnostic textual material which as yet has not been thoroughly

[1] S. Giversen does not consider that this place has been satisfactorily proved to be identical with the place at which the discovery was made. No fragments of papyrus, and no remains of the jar in which they were preserved, have been found. Thomasevangeliet (1959), p. 15.

[2] The best bibliography of the extensive literature is in Giversen, op. cit., p. 142-150. Cf. H.-Ch. Puech in E. Hennecke-W. Schneemelcher, Neutestamentliche Apokryphen I (1959), p. 114ff.

investigated. Hence any result which we may reach here can make no claim to lay bare all the secrets which the *Gospel of Thomas* contains. But it will be an attempt to clarify some of the difficult—but exciting—problems surrounding the gospel traditions, and their paths outside the bounds of the four New Testament Gospels; we shall also try to provide a glimpse of the way in which a heretical theology is developed and gospel material transformed in a milieu governed by a different attitude to Jesus and this world from that found in the New Testament. We may also take this opportunity of pointing out that the terms " Gnosticism " and " Gnostic " are used here without further definition to denote all those syncretistic streams in the early Church which differed from the main traditions, being dominated by a different idea of God, a different concept of the world and man, and a different teaching on the Saviour, and which finally led to a split with the Church. It is terribly difficult on these matters to draw the line between orthodoxy and heterodoxy, due to our basic inability either to find a common denominator for " Gnosticism " or to decide the date at which we can really begin to talk about " Gnosticism."

Several scholars have been working independently on the *Gospel of Thomas*, and as a result many of the related texts have been discovered and used more than once; it is consequently impossible to refer in the footnotes to all who have dealt with the same text. Nor have we been able to cite all the smaller published works, or anything printed in the latter part of this year. The translation of the Coptic text of the *Gospel of Thomas* which we use is largely built upon Professor Torgny Säve-Söderbergh's Swedish translation in *Symbolæ Biblicæ Upsalienses* 16 (1959). I should also like to express my thanks to Professor Säve-Söderbergh for many suggestions, and for the excellent co-operation which I experienced in his seminar on the Coptic Gnostic texts from Nag-Hamadi, which has been working now for a couple of years. The Coptic text used is taken from photographic copies of Nag-Hamadi MSS. published through Pahor Labib in *Coptic Gnostic Papyri in the Coptic Museum at Old Cairo* (1956). Other interpretations of the text have been made subsequently in accordance with the English edition of the gospel. *The Gospel according to Thomas, Coptic Text Established and Translated* by A. Guillaumont, H.-Ch. Puech, G. Quispel, W. Till and Yassah Abd al Masih (1959).

BERTIL GÄRTNER

Uppsala
December 15th, 1959

PART ONE

The Literary Character of the Gospel of Thomas

I

THE LITERARY FORM OF THE SAYINGS OF JESUS

THE TASK of determining the number of sayings of Jesus in the *Gospel of Thomas* is not easy, since the text of the manuscript is continuous, and it is consequently difficult to draw the line between one saying and another. This difficulty is also noticeable in the translations so far published, when it has come to numbering the sayings.[1] Often the interpretation of certain sayings has had to be left open, since it is not possible to know whether they belong together or not. However, the numbering which it seems best to follow is that of the first edition of the text, which numbers 114 logia.[2] Most of these are introduced by the words "Jesus said," "Jesus said to his disciples" or just "He said." Sometimes it is the disciples who ask Jesus a question: "The disciples said to Jesus" (sayings 18 and 20) or "His disciples asked him (and) said to him" (6), a question later answered by Jesus, his answer being introduced by the usual formula "Jesus said." On two occasions it is Mary (21) or Salome (61b) who puts questions to Jesus, and the last saying in the Gospel names Simon Peter as the questioner (114). On two further occasions the opponents of Jesus seem to be lurking behind the questioners: "They said to him . . ." (91 and 100). On a very few occasions there is a brief description of the situation which called forth the

[1] J. Leipoldt, Ein neues Evangelium?, Theol. Lit. Zeit. 7:1958; T. Säve-Söderbergh, Evangelium Veritatis och Thomasevangeliet, Symbolæ Bibl. Upsalienses 16 (1959) (Swedish); J. Doresse, L'Evangile selon Thomas (1959); S. Giversen, Thomasevangeliet (1959) (Danish).

[2] Guillaumont-Puech-Quispel-Till-Yassah Abd al Masih, The Gospel according to Thomas (1959).

saying: "Jesus saw some children who were being suckled. He said to his disciples . . ." (22), "A woman in the crowd said to him . . ." (79), and "They showed Jesus a gold coin and said to him . . ." (100). Occasionally a saying of Jesus may occur twice, in different forms (56 and 80, 87 and 112).

If we consider the sayings of Jesus in their outward form, with a view to deciding in which literary categories they appear, we find that they mainly follow those categories which we meet in the New Testament Gospels. Thus parables take a prominent part in the *Gospel of Thomas*; there are 14 examples, of which the majority are known from the synoptic Gospels. We have, for example, "The Parable of the Sower" (9), Matt. 13.3-9 par., "The Rich Fool" (63), Lk. 12.16-21, "The Wedding Feast" (64), Matt. 22.1-9 par., and "The Wicked Husbandmen" (65), Matt. 21.33-39 par.[1] There are in addition a number of examples of imagery and metaphor,[2] among which occur "The City on the Hill" (32), Matt. 5.14, "Old Wine in New Wineskins" (47), Lk. 5.37-39, "The Mote and the Beam" (26), Matt. 7.3-5, and "The Harvest and the Labourers" (73), Matt. 9.37f.

Another familiar form in which sayings of Jesus occur in the canonical Gospels is the "beatitude," a form which recurs frequently in the *Gospel of Thomas*. Four of the New Testament Beatitudes are found here (54, 68, 69 a and b), but in a considerably altered form, e.g.,

> Jesus said:
> Blessed are you when they hate you and persecute you,
> And find no place there where you have been persecuted.
>
> Logion 68

Seven of them are unknown in the New Testament,[3] e.g.,

[1] Other parables, Nos. 8, 20, 21a, 57, 76, 96, 97, 98, 107 and 109.
[2] Cf. R. Bultmann, Die Geschichte der synoptischen Tradition (1931), p. 181ff.
[3] Logion 7, 18, 19, 49, 58, 103.

... Blessed is he who shall stand (upright) in the beginning
And he shall know the end,
And he shall not taste death.

Logion 18

Similarly, there is the characteristic cry of "Woe!" in two of the sayings (102 and 112), neither of which has a counterpart in the New Testament; nor are they connected with any of the Beatitudes as recorded by Luke.

Jesus said:
Woe unto them, the Pharisees,
For they are like a dog sleeping in the cattle manger,
Which neither eats (itself) nor lets the cattle eat.

Logion 102

Among those sayings which R. Bultmann in his book "Geschichte der synoptischen Tradition" includes under the heading "Mahnworte,"—exhortations to watchfulness, and thus sayings with a certain apocalyptic character—there is only one which appears in the *Gospel of Thomas*, that on "The Householder and the Thief," in Matt. 24.43-44: "If the owner of the house knows that the thief is coming, he will watch before he comes..." (21b). The purely apocalyptic sayings from the New Testament are missing, with one exception, Matt. 26.61 par., the form of which is, however, entirely altered, and the content of which has lost its apocalyptic emphasis.[1]

Jesus said:
I shall tear [down this] house
And none shall be able to build it up [again].

Logion 71

Since the greater part of the *Gospel of Thomas* seems to present

[1] See below, p. 172f.

Jesus, through his sayings, as the revealer of gnosis, there are very few sayings containing ethical exhortations or rules for the Church. But some of the well-known sayings from the New Testament Gospels, about alms, prayer and fasting, Matt. 6.1ff., do occur (6, 14 and 27), as well as others such as that dealing with the sin against the Holy Ghost (44), Matt. 12.31-32 par.

Another well-known literary form in the New Testament Gospels, which has its counterpart in the *Gospel of Thomas*, is the group of " I-sayings." Sayings of this kind which are echoed in the New Testament are e.g. the saying on the fire which Jesus was to kindle, Lk. 12.49.

> Jesus said:
> I have cast a fire upon the world
> And behold, I am watching over it, until it burns.
>
> Logion 10

A large number of unknown sayings of Jesus also occur in this form, e.g.

> Jesus said:
> I shall choose you, one of a thousand and two of ten thousand,
> And they shall stand (there), as they are a single one.
>
> Logion 23

There are of course several other literary categories in the New Testament, but the most important ones which can be paralleled in the *Gospel of Thomas* are those named above. The *apophthegmata*, describing scenes which are bound up closely with sayings of Jesus, and which occur so frequently in the New Testament, are conspicuous by their absence. On the other hand, a number of sayings which in the New Testament are connected to some scene are found in the *Gospel of Thomas* as "independent" logia. Also missing are the disputes which take up so much of the New Testament—the Tradition of the Elders, Mk. 7.1-23 and Marriage and Divorce, Mk. 10.2-12. Furthermore, there are no accounts of miracles; nor is there any hint of the historical course of events connected with Jesus: there is thus no narrative material whatever. Neither the Passion narratives nor the Resurrection pericopes, both of which belong to the fixed traditional collections in the New Testament Gospels, have any place. Thus it is only disconnected sayings which are set out in this gospel, and most of the literary categories represented can also be seen in the New Testament. But we may go further, and observe that some of the sayings of Jesus in this gospel have a structure to which it is worth paying close attention, since they can bear witness to the origin of these sayings in a milieu other than that of the New Testament.

In two sayings we come across an indirect dialogue in which answers are given to opponents' arguments. The style is one of discussion and argument, which has as its objective the presentation of items of theological doctrine, which are later rejected.

> Jesus said:
> If they who persuade (lead) you say to you,
> " Behold, the kingdom is in heaven,"
> Then the birds of heaven will precede you.
> If they say to you,
> " It is in the sea,"
> Then the fishes will precede you.
> But the kingdom is within you and it is outside you . . .
>
> Logion 3

Or hypothetical questions are posed (by opponents or in a catechetical form) and answered.

Jesus said:
If they say to you,
" Where have you come from? "
Say to them:
" We have come from the light ..."
If they say to you,
" Are you? "
Say,
"We are his children and we are the elect of the living Father ..."

Logion 50

This form of indirect dialogue and discussion has no place in the Synoptic Gospels,[1] but seems rather to belong to the epistles and tracts. We can in a way say that it forms part of Paul's method of presentation, and quote the Epistle to the Romans, in which he himself makes comments and asks questions which he then goes on to answer; but this is not really the same thing as we find in the *Gospel of Thomas.* In another " gospel " from the Nag-Hamadi library—the *Gospel of Philip*—we encounter this form once more. Thus we read, " Those who say that the Lord first died and (then) arose are wrong. For he first arose and (then) he died ..." 104. 15ff.[2] It is most likely that this stylistic form in the *Gospel of Thomas* has close connections with another literary category in this gospel, which reveals a Gnostic milieu.

On several occasions, sayings are made up of question and answer—questions asked by the disciples, by Mary or by Salome, and answered by Jesus. These questions are mainly to do with points of doctrine, typically Gnostic in emphasis. Almost all the sayings which appear in this form (as well as in the indirect dialogue form) contain material of undoubted Gnostic colouring,

[1] A comparison might possibly be made with Matt. 24. 23, " Then if any one says to you, ' Lo, here is the Christ! ' or ' There he is! ' do not believe it ..."
[2] Cf. 103.23ff.; 121.1ff.

if they are not purely Gnostic pronouncements. Thus in this literary category we are dealing, not with logia which are typical variants of sayings of Jesus found in the New Testament, but with those most easily classified as Gnostic creations or Gnostic revisions. As a typical example we may quote:

> His disciples said to him:
> "On which day shall the rest of the dead come
> And on which day shall the new world come?"
> He said to them:
> "That which you expect has come,
> But you do not recognise it."
>
> Logion 51

The dialogue form is put to constant use in Gnostic writings, and may be said to be a characteristic means of expression in that context. Such is the case with e.g. the Gnostic *Jesu Christi Sophia*, which probably dates from the 2nd century, and which is constructed according to the dialogue pattern common in the so-called Gnostic "gospels."[1] This is a good example of the way in which the most secret knowledge was conveyed through questions and answers put to, and given by, Jesus. In the very beginning of *Jesu Christi Sophia* the risen Jesus appears as the one who is able to answer all the most profound questions—on the secret of revelation, and the way of saving knowledge—only after his "human" existence. The same applies to *Pistis Sophia*, the various parts of which date from the 3rd century, though in this instance the dialogue takes an even more developed form. We may also mention the *Apocryphon of John* (particularly in its later part) which would seem to belong among the most ancient of Gnostic scriptures, dating perhaps from the first years of the

[1] See further Puech in Hennecke-Schneemelcher, Neutest. Apokryphen, p. 170f.

2nd century,[1] and the as yet unpublished *Apocryphon of James* from Nag-Hamadi.[2]

There is thus no doubt that the question-and-answer form occupies a key position in Gnostic literature. The style is often extremely naïve: the questions are artificial, and exist only in order to allow the Gnostic " revealer " to share his teachings on the position of Christ in the world-all, or the ascent of the soul to the world of light. This dialogue form appears even in such apocryphal scriptures as the *Apocalypse of Peter* and *Epistula Apostolorum*, which date from the beginning or the middle of the 2nd century, and which cannot be said to be directly Gnostic. The greater part of the latter writing consists in fact of profound questions and answers, introduced by the words, " We said to him "—" He said to us." The disciples ask doctrinal questions, and Jesus answers them. In this case we might go so far as to say that the dialogue is entirely dominant. The same applies to another of the Nag-Hamadi scriptures, the " *Dialogue of the Saviour*," which may be classified as a " gospel " in dialogue form.[3] The few remaining fragments of the *Gospel of the Egyptians* seem to indicate that it may have contained similar " dialogue-sayings."[4]

Some small insight into the way in which this dialogue style was used in Gnostic circles is provided by a comparison between two closely related Nag-Hamadi scriptures, *Jesu Christi Sophia* and the *Letter of Eugnostos*. Though from the point of view of content they bear a remarkable resemblance to each other, in their literary form they differ considerably. The *Letter of Eugnostos* is made up of a consistent exposition of doctrine in the form of a letter; *Jesu Christi Sophia*, following well-known Gnostic practice, is made up of an exposition in dialogue form set in a

[1] Puech in Neutest. Apokryphen, p. 242f.
[2] Puech in Neutest. Apokryphen, p. 248f.
[3] Puech in Neutest. Apokryphen, p. 173f.
[4] Cf. M. R. James, The Apocryphal New Testament (1953), p. 10ff., and W. Schneemelcher in Neutest. Apokryphen, p. 109ff.

narrative framework, consisting mainly of a prologue and an epilogue. H.-Ch. Puech considers, and I think it probable, that this latter document is an edited form of the letter, in which the more continuous epistle-style is exchanged for a longer dialogue. Thus the author of *Jesu Christi Sophia* has transformed a letter into a conversation, broken up the exposition into short sections and placed their content in the mouth of the Risen Lord as answers to questions put to him.[1] A number of the sayings in the *Gospel of Thomas* which have this typical question-and-answer form may be understood as resulting from a similar editing process; in this way Gnostic points of doctrine have been made into independent sayings, in which Jesus answers questions vital to the Gnostics. Those of the logia in the *Gospel of Thomas* which seem to take such a literary form, and would thus be of more recent origin, are just those which are distinguished by the nature of their contents as more obviously Gnostic. A further question is, however, whether this literary form, evidently used for preference in Gnostic literature, has an intimate connection with the Gnostic understanding of Jesus as mediator of a profound and secret revelation.

It would obviously be untrue to say that this building-up of sayings according to a pattern—questions asked by the disciples, leading to an answer from Jesus in which he presents his teaching—is to be found only in Gnostic literature. It has its counterpart in other literature, and occurs to some extent in the New Testament, particularly in Matthew and John. As an illustration we may quote Matt. 18.21-22, "Then Peter came up and said to him, 'Lord, how often shall my brother sin against me, and I forgive him? As many as seven times?' Jesus said to him, 'I do not say to you seven times but seventy times, seven.'" Behind such questions and answers can be seen, time and time again,

[1] Puech in Neutest. Apokryphen, p. 172f. There are other similar examples of how a doctrinal exposition was placed in the mouth of Jesus, or made into a dialogue, according to J. Doresse, L'Evangile selon Thomas, p. 5.

how the evangelist throws light on questions current in the early Church, by means of questions asked by the disciples or by opponents, and answered in sayings of Jesus. But although in their outward form the examples from the New Testament resemble closely their Gnostic counterparts, the themes treated in them are given a quite different orientation. Despite this, however, the questions and longer answers given by Jesus in John 13.36-14.24 provide valuable comparative material. In this passage, Jesus' farewell discourse, questions of a different kind are asked. Simon Peter asks, "Lord, where are you going?" 13.36; Thomas says, "Lord, we do not know where you are going; how can we know the way?" 14.5; Philip prays, "Lord, show us the Father, and we shall be satisfied." 14.8; Judas asks, "Lord, how is it that you will manifest yourself to us, and not to the world?" 14.22. This form and the content of these questions, which to some extent separates John from the synoptics, is also evidence that John originated in a gnosticising milieu, in which it was vital to present the Gospel in a form in which it could make its proper impact.

We might thus say that the *Gospel of Thomas* is in many cases not far removed from the canonical Gospels, at least as far as its literary form is concerned. What distinguishes them is that the former lacks several of those forms of expression which are found in the New Testament, and seems to show a marked preference for the dialogue form, so much favoured among Gnostics. This may indicate that the gospel originated, and that some of the sayings were shaped, in a Gnostic milieu. There are a number of other observations which may be made in this connection, and which point in the same direction. For instance, we have remarked that "beatitudes" occur on a number of occasions, although their content goes far beyond the doctrines of the New Testament. Now the "beatitude" was also a favourite form among the Gnostics; the "beatitudes" of Jesus were for Marcion the vital criterion of Christ's message, for there, as nowhere else, he found expressed the love of the Saviour-God. It was indeed the poor, the despised, the hated and the persecuted who accepted the Gospel.[1]

[1] See A. v. Harnack, Marcion. Das Evangelium vom fremden Gott, Texte und Untersuchungen z. Gesch.d.altchr.Lit. 45 (1921), pp. 114 and 167.

II

THE LITERARY FORM OF THE GOSPEL OF THOMAS

As WE have already mentioned, the *Gospel of Thomas* is made up of independent sayings of Jesus, arranged consecutively, and introduced for the most part by the phrase, "Jesus said." On a number of occasions a saying of Jesus is introduced as the answer to a question, or takes the form of a brief dialogue. But there is not a single narrative episode from the life of Jesus, nor is there any material which has to do with his birth, his ministry, his works, his conflicts with the Pharisees, or his suffering, death and resurrection. This is, then, not a gospel of the New Testament type, but purely and simply a collection of sayings. These are, however, not collected under various headings, as is the case in Matthew, for example, in which sayings of Jesus are without historical elaboration brought together into discourses, the contents of which form near-unities under such headings as eschatological-apocalyptic sayings, ethical exhortations and parables on the Kingdom of Heaven.

As far as can be seen, the sayings in the *Gospel of Thomas* are not arranged according to any system. It is only here and there that certain sayings clearly belong together, either because of the "key-word" principle, or because they deal with questions of similar character. As an example of the way in which the key-word principle works may be mentioned (28) and (29), in which the relevant word is *sarx*, and (50) and (51), in which the key-word is *anapausis*, rest.[1] On the second point, there is a corres-

[1] Cf. G. Garitte, Le premier volume de l'édition photographique des manuscrits gnostiques coptes et l' "Evangile de Thomas," Le Muséon 70 (1957), p. 63f.

pondence between (25) and (26); a common subject at the core of these two sayings, i.e. relationship to one's brother. Sayings (49) and (50) are also connected, the common factor being a treatment of the Gnostic's place of origin. One wonders sometimes whether the relationship between certain sayings of Jesus is evidence that they were taken from the same written source, but this is much more difficult to prove, since only fragments of the apocryphal gospels concerned have been preserved.

This unsystematic compilation of sayings, is, in general, evidence that the person who finally " composed " the gospel had no intention of giving a systematic account of those doctrines which he considered important: all he did was collect them. The varying character and content of these sayings indicates, too, that it is a typical collection.

But a collection of sayings of Jesus such as the *Gospel of Thomas* is far from being a normal occurrence. The other apocryphal gospels—known either from fragments or more extensively—are written more in a narrative form, following the example of the canonical Gospels. Those apocryphal gospels usually referred to as Jewish-Christian are, as far as we can see from the scarce material, mainly narrative.[1] The *Nazarene Gospel* has clearly been built up, as far as content, scope and arrangement are concerned, on the pattern of the canonical Matthew, and is so clearly of synoptic type that it has even been called a "second Matthew." The *Ebionite Gospel* is also of this kind, and also bears a close relationship to Matthew. The *Gospel according to the Hebrews* differs in form from the canonical Gospels, but contains narrative material, such as accounts of the Last Supper and the Resurrection. The same is true of the other "gospels": The *Gospel of Peter*, The *Book of James* or *Protevangelium*, *Thomas's account of the childhood of Jesus*, and others.

Unfortunately we know far too little about the *Gospel of the*

[1] For these gospels, see Hennecke-Schneemelcher, Neutest. Apokryphen.

Egyptians to be able to make any categorical statements about its appearance. However, the fragments which have been preserved contain a number of logia, in a form which resembles the question-and-answer style of the *Gospel of Thomas*; this gospel may possibly have consisted of compiled doctrinal material and sayings of Jesus, but that is purely a hypothesis. It we want to find a parallel to the structure and characteristic composition of the *Gospel of Thomas*, we must turn to a document found in the Nag-Hamadi library: the *Gospel of Philip*. Here we find once more a method of putting together passages which have apparently been taken from tracts; on rare occasions we can discern some direct connection between passages. A proportion of the collected material seems to consist of doctrinal proverbs and phrases, whilst the longer passages give the impression of being typically Gnostic, wellnigh incomprehensible accounts of creation and man, salvation and sacraments.[1] But in this gospel there are, with very few exceptions, none of those sayings of Jesus which are so typical of the *Gospel of Thomas*; for this reason we must treat the *Gospel of Philip* rather as a compendium of doctrinal passages drawn from Gnostic sources.

The only documents which correspond directly to a logia-collection such as the *Gospel of Thomas* are the *Oxyrhynchus Sayings of Jesus*, Papyri Nos. 1, 654 and 655, but these are in point of fact a Greek version of the same document as the *Gospel of Thomas*. Even if the interpretation of such disagreements as exist between the *Gospel of Thomas* and the three fragments gives rise to some discussion, that in no way alters the fact that we are here dealing with two very similar versions of the same basic document.

We must conclude that the *Gospel of Thomas* seems to be unique in literary form. Those writings which bear some resemblance to it, the *Gospel of Philip* and possibly the *Gospel of*

[1] See the German translation by H.-M. Schenke, Das Evangelium nach Philippus, Theol.Lit.Zeit. 1:1959.

the Egyptians, both belong in Gnostic circles. We also know, thanks to indications given in the Church Fathers, that in the early Church there flourished a number of " written " gospels, which were denounced as forgeries. Origen, in his first homily on Luke's Gospel, accuses those who compile gospels recklessly and without spiritual gifts, naming several of those which he has read, but rejecting all of them. It does not appear likely, from this statement, that any of these gospels was made up exclusively of sayings of Jesus. Irenæus, in *Adv. haer.* I, 8, 1, gives a number of interesting items of information on the way in which certain Gnostic groups made use of sayings of Jesus; it is quite possible that the existence of collections of sayings can be discerned in this context. Irenæus in fact writes that these groups commit offences against the order and context of Scripture, that they alter and rearrange, that they disturb the entire meaning of the Word of God, and that their arrangements of the text are responsible for leading many astray. We have, though, no definite proof of the existence of other similar collections of sayings of Jesus.

We have, however, one clue pointing to the origin of a gospel-form of this type, namely the constantly recurring introductory phrase "Jesus said." Many of the *agrapha* which we come across here and there in the writings of the Fathers, as well as in other Christian literature, are introduced by a similar form of words, " He said," " The Lord said," " The Saviour said "[1]—evidently a common way of identifying logia as originating from Jesus. This naturally applies also to quotations from the canonical Gospels. Similarly with those extracts from the Valentinian scriptures which we have at our disposal: sayings of Jesus are there frequently introduced by the same quotation formulæ.[2] Thus, when sayings of Jesus are presented in a con-

[1] See A. Resch, *Agrapha*, Aussercanonische Schriftfragmente (2. Aufl.), Texte und Untersuchungen z. Gesch.d.altchr.Lit. 30 (1906).

[2] A large number of examples are given by Carola Barth, Die Interpretation des Neuen Testaments in der valentinianischen Gnosis, Texte und Untersuchungen z.Gesch. d.altchr.Lit. 37 (1911), p. 28ff.

tinuous text, they are often introduced by the phrase " Jesus said," a form of words which has clear connections with a " homiletic style " or a presentation of doctrine. It is also reasonable to suppose that this admittedly stereotyped form was used in order to reinforce the authority of some of the more " dubious " sayings of Jesus—as with some of the logia in the *Gospel of Thomas.*

In the Synoptic Gospels, these very words—" Jesus said " or " He said "—are often used to introduce sayings of Jesus. Despite this, a deliberate collection of such sayings, introduced by this stereotyped formula, occurs only once, in Mk. 4. When Matthew and Luke bring sayings of Jesus together into discourses, an attempt is usually made to present the material consecutively. But in Mk. 4, parables and sayings are put together, the sayings are introduced by " He said to them," vv. 13, 21, 24, 26 and 30, and no description of the situation leading to the logia is given.

Bearing this in mind, it would be very easy to bring in the source Q, behind Matthew and Luke, as an excellent piece of comparative material for the *Gospel of Thomas.* But there has never been any substantial measure of agreement about the nature of this hypothetical collection of logia, and the extent of Q itself is correspondingly vague as a result. Furthermore, it must be pointed out in this context that Q is generally supposed to have contained a large amount of narrative material[1]—which is far from being the case with the *Gospel of Thomas.* The unique form of the *Gospel of Thomas* seems to indicate that its background differed considerably from that which lay behind the collections of sayings of Jesus which are thought to have existed in the beginning of the gospel tradition.

An analysis of some of these sayings of Jesus may throw some light on this background. Thus in logion 100 we read:

[1] Cf. T. W. Manson, The Sayings of Jesus (1950), p. 39-148; F. C. Grant, The Gospels, their Origin and their Growth (1957), p. 59ff.

They showed Jesus a gold coin and said to him,
" Those who belong to Cæsar demand tax from us."
Jesus said to them:
" Give Cæsar the things which belong to Cæsar,
Give God the things which belong to God,
And give me what is mine."

The counterpart of this saying is to be found in all three Synoptic Gospels, Mk. 12.13-17 par.; this version differs considerably from that of the Synoptics, however. It has for the most part been stripped of its situation and the polemical context in which it appears in the Synoptics. There is only the barest reference to the fact that the saying has anything whatever to do with the payment of taxes: " They showed Jesus a gold coin and said . . ." Nor is there any reference to the image and inscription on the coin, upon which Jesus' answer depended. Furthermore, the question put to Jesus is different. In the Synoptics we read, " Is it lawful to pay taxes to Cæsar, or not? " The form of Logion 100 demonstrates that the point at issue is something other than the attitude of the Messiah to Israel and the occupying forces. The question as we have it in the Logion fits in very well with Clement of Alexandria's interpretation of " Cæsar " as " the temporary Archon "[1] (an expression which in *Heracleon fr.* 34/40, stands for the Demiurge). This explains the form in which we have the logion, as well as the addition, " And give me what is mine."

Similar observations can be made about Logion 99, which deals with Jesus' mother and brothers who come seeking him, Mk. 3.31-35 par. The version of the *Gospel of Thomas* is noteworthy because of the simplification of the surrounding narrative and the saying itself, as well as for a typical addition which is made. A similar abbreviation is to be found in Luke 8.19-21,

[1] Clement Alex., *Eclogae ex scripturis propheticis* 24.

though on a smaller scale and without any additions to the text. We might produce a number of examples from the *Gospel of Thomas* which demonstrate the way in which sayings of Jesus are almost entirely detached from their Synoptic framework—a circumstance diametrically opposed to that which Bultmann considers to have happened in the case of the Synoptics, in which originally isolated sayings have been brought together with a variety of connecting narratives. But at the same time, these logia in the *Gospel of Thomas* show that tentative re-expressions had been made; the impression which we gain from this is that the sayings of Jesus had been "stripped" and altered, in a milieu far different from that of the main stream of the Church. The object of all this seems to have been to render them more convincing as proofs for a different theological interpretation than the New Testament provided.

The "narrative" sections in the Gospels were relatively unimportant in this milieu: it was the sayings themselves which were vital.[1] Once more we may refer back to Irenæus (*Adv. haer.* I, 8, 1), who says that the Gnostics were very fond of removing discourses, sayings and parables from their proper contexts and trying to adapt them to their myths. It may well be the case that the *Gospel of Thomas* was collected by someone who picked sayings of Jesus out of various gospel traditions, tracts and homiletical traditions; in the latter case it would be quite usual to refer to sayings without giving any hint of their place or context in the gospels—which applies equally to the Fathers in their quotations from the canonical Gospels. A consideration of this background makes it easier to understand how the *Gospel of Thomas* came to take the form of a collection of sayings of Jesus, and nothing more.

[1] See below, p. 75.

III

CONFLATIONS OF SAYINGS OF JESUS

CHARACTERISTIC of many of the logia in the *Gospel of Thomas* is the fact that they combine different New Testament sayings of Jesus in a way for which, however, we have no equivalent in the New Testament. For example, Logion 14 is a combination of sayings from the Sermon on the Mount, Matt. 6, from the Commissioning Discourses, Lk. 10 and Matt. 10, and from the pronouncement on purity and impurity, Mk. 7.15.

> Jesus said to them:
> If you fast (Matt. 6.16), you will create a sin for yourselves.
> If you pray (Matt. 6.5.), you will be condemned.
> If you give alms (Matt. 6.2), you will do evil to your spirits.
> And when you go into every country and wander in the Kingdoms (Matt. 10.11),
>
> If they receive you,
> Eat what is put before you,
> Heal the sick among them (Lk. 10.8-9, Matt. 10.8).
> For that which enters your mouth shall not defile you.
> But that which comes out of your mouth,
> That it is which shall defile you (Mk. 7.15, Matt. 15.11).

This combination of sayings of Jesus is new, and one wonders what can have given rise to such a construction, since in the New Testament there is no connection between the three sections. It is naturally very difficult to make any definite pronouncement regarding such a form, but it is most likely that these sayings were combined in this way for a very definite theological reason. The theme appears to be concerned with the proper attitude to important aspects of the religious life, an attitude which has as its background the stressing of the inward, the "finer" and the more spiritual in man, as opposed to the outward. In Matt. 6, rules are given which condemn hypocrisy in almsgiving, prayer and fasting, all of which are introduced by the same formula: "When you give alms . . ." "When you pray . . ." "When you fast . . ." But this introduction is followed in Logion 14 by totally different words; a new interpretation has been made—through a complete alteration. The words of Jesus to the disciples in Lk. 10 have taken on a new implication through the addition of the saying on purity and impurity. It is this latter aspect which may have given rise to the combination of "Eat what is put before you," and ". . . that which enters your mouth shall not defile you." Thus we have a "new" logion about alms, prayer, fasting and "clean and unclean," very probably bound up with a "Gnostic"—or at least, an ascetic—interpretation of the relationship of man to the material world.

Another typically new combination of sayings of Jesus is found in Logion 39.

> Jesus said:
> The Pharisees and the scribes have received the keys to knowledge.
> They have hidden them. Nor have they entered;
> And those who would enter, they would not allow.
> But you shall be wise as serpents and harmless as doves.

Here we have a conflation of Jesus' words condemning the Pharisees, in a form which is a blend of Lk. 11.52 and Matt. 23.13, and the Logion about serpents and doves, Matt. 10.16.[1] From the

[1] Texts combining Lk. 11. 52 and Matt. 23. 13 also occur in the *Pseudo-Clementines* as

point of view of the New Testament, as far as one can judge, this conflation is tendentious. Evidently the "serpent and dove" saying has been interpreted in such a way as to make a combination with the warning to the Pharisees quite possible, though in the *Gospel of Thomas* this warning has become a general statement. " Knowledge " is probably the element which holds the two sayings together. This point of view gains in probability when we remember that the *Pseudo-Clementines* used Lk. 11.52 and Matt. 23.13 when discussing gnosis, and that the Valentinians made the saying on doves and serpents the basis for a discourse on gnosis and its gifts.[1] We might say, then, that this combination gives some indication of the direction in which the interpretation of Logion 39 leaned when it was first introduced into the *Gospel of Thomas*.

In certain of the parables, we find a concluding saying of Jesus which had no connection whatever with the original parable, but which has obviously been brought in with a view to interpretation, additions of this kind having been made in order to emphasise the meaning of the parable. A typical example of this procedure is found in Logion 76.

> Jesus said:
> The Kingdom of the Father is like a merchant who had a load of merchandise.
> When he found a pearl, the merchant sold his goods,
> For he was a wise man (and) bought this single pearl.
> You also ought to seek for his treasure, which is not destroyed (but) endures,

---

well as the saying that the keys " have been hidden " by the Pharisees. See further G. Strecker, Das Judenchristentum in den Pseudoklementinen, Texte und Untersuchungen z.Gesch.d.altchr.Lit. 70 (1958), p. 126; G. Quispel, The Gospel of Thomas and the New Testament, Vig.Christ. 11 (1957), p. 190.

[1] *Pseudo-Clementines*, Hom. III, 18; XVIII, 15, 7ff.; Tertullian, *Adv. Valent.* 3.

In that place where the moth does not come in and devour
And no worm destroys.

Here there has taken place a conflation of the parable of the "Pearl of great Price," Matt. 13.45f., and Jesus' saying on treasure in heaven, Lk. 12.33f. and Matt. 6.19-21. Now when we compare these logia from the *Gospel of Thomas* with their New Testament counterparts, we find several distinguishing features, the character of which makes one wonder whether the sayings concerned may not have undergone some process of correction from the Gnostic viewpoint. The combination we have here is otherwise unknown, but its existence is understandable in a milieu in which it was thought desirable to support theological contentions other than those governing the New Testament. It is a moot point whether this may not be a quotation made from memory. The form of the parable shows that we are dealing here with a retelling of a familiar story, and the saying on treasure in heaven combines texts from Matt. and Lk. without actually following either. Since the parable of the Pearl of great Price is combined directly with the parable of the treasure in the field, it is understandable that the word "treasure" has awakened associations, which have then led on to the saying concerning treasure in heaven. The determinative factor for these conflations seems in each case to be the content of the sayings. We are thus enabled, through studying the way in which sayings of Jesus were combined, to obtain a certain degree of insight into theological ideas and interpretations current in the circle which was responsible for the *Gospel of Thomas*.

If we want to find some equivalent for this combination of different sayings of Jesus, the New Testament naturally provides us with a number of examples. The combined sayings which we find there are evidence of a similar, though more moderate, procedure, particularly as a result of editing done by the different evangelists. For example, the saying about the salt which lost its savour occurs in one context in Matthew, in another in Luke, and in a third in Mark. Similarly, the parable of the lost sheep in Matt. 18 and Lk. 15 occurs in passages with quite different themes. Nevertheless, these logia are introduced within the framework of a certain overall interpretation, and are not so closely bound up with other sayings of Jesus as is the case in the *Gospel of Thomas*. There we, in fact, encounter a degree of freedom in combination which is not only evidence of different shades of interpretation but also of definite and thorough-going interpretations, aimed at stressing a " deeper " understanding of the sayings.

The " meditative "—if we may be allowed to use the word—combination of sayings which we have in the *Gospel of Thomas* is far from usual. But we do find something similar in the Gnostic *Gospel of Mary*, which dates from the 2nd century. There can be observed how certain theological ideas draw logia together, so that one saying of Jesus is added to another. Eight lines of this Gospel serve to combine a large number of sayings: a number are merely hinted at, but the hints are sufficiently broad to leave no doubt as to which Biblical texts are referred to.

> Peace (be) with you (Lk. 24.36, Jn. 20.19).
> My peace I bring to you (Jn. 14.27).
> Be on your guard, so that no one leads you astray with the words (Matt. 24.4):
> " See, here! " or " See, there! " (Matt. 24.23).
> For the Son of man is within you (Lk. 17.21).
> Follow him! They who seek him shall find him (Matt. 7.7).
>
> *The Gospel of Mary* 8, 14-21

A somewhat different principle for the conflation of different logia is given, e.g. by the *Pseudo-Clementines*, in which we occasionally come across a whole series of sayings of Jesus. Here, however, it is more a matter of a collection of proof-texts, gathered in support of some thesis. For example, the Apostle seeks to prove the existence of the evil one by quoting texts from Matt. 12.26, Lk. 10.18, Matt. 13.39, a possible agraphon, Matt. 5.37 and others.[1] Even if it is not exactly this process which takes place in the *Gospel of Thomas*, we still gain a valuable insight into the way in which later theological discussion was carried on, and doctrinal statements were made.

This also applies very well to the Valentinians, who favoured combinations of different sayings of Jesus, with particular preference for Luke's Gospel. As an illustration of this, we have the coupling of Lk. 15.4-7, the parable of the lost sheep, with Lk. 19.10, " For the Son of man came to seek and to save the lost."[2] Or we might mention the four sayings—with approximately the same content—from the Synoptic Gospels which are found together in a fragment of Heracleon.[3] But the same phenomenon also occurs in the Fathers, and must thus have been a widespread custom.

An additional point to which we must pay the closest attention in this context is the constant occurrence in the *Gospel of Thomas* of " compound texts " which stand in close relationship to the conflated sayings we have been considering. In a large number of those logia into which New Testament sayings of Jesus are introduced—in fact, in the majority of them—there occurs a

[1] *Pseudo-Clementines*, Hom. XIX, 2, " And I know that He has said somewhere else: If Satan casts out Satan, he is divided against himself. How then is his kingdom to stand? And He pointed out that He saw the evil one like lightning falling down from heaven. And elsewhere He said: He who sowed the bad seed is the devil. And again: Give no pretext to the evil one. Moreover, in giving advice, He said: Let your yea be yea, and your nay nay. For what is more than these is of the evil one."

[2] See further Th.Zahn, Geschichte des neutestamentlichen Kanons I (1888), p. 740ff.

[3] Clement Alex., *Strom.* IV, 70.

mixture of the parallel synoptic texts which is most striking. We may take as an example Logion 33.

> Jesus said:
> That which you hear with one ear (or) the other ear,
> Preach upon your rooftops.
> No one lights a lamp and puts it under a bushel,
> Nor does he put it in a hidden place,
> But sets it upon the lamp-stand,
> So that every one who comes in or goes out
> May see its light.

Here two sayings have been coupled together, the latter interpreting the former; but at the same time we notice that the Matthean and Lukan versions have become intertwined, and are now typical " compound texts." In the latter part of the logion, Lk. 8.16, 11.33 and Matt. 5.15 have been combined, with certain small additional variants, which have no equivalent at all in the New Testament. But this is no novelty; on the contrary, it is a quite well-known occurrence, as other documents prove.[1] For example, in the *Pseudo-Clementines*, Hom. III, 51, 3, there is a " compound " of Matt. 24.35 and 5.18, " The heaven and the earth shall pass away, but one jot or one tittle shall not pass from the law." This blend of the two texts in question has been interpreted as an emphatic statement on the eternal validity of the law and possibly as a manifestation of the author's habit of " free, tendentious quotation."[2]

Such texts as this are also supported in the Fathers. One passage in Origen, which has almost the character of a mosaic, puts together Matt. 6.25-26 and Lk. 12.24, 29, after which he quotes Matt. 6.28 word for word (*Contra. Celsum.* VII, 2, 4), though farther on in the same work he does quote " word for

[1] Cf. e.g. *Pap.Egerton* 2, expounded by J. Jeremias in Neutest. Apokryphen, p. 59f.
[2] Strecker, Das Judenchristentum in den Pseudoklementinen, p. 126. Here are reproduced the most important compound texts.

word " after the New Testament. Clement of Alexandria makes use of the same process when he interweaves Lk. 12.22ff. and Matt. 6.25ff. (*Paidag*. II, 10, 102). It would be easy to multiply examples, but these suffice to show that " compounds " of synoptic sayings were a general occurrence; it has even been suggested, when discussing Clement and Origen, that there was an Alexandrian school responsible for this tradition.[1] "Compound texts " of this type occur in the writings of the Valentinians as well—further proof that this was a current technique.[2] Behind this " free " attitude to the various gospel traditions of the New Testament there may have been, at least as far as the Fathers were concerned, a less carefully thought-out attitude to the actual words of the canonical Gospels. They considered themselves far less tightly bound to the precise formulation, than to the *content* of the text. When we consider the Gnostics, we notice that there may also have been, at the back of their quotations, some attempt at a harmonisation of the text of the New Testament. This may well be an expression of the same striving which gave rise to Marcion's single gospel and the Diatessaron of Tatian. This tendency towards a harmonisation of the Gospel can occasionally be traced even in Origen, as well as a deliberate avoidance of literal quotation in the interests of reaching the real meaning of the texts in question.

The occurrence of these " compound texts " in the *Gospel of Thomas* must be treated as one element in a process which can be proved to have been very common during the 2nd and early 3rd centuries. Furthermore, we ought to take into consideration that these logia may reflect various attempts at harmonising the

[1] See e.g. P. Koetschau, Bibelcitate bei Origenes, Zeitschr.f.wiss. Theol. 43 (1900), p. 331ff.; E. Hautsch, Die Evangelienzitate des Origenes, Texte und Untersuchungen z.Gesch.d.altchr.Lit. 34 (1909), p. 5ff.

[2] Zahn, Geschichte des neutestamentlichen Kanons I, p. 741; R. M. Grant, Notes on the Gospel of Thomas, Vig. Christ. 13 (1959), p. 174ff., has pointed out the same tendency among the Naassenes. Cf. G. Bardy, Les citations bibliques d'Origène, Revue Biblique 16 (1919), p. 106ff. and E. Massaux, Influence de l'Evangile de saint Matthieu sur la littérature chrétienne avant saint Irénée (1950), p. 466ff.

Gospels. We must naturally not ignore the possibility that certain logia may be expressions of a gospel tradition outside that of the New Testament. But with the background of these " compound texts " in the early Church, we must be very cautious in passing judgment, particularly in those cases in which we have no proof available from manuscript traditions.

IV

KNOWN AND UNKNOWN SAYINGS OF JESUS IN THE GOSPEL OF THOMAS

THE MANY logia in the *Gospel of Thomas* may be divided into three groups: first, those which reproduce sayings of Jesus which are preserved in the canonical Gospels, secondly, *agrapha* previously encountered, mainly in patristic literature, and thirdly, hitherto unknown sayings. Of these three groups, the first is by far the largest, in fact comprising about one-half of the 114 logia. As we have shown in the preceding chapters, these logia contain phrases or parts of canonical sayings of Jesus, frequently in a form which seems to indicate a " mixing " of synoptic versions. Other sayings agree more directly with the New Testament, but these are few in number. What is particularly surprising is that there is scarcely a single complete saying of Jesus which is identical with its synoptic counterpart in every detail. The *Gospel of Thomas* is to a greater or lesser extent made up of variant readings. One of the logia which approximates most closely to the New Testament is

> Jesus said:
> Blessed are the poor, for yours is the kingdom of heaven.
> Logion 54

The text is close to that of Luke, 6.20, but instead of " the kingdom of God " has " the kingdom of heaven," in common with the Matthean version. A possible explanation of this may have been an unwillingness to use the expression " the kingdom of God," which is not found at all in the *Gospel of Thomas*. This reading may also be explained as reflecting the texts of Tatian and Marcion.[1]

The differences between the New Testament and the *Gospel of Thomas* may to some extent be illustrated by reference to the parables. Here we may make the preliminary observation that some are shorter than the New Testament versions, others are expanded, whilst others again correspond quite well. The first two groups can be more closely illuminated by quoting the parable of the wheat and the tares.

> Jesus said:
> The kingdom of the Father is like a man who had [good] seed.
> His enemies came by night (and) sowed weeds among the good seed.
> The man would not allow them to pull up the weeds.
> He said to them:
> By no means may you go and pull up the weeds
> And pull up the wheat together with it,
> For on the day of harvest the weeds shall be revealed.
> (Then) shall they pull it up and burn it up.
>
> Logion 57

This parable occurs only in Matt. 13.24-30, where it is quoted in more detail, and in an extended form, and it would be easy to draw the conclusion that the shorter form is older and more primitive, the more developed form having grown up gradually. But in this case the solution is not so simple; a closer examination of Logion 57 shows in fact that we are dealing here with a compressed version of what was originally a longer text. It is here sufficient to point to the gap in presentation which occurs between the statement that the enemy " sowed weeds among the good

[1] The reading is supported, and v.Soden refers to such a possibility, Die Schriften des Neuen Testaments II (1913), p. 266. Cf. Tertullian, *Adv. Marcionem* IV, 14.

seed " and the next line, " The man would not allow them to pull up the weeds." It would have been natural at this point to introduce a line pointing out that after a time, both wheat and weeds began to grow together, and that it was then that the man was faced with the problem of what to do about it, to " pull up " or " let grow together." Furthermore, after the " gap " the word " they " is suddenly introduced, referring to no previously named person. The narrative pre-supposes a longer version, and the conclusion has also been altered, the emphasis having been placed on the fate of the weeds. The impression which we gain from this form is that we have here a summary of the Matthean parable, rather than an independent tradition or version;[1] the alteration of the parable may possibly be explained as expressive of a desire to stress something special, the consequence being that " uninteresting " parts are dispensed with. This is of course usual in a homiletical context.

One example of how a parable is filled out is provided by the parable of the Marriage Feast, Lk. 14.16-24 (Matt. 22.1-10).

> Jesus said:
> A man had guests, and when he had prepared the feast, he sent his servant to invite the guests. He went to the first (and) said to him, " My master calls you." He said, " I am owed money by some merchants. They are coming to me this evening. I shall go and give them my provisions. I decline the invitation to the feast." He went to another (and) said to him, " My master has called you." He said to him, " I have bought a house and they have fixed a date for me. I have not time." He went to another (and) said to him, " My master has called you." He said to him, " My friend is to be married and it is I who shall

[1] It is more difficult to assess the relation between Logion 63 and Lk. 12. 16-21, of which the former is considerably shorter.

arrange the banquet. I cannot come. I decline the invitation to the feast." He went to another (and) said to him, "My master calls you." He said to him, "I have bought an estate and must go to collect the rent. I cannot come. I decline." The servant came (and) said to his master, "Those whom you have invited to the feast have declined to come." The master said to his servant, "Go out into the streets. Those that you find, bring here, so that they may feast. Merchants and traders [shall] not [enter] into my Father's dwellings."

Logion 64

This parable occurs largely in the same form as in Luke, but there are four examples given here of how the invited guests present their excuses, as against three in Luke, and the examples here are different. Luke gives three examples of hindrances: one has bought a field, another an ox, and a third had just been married. In Logion 64 it is not only the various excuses which are of interest; instead the emphasis has been laid on the fact that those who declined to come to the feast were engaged in the pursuit of commerce. The examples have therefore been given a new content: the man who had "married a wife" has become the one responsible for the arrangements at someone else's wedding. Examples have been multiplied and extended around this theme, and the special theme itself has a definite form. The conclusion of the parable has also been altered from the general statement in Luke—"None of those men who were invited shall taste my banquet."—to "Merchants and traders shall not enter into my Father's dwellings." Other details in Luke have disappeared, particularly the important detail that it is the under-privileged members of society who are invited as replacements, since they were without importance in this other context.

It is, however, difficult to say what this "other context" may have been. The polemic against "merchants and traders" has no parallel in the New Testament, and is otherwise not easy to support.[1] A very general reference may of course be made to the hostile attitude to commerce shown in Jewish wisdom literature, where it is frequently said that a variety of sins follow upon the acquisition of money, e.g. Ecclesiasticus 26.29ff.; similar tones are heard in the *Testament of Issachar*, 3ff. But it was not merely in certain Jewish circles that commerce was looked upon with suspicion and a word of warning; in the ancient world in general, commerce was considered to be a socially inferior occupation, and virtually synonymous with swindling.[2] It is therefore not surprising to find this attitude in the atmosphere of "world-renunciation" which surrounded many of the logia in the *Gospel of Thomas*. Nor is it out of the question that there may lie hidden some deeper meaning behind the expression "merchants and traders," though this is far from easy to demonstrate.

Of the other parables, all of those which have equivalents in the New Testament are altered except one, the Parable of the Sower, Logion 9, which agrees with Mk. 4.1-9 par.; this is apart from some small variant readings, which all have well-known parallels. The other "altered" parables contain so many different details that it is very hard to believe that they reproduce valuable independent traditions; the impression given is that they are of more recent origin.

The second group of sayings of Jesus in the *Gospel of Thomas* is made up of *agrapha* already known from patristic literature, from fragments of other apocryphal gospels or from other literature.[3] One such saying of Jesus which has often been quoted

[1] A comparison might possibly be made with Rev. 18. 3, 11ff.

[2] See further, on this problem in general, G. Boström, Proverbiastudien, Lunds Univ. Arsskrift (1934), p. 53ff.

[3] See, above all, Resch, *Agrapha*; J. Jeremias, Unbekannte Jesusworte (1951) and Hennecke-Schneemelcher, Neutest. Apokryphen.

is that in Logion 82, known earlier in Origen's exposition of the Prophet Jeremiah, III, 3, "I have read somewhere that the Saviour said—and I question whether some one has assumed the person of the Saviour, or called the words to memory, or whether it be true that is said—but the Saviour himself says:

> He that is near me is near the fire.
> He that is far from me is far from the kingdom."

Other sayings of Jesus are known—entire or in part—from quotations in Irenæus, Clement of Rome, Clement of Alexandria, Origen, Hippolytus, etc. Similar sayings, as well as parts of logia from the *Gospel of Thomas*, are to be found in other apocryphal acts, and in fragments from the *Gospel according to the Hebrews* and the *Gospel of the Egyptians*. A large group of sayings is also known from the *Oxyrhynchus Papyri*, and a number of logia have been found more recently in Manichæan and Gnostic documents. The majority of passages in which these sayings of Jesus are to be found have already been noted down, and it will suffice for our purposes merely to record that fact.[1] It is a matter of a group of some 20 logia (Puech enumerates 18) over and above those found in Oxyrhynchus.

The third group of sayings of Jesus in the *Gospel of Thomas* is made up of those hitherto entirely unknown. It is very difficult to pass any overall judgment upon them, since they vary considerably. It seems, however, possible to say that the majority of them, in the form in which we have them, cannot be genuine sayings of Jesus, since they bear such obvious traces of the religious ideas which characterised the Gnostic groups using this gospel. In many cases, as we shall see later, a glimpse shows how foreign they are to the New Testament. But other sayings cannot without more ado be labelled as genuine or spurious: it is quite

[1] H.-Ch.Puech, Une collection de paroles de Jésus récemment retrouvée: L'Evangile selon Thomas, C. R. Académie des inscriptions et belles-lettres (1957), p. 165f., and in Neutest. Apokryphen, p. 212ff. Cf. J. Doresse, L'Evangile selon Thomas, p. 121ff.

out of the question to judge them—and their relation to Jesus—with absolute certainty; this problem has already been dealt with in our consideration of the known *agrapha*.[1] What we can do, however, is to investigate the extent to which they contradict the content of the New Testament Gospels, and the picture of Jesus given there; in this way we can determine their age and milieu. We may naturally wonder whether it might not be possible that some of the logia in the *Gospel of Thomas*, although their expressions and contents are foreign to the New Testament, may be genuine sayings of Jesus. Such an assertion would, however, be extremely hazardous, and quite impossible to prove. It must remain a hypothesis.

If we would quote examples of sayings which appear substantially to agree with the New Testament, and which may belong to a traditional source of sayings running parallel to the New Testament, there are very few from which to choose, and closer analysis may reveal even these to have a different character. My own personal choice would be e.g.:

> His disciples said to him:
> "Who are you, that you tell us this?"
> <Jesus said:>
> " From what I tell you, you do not know who I am.
> But you have become like the Jews,
> For they love the tree (and) hate its fruit,
> And they love the fruit (but) hate the tree."
>
> Logion 43

Certain of the details in this saying, such as the use of the term Ἰουδαῖος, " the Jews," appear to be more recent, since in the synoptics the word is seldom used, and never by Jesus. It is not until the Gospel of John that it begins to be used more frequently, but then only in one actual saying of Jesus, 4.22,

[1] See Jeremias, Unbekannte Jesusworte, p. 26ff.

which is typically enough in the course of a conversation with a non-Jew.[1] It therefore jars somewhat in Logion 43. But otherwise the paradoxical statement on the fruit and the tree seems to me to be quite in line with Jesus' way of expressing himself, according to the New Testament.

Another saying which should be included in this group is one which we have already quoted, Logion 102, about the dog in the manger. On the other hand, we can be far from certain about the first part of Logion 47:

> Jesus said:
> It is not possible for a man to ride two horses
> Or to draw two bows . . .

One is tempted to wonder whether this may not be a question of a typical development in line with the other parts of the Logion, ". . . and it is impossible for a servant to serve two masters." It is easy enough, using contrasting pairs, to ring the changes on a theme such as this, and we are in no position to be able to solve the problem with any degree of certainty.

Similarly with the two following proverb-like statements, the first of which we have in the New Testament.

> Jesus said:
> No prophet is well received in his own town.
> The doctor does not cure those who know him.
>
> Logion 31

The first saying, on the prophet, is shorter here than in Mk 6.4 and Matt. 13.57, but agrees entirely with Lk. 4.24. Furthermore, the term δεκτός, " well received " in Luke is a link with Logion 31. But this saying has a supplement, a proverb about the doctor and his patients, which has no equivalent in Matt. and Mk. Now it may be considered that Logion 31 is the original

[1] See further art. Ἰουδαῖος by W. Gutbrod in Theol. Wörterb. III, p. 370ff.

form of the saying on the prophet and his home,[1] and that the "doctor" saying may be genuine. It is, however, of interest to note that in Lk. 4, the pericope of Jesus in his home town, Jesus repeats an accusation which was thrown at him in Nazareth, "Doctor, heal yourself!" The reason for this accusation was evidently that he had worked no miracles of healing in his home town, though he had done so in Capernaum. Luke places the "doctor, heal yourself" passage and the saying on the prophet in close connection, in just the same way as they are linked together in Logion 31. We may therefore draw the conclusion, either that the *Gospel of Thomas* reproduces the original tradition used by Luke, or that the pericope in Luke was known to the editor of the *Gospel of Thomas*, who brought the two proverbs together and removed them from their framework. In this process the proverbs took on another form, in connection with the group of variant readings to which proverbs always give rise. As we see, the problem is not at all easy to solve.

It goes without saying that when we are considering this group of "genuine" sayings of Jesus, there may have existed—purely hypothetically—in or behind most of the logia, sayings of Jesus considerably more "primitive" in character than those we have in the logia themselves. These "primitive" sayings may then, in the heretical milieu in which they existed, have been altered or "gnosticised." But in the majority of cases it seems to be an altogether hopeless task to marshal sufficient adequate reasons for digging out any such "original sayings."

[1] Bultmann, Die Geschichte der synoptischen Tradition, p. 30f.

V

THE DIFFERENT TRADITIONS IN THE GOSPEL OF THOMAS

One soon discovers when studying this Gospel that it includes a mass of varied material. The sayings show traces of editing, and seem to be drawn from different traditions. The overall impression is clearly one of being a composite work. It seems to me quite unthinkable that in the *Gospel of Thomas* we should be dealing with a unified and consistent traditional source: instead we find logia which appear to be later Gnostic constructions, logia taken from those gospels which are in general ascribed to Jewish-Christian circles, and finally, all those manifold variations, conflations and alterations of Synoptic sayings of Jesus, with which we have already dealt.

When we attempt to distinguish the different stages of development of these sayings, and to trace Jewish-Christian or primitive Christian traditions behind the Gnostic forms, we run into unforeseen difficulties, however; it is in fact impossible, at the present stage of research, to come to any definite conclusion about the material as we now have it. What we can do, though, is to point out certain tendencies and lines of development which are important for our estimation of the gospel.

All seem to be agreed upon one point: that the *Gospel of Thomas*, in the form in which we have it, is a document embellished from a Gnostic source, arising out of a milieu which has set its mark very decisively upon the sayings. But behind all this it has been thought that there are extraordinarily valuable remnants of a gospel tradition which flourished alongside the canonical Gospels, the roots of which stretched far back in time —indeed, as far as certain circles within the early Church in Jerusalem. The principal exponent of these views is G. Quispel,[1] who writes: " The importance of the *Gospel of Thomas* lies in the fact that it contains an independent and very old gospel tradition. When I say independent, I mean that some sayings of the *Gospel of Thomas* were not taken from our canonical Gospels, Matthew, Mark, Luke and John, but were borrowed from another source."[2] This ancient source, according to Quispel, goes back to an Aramaic tradition, about which it is very difficult to be precise, namely, " the Jewish-Christian gospel tradition." There was in Jerusalem a group which did not make a break with the observances of the Jewish law; they continued to live apart from " the growing Catholic Church," and maintained their own gospel traditions. The *Gospel of Thomas* exhibits in several cases " a very close affinity to the fragments of this Jewish-Christian tradition," which was not one of the sources for the canonical Gospels. Quispel goes on to say that it is possible to find traces in the *Gospel of Thomas* of the Aramaic tradition from which the hypothetical source Q was derived, in a " revised and secondary form." Thus the new Gospel should contain a good deal of material of the same historical value as the synoptics. " They (these new sayings of Jesus) may have been transmitted in a Palestinian milieu quite isolated from the rest of Christendom and not influenced by the trends of Pauline theology. And we must not exclude the possibility that these people may sometimes have preserved the words of Jesus in a form more primitive than that found in the canonical Gospels."[3]

Unfortunately, these theses of Quispel are built on far too many hypothetical suppositions, and therefore cannot win much

[1] G. Quispel, The Gospel of Thomas and the New Testament, Vig.Christ. 11 (1957), p. 189-207, and idem, Some Remarks on the Gospel of Thomas, NT Studies 5 (1959), p. 276-290.

[2] Quispel, Some Remarks, p. 277.

[3] Quispel, The Gospel of Thomas, p. 205.

credence—at least with the insufficient evidence so far produced in their support. No one would deny that there may be old and valuable traditions in the *Gospel of Thomas*, but there are many difficulties to be overcome before that conviction can be said to have been proved. We know nothing whatever definite about the " independent traditions " which the Jewish-Christian group in Jerusalem are said to have possessed. Nor can we talk about a Jewish-Christian gospel tradition as a well-determined fact, if by " Jewish-Christian " we mean the groups of those " obedient to the law " in the Jerusalem Church prior to A.D. 70. Then we know very little about the Aramaic tradition which may lie behind the extremely hypothetical source Q. The difficulties surrounding any attempt to determine the extent of the so-called Jewish-Christian groups over against the Gentile-Christian are many and great, at least if we concern ourselves with the years between A.D. 50 and A.D. 70. What became of these Jewish-Christian groups after 70 is also very largely unknown.[1] The result of all this is that any talk of a Jewish-Christian tradition in the *Gospel of Thomas* must be very vague. What can be said about those " Jewish-Christian " gospels, fragments of which are preserved—the *Gospel according to the Hebrews;* the *Gospel of the Nazarenes*—is that the picture of these gospel traditions which we gain from them is just as indistinct as the reports given by the Church Fathers on them.[2] As early as the New Testament period one notices a tendency on the part of Jewish-Christian elements to align themselves with gnosticising tendencies, as a result of which a great deal of Jewish Christianity during the 2nd century —as far as our meagre information goes—shows itself to be highly syncretistic in character. The Jewish Christianity of the *Pseudo-Clementines*—despite an anti-Gnostic tendency—has been very

[1] Cf. J. Munck's critical account of the way in which the term " Jewish-Christian " was formerly used, in his address, " Jewish Christianity in Post-Apostolic Times," at the fourteenth general meeting of SNTS 8/9–59. Published in NT Studies 6(1960).

[2] See P. Vielhauer in Neutest.Apokryphen, p. 75-108.

much influenced by both Gnostic and Hellenistic ideas, and serves to point to the way in which Jewish Christianity developed.[1] In this investigation, in order to distinguish as far as possible this development within Jewish Christianity, and to retain terminological clarity we shall use the term " later Jewish Christianity " to indicate this late 1st and early 2nd century syncretistic stream; the most primitive form of Jewish Christianity, from the era of the early Church, will be referred to as " early Jewish Christianity."

It is probable that it is precisely these circles, influenced from one side and another, who preserved the apocryphal gospel traditions which were later assembled by the " Editor " of the *Gospel of Thomas*. The sources which this " Editor " had at his disposal may very well have been made up of an extensive body of material which has been preserved only fragmentarily. It is interesting to see how soon these later Jewish-Christian traditions disappeared; its remnants have been preserved only in isolated fragments of the Fathers or the Gnostics. When eventually later Jewish Christianity became a sect, and disappeared beyond the bounds of " the great Church," these apocryphal gospels lost their *raison d'être*. No single group had any real interest in maintaining them, and it is typical that they are encountered in collections such as the *Gospel of Thomas*, and—more by chance—in Christian Gnostic circles, where they were taken over, made use of, and developed.

There are, however, very few examples of directly "Jewish Christian " logia in the *Gospel of Thomas*. Perhaps the most striking is the saying about James.

> The disciples said to Jesus:
> " We know that you are going to leave us.
> Who shall (then) be great over us ? "

[1] Strecker, Das Judenchristentum in den Pseudoklementinen, p. 213ff.

Jesus said to them:
" Wherever you have come, you shall go to James, the righteous one,
For whose sake heaven and earth came into being."
Logion 12

Here it is James " the brother of the Lord " who is represented as the central figure among the faithful after the departure of Jesus. Here we are evidently dealing with a manifestation of a tradition, held by certain groups within the early Church, representing James as the leader of the Church—to some extent in opposition to Peter and John, whom the New Testament describes as the leaders. In the *Gospel according to the Hebrews* we can see how the interest centres upon the person of James in particular: he is said to have been present at the Last Supper, and to have been the first to whom the Risen Christ showed himself.[1] That it is " the brother of the Lord " who is referred to in Logion 12 when James is mentioned is clear from the epithet, " the righteous one," a not unusual title.[2] The expression, " for whose sake heaven and earth came into being," is also evidence of a Jewish form of expression.[3] James (though whether " the brother of the Lord," the son of Alphæus or the son of Zebedee is meant is not always easy to say) also plays an important part in several of the scriptures from the Nag-Hamadi library, where he appears, sometimes as leader of the college of Apostles in Jerusalem, sometimes as one of the three who received a secret revelation from the Risen Jesus. These traditions, in which James assumes such importance, may very well be evidence of the way in which Jewish-Christian ideas were absorbed by the extreme syncretism of the Gnostic milieu.

[1] Neutest. Apokryphen, p. 104ff., James, p. 8ff.
[2] E.g. Origen, *Contra Celsum* I, 47, and II, 13; Eusebius, *Hist.eccl.* II, 23, 4ff.
[3] It is a title of high honour which is here accorded to James. It is normally applied e.g. to the Torah, David, the Messiah, Israel and in the NT to Jesus, Col. 1. 16. Cf. the *Apocryphon of James*, dealt with by Puech in Neutest. Apokryphen, p. 245ff.

Another logion which in expression can be characterised as generally Jewish-Christian is this:

> <Jesus said:>
> If you do not fast from the world
> You shall not find the kingdom.
> If you do not keep the Sabbath as Sabbath
> You shall not see the Father.
>
> Logion 27

Here we have fasting, and keeping " the Sabbath as Sabbath,"[1] set down as conditions for " seeing the Father," i.e. conditions of salvation. But even though fasting is on this occasion given a positive evaluation, we have already quoted a saying in which four important Jewish commandments—on fasting, prayer, alms-giving and the observation of purity—are rejected. The question now is whether it is only in its outer form that Logion 27 may be said to be largely Jewish-Christian. The concept of " fasting from the world " has no support in the New Testament, and little in Judaism if we make an exception of certain ascetic groups. But on the other hand, it fits in admirably with the Gnostic's negative attitude to the world and the body. This double attitude to fasting in the two sayings may be understood as an example of the way in which the *Gospel of Thomas* contains material from different traditions; it may, however, point to two distinct meanings given to " fasting." In this saying, the injunction to " keep the Sabbath " appears to point to a Gnostic interpretation, of quite different content from the common Jewish keeping of the Sabbath.[2] Logion 27 is thus rather ambiguous, and it is very difficult to decide what is " Jewish-Christian " about it, and what belongs to the syncretistic interpretations of later Jewish Christianity or Gnosticism.

[1] For the Greek text of *Ox. Pap.*, cf. H. G. E. White, The Sayings of Jesus from Oxyrhynchus (1920), p. 27f., and for the Coptic, cf. Giversen, p. 67.
[2] See e.g. *The Gospel of Truth* 32.18ff.

It is also noteworthy that the *Gospel of Thomas* contains material which seems to have a polemic purpose, directed against certain doctrines of "Jewish Christianity." We have already pointed out that a negative attitude to fasting and almsgiving enters upon the scene; in Logion 53, circumcision is rejected.

His disciples said to him:
"Circumcision, is it of value, *ὠφελεῖν*, or not?"
He said to them:
"If it were of value,
Their Father would have created them circumcised from their mother's womb.
But the real circumcision in the Spirit has become of full value."

It is a hazardous undertaking to try and determine the origin of the contents of this logion. Paul polemises against circumcision, particularly in the Letter to the Romans, from which (2.25) we may observe that the expression, "circumcision is of value, ὠφελεῖν," is identical with Logion 53. The question of "value" is otherwise a form of words belonging to the didactic style of theological statement, and clearly corresponds to Jewish didactic usage.[1] We may compare this saying with a passage in the *Odes of Solomon*, where "circumcision" represents baptism; the difficulty is, however, that of knowing whether this passage is based on Christian, later Jewish-Christian or Gnostic ideas. The passage in question reads: "My heart was circumcised and its flower appeared; and grace sprang up in it: and it brought forth fruit for the Lord, for the Most High circumcised me by his Holy Spirit . . ." Ode XI, 1f.[2] (Circumcision is also interpreted in the same way in Col. 2.11.) But Logion 53 does not seem to be concerned with baptism; it rather, in common with the previous

[1] Cf. O. Michel, Der Brief an die Römer (1955), p. 75f.
[2] R. Harris–A. Mingana, The Odes and Psalms of Solomon II (1920), p. 265 and 268. Cf. J. H. Bernard, The Odes of Solomon, Texts and Studies VIII (1912), p. 72f.

Logion, 52, which is directed against the Old Testament revelation in general, polemises against those who would retain circumcision.[1]

The *Gospel of Thomas* is thus ambiguous in the sense that it contains on the one hand expressions and ideas which may have emanated from Jewish-Christian sources in general, though turned in the direction of syncretism, and on the other hand traditions which polemise against precisely the same ideas. This is a further indication of the difficulty which we have in determining the content of many of its logia. Yet another illustration of this difficulty is given when we consider the " additions " made to the sayings of Jesus, which have no equivalents in the canonical Gospels or the more important manuscript traditions, and which undeniably add a touch of Gnosticism to them. At this point we might put forward a comparison with the *Gospel of Peter*, which in many cases, when making use of New Testament material shows small alterations; one notices as a result an undertone from some unfamiliar milieu, Gnostic in character. The gospel narratives of the New Testament have been preserved as a basis, but at the same time the interpolations are noticeable.[2] The same applies to the *Gospel of Thomas*. We read, for example:

> Jesus said:
> [The foxes have their holes]
> And the birds have [their] nests,
> But the Son of man has no place to lay his head and rest.
> Logion 86

As usual, this saying of Jesus has become separated from its situation, Matt. 8.20 and Lk. 9.58, but is otherwise identical with the New Testament saying. It is, however, striking that the latter places a full stop after the words " lay his head," while Logion 86 adds the words " and rest." It is not necessary to see this as being

[1] See below p. 150ff.

[2] Chr. Maurer in Neutest. Apokryphen, p. 119ff. Cf. L. Vaganay, L'Evangile de Pierre (1930), p. 83ff.

a conscious reflection, but it is nevertheless most natural to see the additional phrase as being an embellishment based on theological ideas; " rest " as an expression of " the state of blessedness " plays an important role, particularly in relation to later Jewish Christian and Gnostic traditions. The important term " rest " in fact occurs several times in the *Gospel of Thomas*.[1]

There are many more examples of similar " additions," which belong to no textual tradition but should rather be taken as being a conscious interpretation building in a direction foreign to the New Testament. These tendencies are a warning to us, not to be over-hasty in making the many variations and divergences from the New Testament found in the *Gospel of Thomas* into important traditions. But there is a great deal of importance in the suggestion made first and foremost by Quispel, that certain expressions in a number of logia of the *Gospel of Thomas* have equivalents in the *Pseudo-Clementines*; this he interprets as evidence that a certain distinctive type of saying of Jesus existed in a " Jewish-Christian " milieu, and has manifested itself in these two " collections."[2] In addition, Quispel found " more than 100 parallels " between the logia of the *Gospel of Thomas* and the Diatessaron.[3] This agreement leads Quispel to the conclusion that there flourished, within a " Jewish-Christian " milieu, an original Aramaic tradition, which Tatian utilised by the side of the four canonical Gospels (the fifth source) when he compiled his Harmony of the Gospels. This Aramaic tradition can also be traced in the *Gospel of Thomas* and the *Pseudo-Clementines*, and it should be placed side by side with the above-mentioned ancient " Jewish-Christian " traditions which Quispel considered to have flourished independently of the main stream of gospel traditions, and to date back to the early Church. " They may be traced back

[1] See below p. 265f.

[2] G. Quispel, L'Evangile selon Thomas et les Clémentines, Vig.Christ. 12 (1959), p. 181ff.

[3] G. Quispel, L'Evangile selon Thomas et le Diatessaron, Vig.Christ. 13 (1959), p. 87ff.

to the descendants of the primitive community of Jerusalem, who lived on in the Near East almost completely isolated from the Gentile Christian developments."[1] When we remember that the existence of certain Aramaisms in the *Gospel of Thomas* can be demonstrated,[2] there is evidently a great deal to be said for an " Aramaic " gospel tradition.

It is, however, extremely difficult to be factual about this " Aramaic gospel tradition," since the material is diffuse and contradictory. In order to give some idea of the difficulties which are encountered, I should like to make some reference to another connection, which must not be overlooked when these primitive traditions are to be evaluated.

The most recent investigation of the Biblical quotations in the *Pseudo-Clementines* regards it as being less probable that " a Jewish-Christian gospel " is there quoted.[3] Many of the readings which have earlier been counted as being traces of a " Jewish-Christian " gospel tradition can be more conveniently explained in other ways. An analysis of style and context can to some extent demonstrate that the variants we have here can be ascribed to quotation from memory. Thus some of the Scripture passages are freely reproduced, and we have to reckon partly with stylistic alterations, which are due particularly to a closer approximation to the theme of the consecutive presentation, partly with deliberate re-expressions, e.g. the selection of parts of some sayings in order to stress other aspects. In addition we have the above-mentioned tendency to interweave quotations from the Synoptic parallels or to make new combinations of sayings of Jesus. But in some cases we cannot deny that there are traces, as Quispel showed, of an apocryphal gospel tradition, though to evaluate it is no simple matter.

[1] G. Quispel, Some Remarks on the Gospel of Thomas, NT Studies 5 (1959), p. 290.

[2] A. Guillaumont, Sémitismes dans les logia de Jésus retrouvés à Nag-Hamadi, Journal Asiatique 246 (1958), p. 113-123, considers that the agreements between the *Gospel of Thomas*, the Diatessaron and Syriac translations are evidence of Syrian origins.

[3] Strecker, Das Judenchristentum in den Pseudoklementinen, p. 136.

It is most interesting to assemble the source material which is considered to contain these distinct apocryphal traditions. Hitherto it has been pointed out that the variant sayings of the *Gospel of Thomas* have to a certain extent been encountered as well in the Diatessaron, in the *Pseudo-Clementines* and in the so-called "Western Text of the Gospels."[1] If we consider these, remembering that the variants of the *Pseudo-Clementines* and Justin have much in common, we get a " definite milieu " for many of these readings. Thus it can be demonstrated that there are well-defined lines of connection between Marcion, Tatian, Justin and the *Pseudo-Clementines.* Tatian spent some time in Rome, the implication being that he came into contact with the teaching of Marcion. The two in fact shared certain basic theological truths: an ascetic groundwork, teaching on the Demiurge, a critical attitude to the Old Testament, etc.[2] It has also been pointed out that there are several resemblances between the Diatessaron of Tatian and Marcionite readings,[3] Furthermore, Justin was Tatian's teacher, and it is not surprising that the links between the two are capable of further reinforcement. The relationship of the Diatessaron and the " Western Text " can also be demonstrated. When we find that many of the readings of the *Gospel of Thomas* are so close to the Diatessaron, the *Pseudo-Clementines* and the " Western Text," it seems quite clear that we are here dealing with a common textual tradition, which might easily be condemned as " heretical." This does not mean that Tatian was a Marcionite, or that the textual tradition in its entirety was tendentious, but we ought nevertheless to take into account that much of it originated from circles which showed a heretical attitude, and that it later flourished in a milieu characterised by heretical tendencies. At this period, during the middle and later

[1] Quispel. Some Remarks on the Gospel of Thomas, NT Studies 5 (1959), p. 282.
[2] Harnack, Marcion, p. 236f.
[3] See e.g. H. Vogels, Der Einfluss Marcions und Tatians auf Text and Kanon des NT, in synoptische Studien—A. Wikenhauser—(1953), p. 278ff.

parts of the 2nd century, there was naturally no clear distinction between what was heretical and what belonged to the doctrine and tradition of the great Church; we are dealing only with tendencies and currents of thought. When we remember that careful quotation of the canonical Gospels was not always the rule, as we have already pointed out, but that they could be quoted relatively freely, combining sayings of Jesus with one another or adding to the texts, it is reasonable to suppose that many of the readings which now exist in these documents are more recent variants.

But since so many identical readings occur in this group of scriptures, we must still reckon with the fact that, alongside all tendencies towards re-expression, there must have been a gospel tradition "at ground," such as e.g. the much discussed "fifth source" for the Diatessaron, the *Gospel according to the Hebrews* or whatever it may be called. But this tradition is so much hidden by the mists of time that it is impossible to trace.[1] In addition, Aramaisms which have been found in these traditions give rise to the thought that an Aramaic source must have existed, though we know nothing about its age, and we are in no position to be able to evaluate its traditions, since no one has seen more than a few variants which may have originated there. If we attempt to retrace our steps in time to the beginning of the 2nd century, we find ourselves caught in a tangle of hypotheses.[2] It is consequently very risky to make any definite pronouncements on the gospel traditions in the "earliest form" of the *Gospel of Thomas*, and we must issue a warning against excessive optimism, and over-readiness to accept the thesis that we are dealing with gospel traditions so valuable that they are to be placed on a par with the Synoptic Gospels. What we have to do is to weigh the

[1] It is naturally often difficult to decide whether the Aramaisms in the *Gospel of Thomas* should be placed in the category of general Semitisms, or whether they are real proof of the existence of an Aramaic "original source."

[2] Cf. the sober presentation and restrained judgment of M. Black, An Aramaic Approach to the Gospels and Acts (1954), p. 199ff.

relative values of, on the one side, tendentious re-expressions of logia in the *Gospel of Thomas*, variations due to quotation from memory or a more liberal attitude to the needs of literal quotation and, on the other, certain variations which may have emanated from a lost gospel tradition which existed parallel to the main stream. In addition, we must remember the important fact that the great majority of the logia which reproduce synoptic material are of a type of compound text which came into existence at a later date, when the three first New Testament Gospels were already known and used. Marcion and Tatian both attempted to present the one Gospel, and it is this attempt which finds its counterpart in the compound texts of the *Gospel of Thomas*.

VI

LUKAN MATERIAL IN THE GOSPEL OF THOMAS

WE HAVE already said that most of those sayings in the *Gospel of Thomas* which reproduce canonical sayings of Jesus, either whole or in part, consist of material from the three synoptic Gospels, blended in such a way as to suggest a Harmony of the Gospels. We can, however, go one step farther with these compiled sayings, and make the interesting observation that they follow the text of Luke rather than Matthew or Mark. It is by no means the case that there is an overwhelming resemblance to Luke, but the likeness is nevertheless sufficiently evident to be worth pointing out. The *Gospel of Thomas* on a few occasions makes use of distinctively Matthean material (e.g. in Logia 76 and 109), and in a number of sayings approximates more closely to the Matthean version, but in the majority of cases it is Luke which predominates. A typical example of this tendency is provided by the latter part of Logion 47.

> . . . and it is impossible for a servant to serve two masters,
> (For) otherwise he will honour the one and treat the other badly.
> A man does not drink old wine,
> And desire at once to drink new wine,
> And new wine is not put into old wine-skins, that they may not burst,
> And old wine is not put into new wine-skins, that it may not be spoiled.

An old patch is not put on a new coat,
Lest it should tear.

In the first section, on serving two masters, the word "servant" shows that the saying stands closest to Lk. 16.13. Similarly in the following sections, on wine and the patched coat: Lk. 5.36-39 provides the best parallels, having in addition the sentence, " And no one after drinking old wine desires new," v. 39, which is not found in either Matthew or Mark. As usual, the order of the saying has been altered—a couple of lines transposed, when compared with Luke; the typical combination of various sayings of Jesus; and an additional item, an augmented parallelism, which has no counterpart in the New Testament.[1]

Several other sayings show this marked preference for Luke in certain details, and this raises the question as to whether there is any special reason for this. It is conceivable, for instance, that the *Gospel of Thomas* and Luke may have made use of a common source unknown to Matthew and Mark. Thus when Luke, in the prologue to his Gospel, mentions that he had investigated the sources for the story of Jesus, and that " many have undertaken to compile a narrative," 1.1, it is not out of the question that he may have known and made use of different traditions from those used by the two other synoptic writers, traditions which crop up again in the *Gospel of Thomas.* But this is a quite untenable solution to the problem, particularly in the light of the blending of synoptic material in the logia. One is rather inclined to believe that the school of thought which collected and shaped the *Gospel of Thomas* had a distinct preference for Luke. Such an attitude is, however, far from usual.

The *Pseudo-Clementines*, for example, show no such tendencies. The preserved fragments of Jewish-Christian gospels—in common

[1] Quispel considers that this logion, with its careful parallelism, shows an earlier form, The Gospel of Thomas and the New Testament, Vig.Christ. 11 (1957), p. 194f.

with other apocryphal gospels—did not have Luke, but Matthew, as their main source and pattern. This latter Gospel provides the "central tradition," and was also given pride of place by many of the heretics of the early Church. Epiphanius tells us that Cerinthus made use of Matthew; Irenæus records that the Ebionites used the same Gospel exclusively.[1] Examples could be multiplied. But there were in the early Church a number of groups which kept mainly to Luke, among which we may mention the Marcionites. Marcion in fact rejected Matthew, Mark and John, and kept Luke as the one and only Gospel, after he had revised it to some extent. In this process he removed the first chapters, which did not accord with his Christological ideas, and made a number of more or less noteworthy revisions, omissions, additions, substitutions and transpositions. His intention was to restore the original Gospel and free it from all judaising tendencies.[2] Irenæus also mentions, when dealing with another group, the Valentinians, that they preferred to use Luke, saying that if they were deprived of Luke, a great deal of their empty doctrine would lose its support.[3] Origen in his turn knew that some heretics kept by choice to Luke, "*innumerabiles quippe haereses sunt, quæ evangelium secundum Lucam recipiunt*," *Hom. in Lucam* XVI.

The tendency of the *Gospel of Thomas* to prefer Luke may well be placed in this context. It seems to me improbable that the logia of the *Gospel of Thomas* should have emanated from a milieu which had no knowledge of the synoptic Gospels; it is much more likely that the synoptic traditions have formed a basis upon which, following the custom of the period, an attempt has been made to weave them together and present the Gospel as a unity. In this milieu, and as a consequence, the greatest affinity was felt to the Gospel of Luke.

[1] Epiphanius, *Panar.haer.* XXVIII, 5, 1; Irenæus, *Adv.haer*, I, 26, 2.

[2] Harnack, Marcion, p. 32ff., and 230*ff. Cf. E. C. Blackman, Marcion and His Influence (1948), p. 42ff.

[3] Irenæus, Adv.haer. III, 14, 3f., "*Et alia multa sunt, quae inveniri possunt a solo Luca dicta esse, quibus et Marcion et Valentinus utuntur.*"

VII

PRINCIPLES DETERMINING THE SELECTION OF MATERIAL

ON READING the *Gospel of Thomas*, one very soon notices its unsystematic construction. Sayings quite different in character follow one another, and theological ideas often give way to one another without there being any golden thread, or obvious principle being followed. This impression is actually due to the character of the gospel as a collected work, in which different traditions and different thought-worlds are represented without having been put together by the organising hand of a strict editor. But when we observe the way in which the " Compiler " of the gospel has brought together material from various sources, one wonders what the principles were on which he worked. For one thing, the material at his disposal must have been considerably more comprehensive than the content of the *Gospel of Thomas* would seem to indicate. The apocryphal gospel traditions which he evidently used contain a mass of narrative material, and also sayings of Jesus for which he found no place. Why, then, has the choice been made, from the point of view of content, on such a narrow basis?

It is striking to see what it is which is missing from the content of the sayings. For instance, there is no Old Testament background, despite the fact that it plays such a vital role in all the important gospel traditions. Those " gospels " in which it is most weakly represented are typical Gnostic products.[1] The idea

[1] The character of the *Gospel of the Egyptians* is much more difficult to determine, as only small fragments are preserved.

of the fulfilment of prophecy—so important in the canonical and Jewish-Christian Gospels—has no overall place in the *Gospel of Thomas*, either. Those Christological ideas which are connected with the question of the Messiah, and the suffering and death of Jesus as the fulfilment of prophetic promises, are of no interest to the " Compiler " or " Editor." The only occasion on which the Old Testament question is taken up is in one logion, where the Old Testament revelation is rejected.[1] Other vital ideas which are neglected are those which have to do with the Atonement and with the Resurrection. The Second Coming and the Last Judgment, though mentioned repeatedly in the canonical Gospels, are evidently of no further interest; consequently the eschatological problem has been pushed into the background, and the gospel may be said to have been " de-eschatologised." There appears to be little or nothing of any relationship to, or compromise with, the main stream of Jewish theology; hence when the ethical sayings of Jesus are reproduced, they are torn from their New Testament context of definite teaching on the Kingdom of God. There is naturally a great deal more which is missing from the *Gospel of Thomas*, when compared with other gospels—all the narrative material, for example—but it will suffice with what we have already mentioned. It is obvious that the gospel has been compiled upon some definite principle which excluded a large quantity of material.

If we approach the *Gospel of Thomas* from another angle, comparing it with Gnostic " gospels " and theological expositions, we notice that its content is—comparatively speaking—restricted. The epic speculations on the origins and spiritual nature of the heavenly world, on æons and angels, are never mentioned, even if a theology containing such ideas may be discerned behind some of the logia; nor is there any description, or explanation, of the created world and its origins. We must, however, assume that

[1] See below, p. 150ff.

such existed, particularly in those sayings which describe the nature of man and his share in the world of light. We seek in vain for a detailed exposition of the doctrine of the nature of man, though the basic point of view of this gospel presupposes ideas totally different from those of the New Testament. Whilst on this point we cannot avoid mentioning that such a limited presentation of the material as we have in the *Gospel of Thomas* is far from typically Gnostic. The Biblical references which we encounter in their literature are taken from both the Old and New Testaments, and the greater part of the material of the canonical Gospels is represented. The essential point for them was not so much to throw out large sections of the New Testament as to interpret sayings and narratives correctly, which task often implies a rather extensive manipulation of the text. Marcion's one and only gospel was certainly pruned, but nevertheless contained a great deal of material which found no place in the *Gospel of Thomas*. The Valentinians maintained—at any rate ostensibly—that the Scriptures were sacred, and they made use of large sections of the New Testament, though this did not stop them from interfering seriously with the text.[1]

Looking now at the content of the *Gospel of Thomas*, it seems first and foremost to be concerned with reproducing certain definite theological themes. What the "Compiler" of the gospel is evidently concerned to support and illustrate is approximately the following: the situation of man in the world, the corruptibility of this world and the human body, the particles of heavenly light imprisoned in the material world and their liberation, the Saviour's task here in the world, the way of knowledge leading to salvation, and the way in which the saved should live in this world. These are the foci of the gospel, and it is these which determined the material which went into its compilation. In this context, the basic view of Jesus is that he is none other

[1] Zahn, Geschichte des neutestamentlichen Kanons I, p. 718ff.

than the true revealer of gnosis, the mediator of saving knowledge.

If we now proceed to the problem of the more immediate motivation for this limitation in the choice of material, our first observation must be that there is, and can be, no overall explanation, since there is still very little which can be said with certainty about the date at which the gospel originated, and which group was responsible for, and made use of it. One can, however, reflect on various aspects of the choice of material, which may illustrate and perhaps explain certain of the points at issue. For example, if we compare the *Gospel of Peter* with the *Gospel of Thomas*, it is clear that the former stands in a much closer relationship to the canonical Gospels than does the latter and, in those fragments which we have preserved, contains a considerable amount of narrative material. But what is interesting, with this in mind, is to see how in the *Gospel of Peter* there is proof of a tendency, when dealing with material, similar to that of the *Gospel of Thomas*, though the tendency is more powerful in the latter, and clearly heretical. This has to do, not only with their method of using and reshaping texts from the canonical Gospels, but also with their content.[1] Without going so far as to say that the *Gospel of Peter* is Gnostic, we can say that it shows tendencies which recur in a more developed form in Gnostic literature. The presentation has in fact begun to be disconnected from " the framework of the Divine act of revelation "; this is the beginning of a process of development which culminates in the incorporation of the story of Jesus into the Gnostic myths.[2] This ties up with the fact that the Scriptural proofs receive a new implication, no longer being characterised by any decisive factors whatever, in contrast to the Gospels, where the basis is the fulfilment of

[1] On this point there are many resemblances, e.g. the combining of gospel-texts, and a freedom over against the synoptic presentations. Further, see Vaganay, L'Evangile de Pierre, p. 66ff.

[2] Cf. Maurer in Neutest. Apokryphen, p. 120.

prophecy. Furthermore, we can see how the Atonement is pushed to one side and the problem of guilt is watered down, showing how in these traditions we are dealing with a different conception of Christ and his work. There is, too, a noticeable tendency towards a Docetic Christology. If all these tendencies are developed, we reach the heretical (seen from the point of view of the New Testament) basis which characterises the *Gospel of Thomas*, and which has in all probability been a decisive factor in the selection of material.

If we now proceed to consider Marcion, seeking for the principles which may have determined his treatment of the New Testament material, there too we come across certain resemblances with the principles of selection which seem to be behind the *Gospel of Thomas*. In his book on Marcion, Harnack has given twelve theological motives which may have given rise to Marcion's deletions and alterations of texts, of which those applicable to the *Gospel of Thomas* are as follows: (1) The Old Testament cannot have prophesied about what happened in Christ. (2) There is an absolute contradiction between the Creator-God and his work of creation, and the Good God and his work of salvation. (3) The Good God is revealed, not as judge, but as the merciful one. (4) Salvation has nothing to do with the body; only with the soul. (5) Jesus had no earthly body and thus was not born. (6) Jesus demands complete detachment from the world and all the works of the Creator-God. (7) Jesus is to return on the last day only to announce the great separation *which has already taken place.*[1] The selection of material in the *Gospel of Thomas* has probably been determined by certain definite theological ideas, and these motives which have been revealed in Marcion may very well be said to apply to this gospel as well. This does not mean to say that it is Marcionite, but it does show a number of resemblances in principle to Marcion;

[1] Harnack, Marcion, p. 60f.

these principles occur, moreover, in other Gnostic literature, such as the *Gospel of Truth*, and that fact tells us something about the milieu in which the *Gospel of Thomas* was compiled.

It would obviously be possible here to go into comparisons with other authors and other literature from this period, but we shall limit ourselves to only one document, the *Gospel of Truth*, which also belongs to the Nag-Hamadi library, and which is usually dated as early as A.D. 140–150. We cannot, of course, draw too sweeping conclusions from the New Testament material provided in this document, since its exposition has a well-defined theme; it is not a gospel in the normal sense, but rather a homily or a doctrinal tract. But what is important in this context is that the motives governing Marcion's principles of selection, as enumerated above, fit this writing admirably. Particularly striking is the way in which the *Gospel of Truth* dispenses with the Old Testament background. Some have claimed to have found references to Old Testament texts, but the passages in question are so generally "Biblical" in expression that it is quite impossible to identify individual underlying texts.[1] This is made even more strange by the fact that the New Testament, to which this "gospel" often alludes, builds upon the Old Testament throughout, on the principle, "promise—fulfilment." In the *Gospel of Truth*, the thought of fulfilment has disappeared, and interest in the Old Testament has lessened correspondingly. It is furthermore quite usual in Gnostic literature to make use of the Old Testament, incorporating its narratives into the Gnostic system. But in the *Gospel of Truth*—as in the *Gospel of Thomas*—the Old Testament is missing, which may have to do with that current of which Marcion is *one* representative.[2] It can also be pointed out that this resemblance between the two writings, in their attitude to

[1] Gärtner, Evangelium Veritatis och Nya testamentet, in *Religion och Bibel* XVII (1958), p. 66ff.

[2] Cf. Zahn, Geschichte des neutestamentlichen Kanons I, p. 588ff., 593f.; Blackman, Marcion and His Influence, p. 113ff.

the Old Testament, and the motives determining their use of New Testament texts, may also depend upon common basic interests. The thesis of the *Gospel of Truth* centres particularly upon the situation of the individual in the world, and with the path he must follow if he would win gnosis and self-understanding, awaken from his ignorance and receive salvation. The same basic theme recurs in the *Gospel of Thomas*. What is missing from the two writings is a direct exposition of the construction of the cosmic world, and its connected myths, so common in Gnostic literature. This overall resemblance is also supported by details, and this document can often help us to a better understanding of a number of the logia in the *Gospel of Thomas*.

We must mention one further small detail. It has already been pointed out more than once that the *Gospel of Thomas* reproduces none of the narrative sections from the canonical Gospels. This can scarcely be explained otherwise than by saying that this has to do with an intense interest in Jesus' teaching. In a Gnostic milieu it is the knowledge mediated by the Saviour which is the essential factor; hence Jesus' earthly life and those of his miracles which have as their object the things of this world lose interest. In the apocryphal *Acts of the Apostles*, and in Valentinian gnosis, we can discern in this question a principle which also seems applicable to large groups of Gnostics, namely, that the earthly life of Jesus, Jesus in his outward manifestation, was nothing more than an illusion.[1] Jesus' high nature implies that he can alter his appearance, and take on many different forms (see e.g. the beginning of the *Apocryphon of John* or the *Acts of John*, 89ff.). His relationship to the human body was not that "he became flesh," but that he manifested himself outwardly as a man, and in various situations could choose whatever form he considered suitable. In line with this, we also read in *Excerpta ex Theodoto* 7 that Jesus' raising of the dead according to the

[1] Cf. F. Torm, Valentinianismens historie og laere (1901), p. 80ff.

Gospels was only of importance as symbolising a spiritual resurrection. In another text, *Fragments of Heracleon* 40, it seems as though it were only the " psychic " who demanded miracles before they would believe; the " pneumatic " required only the word of the Saviour. In the *Letter of Ptolemæus to Flora* it is also said that the word of the Saviour is the guiding principle of all things.[1] The natural consequence of all this is that the suffering and death of Jesus only appeared to have happened, and was of no importance. It may be that it was some such basic principle which determined the choice of material in the *Gospel of Thomas*, ignoring alike the earthly life of Jesus and his works, his suffering, his death and his resurrection.

[1] Epiphanius, *Panar.haer.* XXXIII, 3, 8.

VIII

THE GOSPEL OF THOMAS AND THE GNOSTIC VIEW OF SCRIPTURE

IN ORDER to estimate and understand the divergences between the New Testament sayings of Jesus and those quoted in the *Gospel of Thomas*, with all their deletions, additions, conflations and tendentious alterations, we must pay attention to the general principles determining the Gnostic view of Scripture. When we have once established an extensive degree of liberty in relation to sayings of Jesus from the New Testament, we tend to wonder whether this is due to an overall lack of regard for the gospel traditions, or whether it is one manifestation of a basic view of Scripture. This is not the place in which to conduct a detailed inquiry,[1] but by taking some of the essential ideas from the attitude of earlier Gnosticism to this question, we may possibly throw light upon the *Gospel of Thomas's* version of sayings of Jesus, and upon many of its more noteworthy variants.

According to Harnack, in the middle of the 2nd century it was the fashion to alter and forge authoritative texts; he considers that to be at least a partial explanation of Marcion's extensive reformation of the New Testament.[2] Marcion could see that both the Old and New Testaments were liable to tendentious alteration, and it was therefore up to him to extract the revelation from the Holy Scriptures, by means of a process of getting rid of the false accretions and distortions. He thus considered himself in a sense bound by Scripture and had no wish to propagate his own

[1] See further e.g. R. M. Grant, The Letter and the Spirit (1957).
[2] Harnack, Marcion, p. 65.

traditions, but wished nevertheless to refine, from the New Testament, the one Gospel and the revelation of the Good God according to the Apostle Paul. But if Marcion in his radical way interfered with the New Testament by accepting very few documents—and these in a revised form—Valentinus worked in a much more cunning way, according to Tertullian. " One man perverts Scripture with his hand, another with his exegesis. If Valentinus seems to have used the whole Bible, he laid violent hands upon the truth with just as much cunning as Marcion. Marcion openly and nakedly used the knife, not the pen, massacring Scripture to suit his own material. Valentinus spared the text, since he did not invent Scriptures to suit his matter, but matter to suit the Scriptures. Yet he took more away, and added more, by taking away the proper meanings of particular words and by adding fantastic arguments." *De præscript. haer.*, Ch. 38.

Irenæus on several occasions mentions falsification of the Scriptures as a characteristic of the followers of both Marcion and Valentinus. They recognise the authority of Scripture, it is true, but make irresponsible alterations, rephrasing and rearranging our Lord's words, changing their meaning altogether.[1] From fragments of Valentinian writings preserved in the Church Fathers, as in the case of the Nag-Hamadi *Gospel of Truth*, it is also clear that they did not quote the Scriptures word for word; their method was much more allusive, though the allusions are very clear: so much so, in fact, that their method of expression can be said to be entirely orientated around the Scriptures.[2] Their violent exegetical methods provide another reason for the strangeness of their reproduction of New Testament material. Irenæus gives an excellent and pointed account of this principle, in the form of a picture. Their procedures, he says, are like those

[1] Irenæus, *Adv.haer.* I, 8, 1 and III, 12, 12.

[2] The *Gospel of Truth* has in fact no direct quotations from the NT. See further, Gärtner, Evangelium Veritatis och Nya testamentet, and W. C. van Unnik, The " Gospel of Truth " and the New Testament, in The Jung Codex (1955).

of a man who alters a work of art, a mosaic, made up of a mass of tiny stones, and forming a beautiful picture of a king. By altering the positions of the stones, he creates instead a picture of a dog or a fox, and then produces this badly finished picture, saying that it is the beautiful picture of the king, and thus leading those people astray who are not familiar with the king's real features. "In like manner do these persons patch together old wives' fables, and then endeavour, by violently drawing away from their proper connection, words, expressions, and parables whenever found, to adapt the oracles of God to their baseless fictions." *Adv. haer.* I, 8, 1.

The Valentinians also used other authorities than the New Testament Scriptures. This may sometimes have to do with gospel traditions other than those which occur in our New Testament.[1] But we must remember when considering their use of apocryphal gospel material that in the middle of the 2nd century there was as yet no fixed canon of Scripture. The core of the tradition was provided by the four Gospels, but it is quite certain that there was a mass of other material which even the Fathers could quote without second thoughts. But more important than this apocryphal material—the Valentinians claimed to be the possessors of a secret, unwritten tradition, which had been passed on by word of mouth from the Apostles, and it was with its help that they were able to penetrate behind the literal meaning of the Lord's words and understand their actual meaning. Here we may make a comparison with a passage in the *Acts of Peter*, Ch. 20, which certainly cannot be reckoned as Valentinian, but which still gives us a very good idea of contemporary attitudes to the New Testament and its limited authority. Peter comes into a Church where they are reading from the Gospel scroll. He at once goes forward, rolls up the scroll, and begins to talk about the right conditions which are needed in order to

[1] Irenæus, *Adv.haer.* I, 20, 1f.

understand the written word. It is only through a deeper understanding of the nature of Jesus—his apparent manifestation in human form—that one's eyes can be opened to the Gospel. It is also into this situation that the secret apostolic tradition can be fitted[1]—the same secret tradition as the one which Ptolemæus recommends to Flora in his letter, when she seeks to win deeper knowledge and the spiritual understanding of Scripture.[2] It is this secret tradition which mediates the truth and is the key to the understanding of the sayings of Jesus, and it is therefore not surprising that Gnostic circles had a definite tendency to assert their own traditions, preserved within their own closed circle, as against those of the Church. They even went so far as to support their claims with lists of bishops of their own.[3]

This basic point of view was common among the Gnostics: the Apostles, as long as they were with Jesus on earth, understood neither him nor his message; this could not happen until he had mediated gnosis to them as the Risen Lord, which he did for some time following upon the Resurrection. This is extremely important for the understanding of the *Gospel of Thomas*, and its prologue seems to refer to this, as we shall see later. It seems to me to be important that we have this matter of the Gnostic attitude to Scripture clear in our own minds, for three reasons: first, because it shows us how such an attitude may have contributed to many of the logia of the *Gospel of Thomas*, with all their divergencies; secondly, in order to help us to understand how so much new and unknown material can have been combined with canonical gospel traditions; and thirdly, because it illustrates the deeper, secret tradition which is said to be found in them. It is also said, in *Excerpta ex Theodoto* 3, that the Saviour came to awaken souls and to kindle the spark which is the Divine element

[1] Zahn, Geschichte des neutestamentlichen Kanons I, p. 722f.
[2] Epiphanius, *Panar.haer.* XXXIII, 7, 9.
[3] H. v. Campenhausen, Lehrerreihen und Bischofsreihen im 2. Jahrhundert in In memoriam Ernst Lohmeyer (1951), p. 240ff.

in man, and that when Jesus gave his Spirit to the Apostles after the Resurrection, John 20.22, it meant that, " After the resurrection, when he breathed the Spirit into the apostles, he blew away and separated off the earthly like ash, and kindled the spark and quickened it." Not until they had been changed in this way could the Apostles receive and mediate the true gnosis.[1]

[1] C. K. Barrett, The Apostles in and after the New Testament, Svensk Exeg. Arsbok XXI (1956), p. 34ff.

IX

THE GOSPEL OF THOMAS AND THE OXYRHYNCHUS SAYINGS OF JESUS

THERE HAVE been many theories advanced in order to explain the background of the sayings of Jesus found in the *Oxyrhynchus Papyri.* The three fragments, *Ox. Pap.* 1, 654 and 655, which Grenfell and Hunt discovered in 1897 and 1903, contained 16 sayings of Jesus, more or less damaged, and some wondered whether these might not be fragments of the *Gospel according to the Hebrews* or the *Gospel of the Egyptians.* Others supposed a collection of sayings of Jesus, taken from various documents.[1] No definite conclusions were reached, but when the Coptic *Gospel of Thomas* came to light, the character of the *Oxyrhynchus Papyri* became a little less mysterious. The measure of agreement between the two discoveries is so extensive that we can go so far as to say that they both represent the same gospel. The 16 sayings from *Ox. Pap.* are all found in the *Gospel of Thomas,* even if they differ in a number of details. The order in which the sayings occur also agrees—with a solitary exception—in both versions. Analysis of the language used enables us to state that the Coptic version is a translation from the Greek; thus from the Coptic text we can restore the Greek logia in *Ox. Pap.,* fragments of nearly all of which are preserved.

The Greek and Coptic texts failed, however, to agree on many points; as a result, many wondered whether they might not after all be two versions of one and the same collection of logia.

[1] See further A. de Santos Otero, Los Evangelos Apocrifos (1956), p. 92ff.; W. Schneemelcher and J. Jeremias in Neutest. Apokryphen, p. 61ff.

If this were the case, then the Coptic text would be a further step in the direction of " gnosticising " the sayings, and would have been the object of some editing.[1] The disagreements are best illustrated by placing the most important texts side by side.

1) *Ox. Pap.* 654 (lines 9-21) and Logion 3. The Greek text includes one sentence which is missing from the Coptic, though all that remains of it is the phrase, " that which is under the earth . . ." Since this logion includes several sentences of a similar type, the most obvious explanation is that the shorter Coptic form is a result of an oversight on the part of the translator.

> If they who persuade (lead) you say to you,
> " Behold, the kingdom is in heaven,"
> Then the birds of heaven will precede you.
> (the missing clause)
> If they say to you,
> " It is in the sea,"
> Then the fishes will precede you. . . .

The translator seems often to be unsure of himself, and his knowledge of Greek is not always faultless; it is quite conceivable, therefore, that the close similarity between the sentences has led to the omission of one line. But we must not dismiss the possibility that he may have deliberately omitted something which did not accord with his theology. This may also apply to the next example.

2) *Ox. Pap.* 654 (lines 27-31) and Logion 5. Once again, the Greek text has a longer version than the Coptic. It is in fact the closing sentence which is missing, ". . . and buried, which shall not be awakened (or arise)." An attempt has been made here to explain the missing sentence as a result of conscious theolo-

[1] Puech in Neutest. Apokryphen, p. 212ff.

gical intervention. The resurrection of the body, which the sentence in *Ox. Pap.* was intended to stress, being unacceptable to the circle which used the *Gospel of Thomas*, has been eliminated.[1]

> Jesus said:
> Know that which is before you,
> And that which is hidden to you shall be revealed unto you.
> For there is nothing hidden, which shall not be revealed.
> [Gk. . . . and buried, which shall not be awakened (or arise).]
> Logion 5

But this discrepancy could equally well be ascribed to a careless translator. It is quite feasible to supply γενήσεται and ἐγερθήσεται at the ends of the last two lines; these words are so similar that it would have been an easy matter for the translator to miss a line.

3) *Ox. Pap.* 1 (lines 24-31) and Logia 30 and 77b. This is the only example of the two versions reproducing logia in a different order. *Ox. Pap.* has the following text:

> [Jesus sa]id: [whe]rever there are . . . [ar]e without God,
> And [wh]ere there is o[ne] alone, I s[ay] I am with h[im].
> Lift [up] the stone and there thou shalt find me.
> Cleave the wood, and I am there.

In the *Gospel of Thomas*, the first half of this logion occurs as an independent saying (though in an obscure form), Logion 30.[2] The latter half, though, is connected to Logion 77. Both versions agree in order on both sides of lines 28-31 in *Ox. Pap.*, though we do not know how this affected Logion 77, since this section is not in the Greek text. This makes it extremely hard to decide

[1] See works referred to above.
[2] Cf. Guillaumont, Sémitismes dans les logia de Jésus retrouvés à Nag-Hamadi, Journal Asiatique 246 (1958), p. 114ff.

whether this difference is accidental, or whether it means that the different versions show considerable discrepancies in the order in which the sayings occur. In support of the former contention we might point out that the Greek logion came into being by a process of association, leading from the thought of the first line, that Christ is present everywhere in the world with the "individual," to the pantheistic idea that Christ is everywhere, under the stone or in the wood of the tree. In the *Gospel of Thomas*, this later pantheistic statement has been coupled with another logion expressive of a similar thought.

> . . . I am the All.
> The All has proceeded from me
> And the All has come to me.
> Cleave a tree, and I am there . . .

The common factor uniting these two sayings is thus that of their content.

4) *Ox. Pap.* 655 (fragment 1 a and half 1 b) and Logion 36. The Greek text has a longer passage, built on Matt. 6.25, 28 and Lk. 12.22, 27, which has to do with not worrying about food and clothing, with the lilies of the field, and with the extension of the span of life. The *Gospel of Thomas* here has a much shorter version.

> Jesus said:
> Do not worry from morning to evening
> And from evening to morning
> What you shall put on (be clothed with).
>
> Logion 36

On this occasion it is highly improbable that the Coptic translator has been careless enough to omit everything that is missing, since that would be far too large a slice. But why should the translator have wanted to remove this passage, since it is entirely in line with the main topic: scorn for the body and its life in this world? It is clear from the following logion, in both *Ox. Pap.* and the *Gospel of Thomas*, that it is precisely the theme of scorn for the body which has given rise to the inclusion of the exhortation not to worry about clothes.

> ". . . When you take off your clothes without being ashamed,
> And take your clothes and lay them under your feet
> Like little children, and tread upon them, then [you shall become]
> Children of the Living One, and you shall not be afraid.',
>
> Logion 37

It may have been the keen interest in clothes, and its connection with a negative view of the sexual life, as seen in the following logion, which led the person who edited the Coptic version to cut out the longer passage in the Greek text.

Over and above these examples, there are a number of minor expressions here and there in the sayings which clearly witness to there having been some editing of the Coptic version. Thus a comparison between the Greek and Coptic versions makes it possible for us to say that the latter is not merely a translation, but is also a revised edition, as far as content is concerned. It is impossible to go further than this, and we must be satisfied with that observation, since our material is so fragmentary, and too diffuse to give conclusive proof one way or the other. A number of the above-mentioned discrepancies can very well be put down to mistakes in copying, and need not imply conscious theological alteration. Further, if the Coptic version, when compared with the Greek, has been edited in a Gnostic way, one might have expected to find interpolations and expansions, whereas the opposite is in fact the case. It is shorter overall than the Greek, which seems to me to be evidence that the majority of differences are due to the carelessness of the translator. In whatever way these discrepancies are judged, the same collection of sayings of Jesus seems to be behind both the Greek text and the Coptic *Gospel of Thomas*.

PART TWO

The Theology of the Gospel of Thomas

I

THE THEOLOGICAL THOUGHT-WORLD OF THE GOSPEL OF THOMAS

IF THE *Gospel of Thomas* is to be understood, if its character is to be determined and if the milieu in which it belonged is to be decided, then it is not sufficient merely to investigate its outward form—however carefully—and the possible traditional elements in the individual sayings. These investigations are of course necessary and basic, as we have tried to show in the previous chapters, though it has not there been possible to analyse the logia in detail, and evaluate their elements of tradition in that way. But so much can be said: that the gospel outwardly belongs in a Gnostic milieu, where it also seems to have originated. Further, it has been demonstrated how terribly difficult it is to try and reach behind the details of the gospel, to valuable gospel traditions; this is due to the fact that the logia bear such evident traces of editing, restatement and tendentious presentation. When working with this material, one is very easily tempted to be extremely pessimistic about the possibility of there being anything obtainable from these traditions—apart from sundry details—which might be of some value for our understanding of the canonical Gospels, or which might have any direct relevance to our estimation of pre-A.D. 70 gospel traditions. On the other hand, the *Gospel of Thomas* is extremely important in connection with our knowledge of later currents in the history of the Church, currents which were syncretistic in character, being both Gnostic and—from the point of view of the main stream of tradition—heretical. But in order to reach a right understanding of this side of the *Gospel of Thomas*, we must make clear its theological thought-world, here in Coptic dress. This demands a consideration of the doctrinal opinions which may have been held by the one who brought together a deliberate selection of sayings from various sources, and of the way in which these sayings are to be understood, if we would understand the reasons for the lack of correspondence between these, and the canonical sayings of Jesus. If these questions can be answered, then we may have some positive explanation to offer of the milieu, and perhaps even the period, with which this gospel is connected.

A very rough and ready distinction can thus be drawn between two main queries about the *Gospel of Thomas*: one analyses the history of every logion in tradition, asking whence it can have originated, and what was its original meaning; the other inquires after the meaning of the sayings for the person who gathered them, and how they were interpreted in the milieu which gave them their present form. We shall follow the latter path in our investigations.

There are, however, several reasons why this latter query is difficult to master. In the first place, when we come to interpret texts which existed within a milieu about which we know next to nothing, it is not always particularly easy to know where to start. Since no decision has yet been reached concerning the Gnostic circle which owned and used the Nag-Hamadi library, it is a perilous undertaking to tackle what is possibly the most difficult of all the documents discovered there. Nor is it so certain that the publication of other, previously unknown Nag-Hamadi documents gives us any better basis for the study of the *Gospel of Thomas*, since we are evidently dealing here with the collected scriptures of different Gnostic groups. This difficulty is emphasised by the fact that when we are working with texts such as these, from an unknown Gnostic milieu, we are constantly dealing with words which carry different implications from those which they have in New Testament or " Christian " theology. This can in fact lead the analyst totally astray. But there is one criterion which we can apply in the best cases—the testimony of the individual logia themselves. By bringing together different logia from the *Gospel of Thomas* in such a way that they illustrate and explain one another, we can reach certain main ideas in the gospel, and thus come to its thought-world by this route.

A further difficulty which we have to reckon with is that the gospel is not simple, if by simple we mean that it has been built upon only a few sources, and those all from the same world of ideas. Nor has it been transmitted unmolested. On the contrary, the sayings have been taken from different sources, owing allegiance to different theological systems, in which individual sayings contained teachings which were from the very beginning mutually incompatible. The theological unconcern which marks the choice of sayings in this gospel, and all the possibilities for theological interpretation which were in vogue, though we cannot know what they may have implied, urge us to be careful. The narrowness and conscious limitation of the nature of this selection do, however, bear witness to the existence of a world of theological ideas to which the " Compiler " subjected his choice of sayings, and which he made them illustrate, though in some cases their milieu of origin knew them as having a quite different content.

These are the principal difficulties which meet the student of the thought-world of the *Gospel of Thomas*. In order to " test " the material we can now select various ideas: the idea of God, how the world is comprehended, the way of salvation and its meaning, the view of man, etc. This gospel, however, lacks all teaching on creation-myths and all cosmic speculations—those very points in doctrinal treatises of Gnostic type which normally tell us the milieu in which we find ourselves. In this case Christology is a better guide, since it is normally quite easy to register differences and developments in the view of the Saviour-figure. Those Gnostic ideas with which we are acquainted are—in common with later Jewish Christianity—so distinctive when it comes to the question of Christology, that we ought to be able to make some observations here. But a Gnostic-inspired Christology is always intimately bound up with a mass of other important ideas, and so it is a matter of testing the material at a number of points in order to obtain a clear picture. The Saviour-figure can indeed be understood only from the cosmological aspect, the situation of man in this world and his way out of it. For this reason it is best that we attempt to find some leading points of view on the entire doctrinal system which lies hidden in the *Gospel of Thomas*, but with our inquiry constantly centred on its teaching about the Saviour.

II

THE PROLOGUE

Didymus Judas Thomas

THE PROLOGUE provides an important gateway to the understanding of the *Gospel of Thomas*. It contains first some words linking the gospel with the Apostle Thomas, and secondly, a hint that the sayings of Jesus in this gospel have a deeper meaning, upon the understanding of which depends salvation. These latter words form a saying of Jesus, the first logion. The prologue and this logion thus read:

> These are the secret words spoken by the living Jesus,
> And Didymus Thomas wrote them down.
> And he (Jesus) said:
> He who finds the interpretation, ἑρμηνεία, of these words
> Shall not taste death.

It is already clear from the words of the prologue that we are dealing with a Gnostic gospel tradition, since it is mainly in Gnostic and Manichæan circles that the Apostle plays an important role as bearer of tradition. The Gnostics are believed to have had three major gospels, connected with the names of Thomas, Philip and Matthew (Matthias), and one wonders whether it may not be one of them, the *Gospel of Thomas*, which has been found at Nag-Hamadi.[1] We do not know precisely how we are to

[1] Cf. Puech in Neutest. Apokryphen, p. 199ff.; Doresse, L'Evangile selon Thomas, p. 27ff.

identify the various "*Gospels of Thomas*" mentioned in the Church Fathers. It is, however, not identical with that document which has as its ingress, "The Stories of Thomas the Israelite, the Philosopher, concerning the Childhood of the Lord," and which used to be called the *Gospel of Thomas*.[1] This document belongs in fact to the group of "Infancy Gospels" and must not be confused with the Coptic *Gospel of Thomas*. The traditions for the most part speak of the *Gospel of Thomas* as a gospel for heretics, and in some sources it is stated that the Manichæans also used—or possibly wrote—a *Gospel of Thomas*. H.-Ch. Puech is of the opinion that the newly-discovered gospel is an independent apocryphal work, identical with that document mentioned in old sources as being among the Manichæan scriptures.[2]

According to one tradition, which is recorded in *Pistis Sophia*, Thomas, together with the two other Gnostic tradition-bearers Philip and Matthew, received a commission to take down the sayings of Jesus. "Hear, Philip, you blessed one, that I may talk with you, for you and Thomas and Matthew are those who have been given the task, through the first mystery, of writing down all that I shall say and speak, and all those things which you shall see." Ch. 42.[3] In the *Acts of Thomas*, which on many points shows a remarkable affinity with the *Gospel of Thomas*, Thomas is addressed in the following exalted terms: "Thou twin of Christ, apostle of the Most High and initiate in the hidden word of Christ, who receivest his secret oracles, fellow-worker with the Son of God . . ." Ch. 39.[4] Thus in certain traditions the

[1] See James, The Apocryphal New Testament, p. 49ff.; O. Cullmann in Neutest. Apokryphen, p. 272ff.

[2] Puech in Neutest. Apokryphen, p. 203.

[3] Cf. Ch. 43, where Mary says to Jesus, "Concerning the word which you said to Philip, 'You and Thomas and Matthew, you three, are the ones commissioned by the first mystery to write down all that is said on the Kingdom of light, and witness to it,' listen now, so that I may proclaim the interpretation of that word, that which your power of light once prophesied through Moses, 'Through two or three witnesses shall every thing be determined'; the three witnesses are Philip and Thomas and Matthew."

[4] The English translation of the apocryphal texts corresponds mainly to James, The Apocryphal New Testament (1953).

Apostle Thomas is the one who is particularly trusted, and the one who is the bearer of Jesus' secret teaching. The important fact is not that he is a normal bearer of the gospel traditions, as is the case with the canonical Gospels, but that he has been initiated into the secret knowledge which Jesus mediated and which lay hidden in common words.[1] Jesus has spoken the words to him, and he is therefore their custodian. This position of privilege which Thomas assumed is also noticeable in the introduction to "*The Book of Thomas the Athlete*," which is also from the Nag-Hamadi library. "The secret words which the Saviour spoke to Judas Thomas and which I have written down, I Matthew, who heard them while they talked together."[2]

In the prologue Thomas is also called Didymus Judas, a combination of names which is most familiar in Gnostic contexts. Thomas has the surname Didymus in the New Testament as well, three times in John, but is not called Judas. It is mainly in documents Syriac in language and origin that we encounter the combination Judas Thomas,[3] and in Gnostic or gnosticising circles he has two surnames: Didymus—meaning "twin"—and Judas. Thus in the *Acts of Thomas* the dragon of the underworld addresses him as "twin brother of the Christ": "I know that thou art the twin brother of the Christ," Ch. 31. And at the beginning of the same book, we read: "According to the lot, therefore, India fell unto Judas Thomas, which is also the Twin . . ." Ch. 1.[4]

[1] Cf. Ch. 78, "Why standest thou still, O herald of the hidden one? for thy (Lord) willeth to manifest through thee his unspeakable things, which he reserveth for them that are worthy of him, to hear him."

[2] Cf. Puech in Neutest. Apokryphen, p. 223.

[3] Cf. Puech, op. cit., p. 206.

[4] Cf. *The Book of Thomas the Athlete*, Puech, op. cit., p. 223.

" The Living Jesus "

Another important observation we can make when studying the prologue, and one which connects it with Gnostic or gnosticising circles, concerns the expression: " These are the secret words spoken by the living Jesus." That Jesus is described as " the living," ⲓ̅ⲥ̅ ⲉⲧⲟⲛϩ, corresponding to the Greek Ἰης ὁ ζῶν, in *Ox. Pap.* 654, shows that the sayings of Jesus which follow are to be treated in a very special aspect. The epithet " the living " when coupled with the name of Jesus is largely Gnostic terminology, and refers to the Risen Jesus. Among the many examples illustrative of this practice we may mention the *First Book of Jeû*, in which it is a standing epithet for Jesus: " The living Jesus has through the Father proceeded from the æon of light," " The living Jesus has taught his apostles that doctrine apart from which there is no other . . ." The phrase, " The living Jesus answered and said," recurs frequently.[1] The epithet is also common in Manichæism, as well as in many other texts.[2]

The point in using the term " the living " when speaking of Jesus is evidently to stress that the person referred to has emanated from the heavenly world, from the superior world of light in which truth and life are to be found. It is not the " worldly " Jesus who speaks as " the Living One," but the Heavenly Jesus, who showed himself to his disciples as the Risen Christ. The term " living " occurs also in the *Gospel of Truth* with this meaning, although on this occasion it refers, not to Jesus, but to " the heavenly book," " the living book of the living, that which is written in the thought and understanding of the Father, and

[1] See "Jesus, der lebendige" in the index of C. Schmidt-W. Till, Koptisch-gnostische Schriften I (1954).

[2] The Manichæan Psalm-book, ed. C. R. C. Allberry (Manichæan Manuscripts in the Chester Beatty Collection), e.g. 55.17. Cf. Puech in Neutest. Apokryphen, p. 184, 1, and the " Living Gospel " of Mani, p. 265.

which, ever since before the founding of the all, is by Him in the incomprehensible . . ." 19, 35ff. The expression, " the living " also refers here to something which emanates from heaven and reveals itself upon earth. " The living book of the living " in this text is closely linked with Jesus' work of salvation and his revelation in the heart of the Gnostic. When comparing this with other texts, one is even tempted to wonder whether this is purely and simply an image of Christ, the heavenly being who reveals himself here on earth.

The epithet " the living " occurs both in the Old and New Testaments; this gives rise to the question whether the ideas behind the expression " the living Jesus " must of necessity be Gnostic. However, in the Bible this is a title of honour which is accorded to God and not—though with one solitary exception—to Jesus. It is true that in the Gospel of John " life " is linked with Jesus as the one who reveals the divine and life-giving truth, but Jesus himself is not called " the Living One." He is " the living bread," the Spirit is " the living water," but " the Living One " is none other than God.[1] The only exception to this rule in the whole of the New Testament is Rev. 1.17f., " I am the first and the last, and the living one; I died, and behold I am alive for evermore . . ." This sentence has a formal phraseology, and contains a typical Old Testament title of honour, used of God. Here we see furthermore how the Divine epithet has been transferred from God to Jesus; this phenomenon can also be seen in the Pastoral Epistles, where the same epithet is used both of God and of Jesus. In Rev. 1.17f., the term " the living one," referring to the Son of God, is already in use.[2] That it is only a short step to the application of the Divine epithet to the Risen Lord is further shown by Luke 24.5, where the two angels say, " Why do you seek the living among the dead? " But the

[1] John 4. 10, 6. 51, 7. 38, etc.
[2] Cf. I Pet. 2. 4, where the " living stone " refers to Christ.

distinctive meaning and use which the term " the living " has in Gnosticism is not encountered in the New Testament. The context of the prologue to the *Gospel of Thomas* witnesses to the special use of the expression.

We also find the expression " the living " applied to Jesus in the *Acts of Thomas*, e.g. in Ch. 169; this prompts a reflection which is important not only for an understanding of the transfer of the epithet from the Father to the Son, as we have already noticed in the New Testament, but also for the " levelling out " of the distinction between the Father and the Son, so typical of certain of the apocryphal Acts. In these, it is in fact possible to read that the only God is Jesus Christ: "... Father that hast had pity and compassion on the man that cared not for thee. We glorify thee, and praise and bless and thank thy great goodness and long-suffering, O holy Jesus, for thou only art God, and none else, whose is the might that cannot be conspired against, now and world without end. Amen." *Acts of John*, Ch, 77.[1] Jesus is the Lord of all; consequently he is not called the Son of God, nor is God called " the Father of our Lord Jesus Christ." When the expressions " Father " and " Son " are used, they appear to be almost synonymous, so that " Father " can be an epithet for " God, Jesus ": " O God, Jesus, the father of them that are above the heavens, the Lord of them that are in the heavens . . ." Ch. 112. " The Divine Being," who reveals himself in a cross of light to John on the Mount of Olives, says that the being of God has many names, " sometimes Jesus, sometimes Christ, sometimes door, sometimes a way . . . sometimes Son, sometimes Father, sometimes Spirit . . ." Ch. 98. These names are valid in the eyes of men, but what this being is in itself is incomprehensible. The basic idea behind these forms of expression is that " Father," " Son " and other names are merely

[1] Cf. *Acts of Peter* (The *Vercelli Acts*), 20. See further Fr.Torm, Valentinianismens historie og laere, p. 75ff.

descriptions of one and the same ineffable Divine Being. I consider it important that we bear this in mind when we encounter some obscurity in the relationship between the Father and Jesus in the *Gospel of Thomas*, expressed partly in the ascription of the term "the living" to both.[1]

The Secret Words and their Interpretation

In order further to clarify the meaning of the prologue we must take note of the expression "the secret words," and its connection with the first logion, "He who finds the interpretation, *ἑρμηνεία*, of these words shall not taste death." "The living Jesus" i.e. the Risen Lord, utters "secret words" and says that the person who is able to comprehend their deepest meaning will gain eternal life. Seen from the Gnostic point of view it is extremely important to stress the way in which the Risen Lord mediates true gnosis. It was normally considered in Gnostic circles that Jesus accompanied his disciples and closest associates for an extended period of time subsequent to the Resurrection, during which time he gave them the perfect teaching, the right interpretation of his sayings. The basis of this idea is already to be found in the New Testament. According to Luke 24, the Risen Lord on the road to Emmaus expounded the Old Testament prophecies from the standpoint of his risen existence. In 24.45 we read, referring to the most intimate circle, "Then he opened their minds to understand the scriptures." Such an "opening of the mind" is decisive for the Gnostics, since they sought a deeper understanding of the scriptures. We can also at this point refer to Acts 1.3, which seems to be a relevant basis for the Gnostic view of Jesus, as expressed in later literature, ". . . appearing to them during forty days, and speaking of the kingdom of God." The vital point here for the Gnostics was that

[1] See below, p. 113f.

Jesus, as the Risen Lord, freed from his human bodily appearance, could teach his disciples, and interpret to them. In the *Freer-Logion* we have a supplement to the longer Markan final passage on Jesus after the Resurrection; it takes the form of a conversation between the disciples and their Risen Lord, and though it is not Gnostic in character, witnesses to an interest within the early Church in the period during which Jesus showed himself alive after the Resurrection.[1] This same interest, though more developed in the direction of Gnosticism, forms the basis of the *Epistula Apostolorum*, which contains a long conversation on doctrine between the disciples and the Risen Jesus. In this conversation Jesus reveals great and astounding things, and it is a special revelation from the Risen Lord which is claimed to have been preserved in this document.[2]

The Gnostics did not, however, limit this period of new instruction to forty days, as in Acts; they extended the time. The period which Jesus spent with his people in this new state, as pure spirit, is variously estimated—from 18 months to 11 or 12 years.[3] Irenæus, writing about the Valentinians, says that Jesus " after his resurrection from the dead, according to their claims, went about with his disciples for 18 months."[4] During this time he conveyed to them the final truth. " This he mediated only to those few of his disciples whom he knew to be capable of comprehending so great secrets."[5] In one of the many documents from the Nag-Hamadi Library, the as yet unpublished *Apocryphon of James*,[6] we read that the Risen Lord walked with his

[1] See Jeremias in Neutest. Apokryphen, p. 125f.; James, p. 34.

[2] *Epistula apostolorum* 34, " And we said unto him again: Lord, so many great things hast thou told us and revealed unto us as never yet were spoken, and in all hast thou given us rest and been gracious unto us. After thy resurrection thou didst reveal unto us all things that we might be saved indeed . . ." See further C. Schmidt, Gespräche Jesu mit seinen Jüngern nach der Auferstehung (1919); an English translation in James, p. 485ff.

[3] *Pistis Sophia*, " It happened, however, that after Jesus had arisen from the dead he spent eleven years, during which he conversed with his disciples," Ch. 1. Cf. Schmidt, op. cit., p. 202ff.

[4] Irenæus, *Adv.haer.* I, 3, 2. [5] Irenæus, *Adv.haer.* I, 30, 14.

[6] Puech in Neutest. Apokryphen, p. 245ff.

disciples for 550 days after his Resurrection, and that it is Peter and James who are there entrusted with the secret knowledge.[1]

The introductory lines to *Jesu Christi Sophia* give us a good insight into the Gnostic view of how the Risen Lord reveals himself and passes on secret doctrines to his most intimate disciples: "When, after he had risen from the dead, his twelve disciples and the seven women who had followed him as disciples came up to Galilee, to the mountain which is called the place of maturity and joy, still having no clear knowledge of the true nature of the all, the plan of salvation, holy providence, the virtue of the powers, of all that the Saviour had done with them, and the secret of the holy plan of salvation, then the Saviour showed himself to them, not in his first form, but in invisible Spirit. And his appearance was as the appearance of a great angel of light." 78. This figure of light, which can only be apprehended by the initiated, then reveals to them the great secrets; through this instruction the disciples need no longer remain in uncertainty, but gain an insight into the hidden mysteries. Not until this time were the disciples able fully to penetrate the gnosis without which none can be saved. Thus it is not until Jesus has forsaken his appearance in human form that he is able—as a being of pure light—to pass on divine truth.

The same reason for the final revelation, and the same insight into the secrets, are also encountered in the introduction to the *Gospel of Bartholemew*: "At that time, before the Lord Jesus Christ suffered, all the disciples were gathered together, questioning him and saying: Lord, show us the mystery in the heavens. But Jesus answered and said unto them: If I put not off the body of flesh I cannot tell you. But after that he had suffered and risen again, all the apostles, looking upon him, durst not question him, because his countenance was not as it had been aforetime, but

[1] Cf. *Ascencio Jesajae* IX, 16, where 545 days are mentioned. The important conversations between Jesus and Thomas, in the *Book of Thomas the Athlete*, also take place between Jesus' resurrection and ascension, Puech, op. cit., p. 223.

showed forth the fullness of power."[1] It seems to me very likely that the prologue to the *Gospel of Thomas* must be placed in this or in some similar milieu, when we read about " the secret words spoken by the living Jesus," the interpretation of which gave eternal life.[2]

The consequence of this view of the Risen Jesus as the mediator of true knowledge is that the sayings which Jesus uttered during his time on earth are nothing more than parables, the interpretation of which cannot be known until he has manifested himself as a being of light. This is particularly evident in *Pistis Sophia*, where it is clearly said that Jesus first of all uttered the hidden words—corresponding to the sayings of Jesus in their New Testament version—and that then, after the Resurrection, the disciples were given the power to reveal their secret contents. It is often the case that Mary or one of the disciples refers to some saying of Jesus, remarking by way of introduction, " You once said . . ." But these are only " superficial " sayings; there is a deeper meaning to them, which none but the Risen Lord can reveal, by virtue of the power of light, to " those that are of the light." Thus we find a large number of sayings of Jesus, as well as some Psalms, in *Pistis Sophia*; all are given a " spiritual interpretation." The way in which this process is thought out is well described in Ch. 83, where a distinction is drawn between the people of this world, with their " superficial " way of putting questions to Jesus, and the disciples, who have been given " understanding of the light," the power of " observation " and " a highly exalted mind." This latter quality carries with it the power to ask questions " from knowledge of high things "; the resulting questions are so advanced and full of intelligence that they can only be understood and answered by those who have

[1] For variant texts, see James, p. 167 and F. Scheidweiler-W. Schneemelcher in Neutest. Apokryphen, p. 359ff.

[2] We may also refer to the *Apocryphon of John*, with its revelations mediated by the Risen Lord to the Apostle. See Puech in Neutest. Apokryphen, p. 236ff.

knowledge of the mysteries. This step-by-step development in Jesus' teaching—from the secret and incomprehensible to the knowledge revealed to an intimate circle—can also be illustrated from Valentinian gnosis, e.g. *Excerpta ex Theodoto* 66: "The Saviour taught the apostles in the first place in types and mysteries, in the second place in parables and riddles, and in the third place, when they were alone, plainly and directly."

It is thus the Risen Lord who mediates gnosis in a comprehensible form of the initiated or, as we read in *Pistis Sophia*, Ch. 6, "As from to-day I shall speak with you openly about the truth, from its beginning to its consummation, and I shall speak to you face to face, without parables. From this time I shall hide nothing belonging to the highest and to the regions of truth."[1] Even if we are of the opinion that the teaching in *Pistis Sophia* is much more recent, and far more developed, than the *Gospel of Thomas*, we ought not to lose sight of the fact that the prologue of the Gospel accords very well with this view. Further, the principle of exposition which we encounter in these quotations also agrees with what we know of Gnostic Scripture exposition, with its definite relationship to the Risen Lord's disclosure of secrets. The *First Book of Jeû* also provides an excellent parallel to the prologue of the *Gospel of Thomas*, in its attitude to the revelation given to the disciples. There the disciples exclaim, "Lord Jesus, Thou living one, whose goodness is spread out over those who have found his wisdom and the form in which he appeared. . . . O, true word which teaches us, by knowledge, the Lord's, the living Jesus', hidden knowledge." Ch. 3.[2]

The saying of Jesus which is connected with the prologue—"He who finds the interpretation, ἑρμηνεία, of these words

[1] See further Harnack, Über das gnostische Buch Pistis-Sophia, Texte und Untersuchungen z. Gesch. d. altchr. Lit. 7 (1891), p. 55ff. Cf. The *Manichæan Kephalaia* 16.37f.

[2] Cf. Ch. 1, where the Saviour's divine origin is praised, and where it is said that Jesus received knowledge from the Father, the doctrine, "beyond which there is given none other, which the living Jesus taught his apostles, when he said, 'This is that teaching in which dwells the whole of knowledge.'"

shall not taste death"—also fits in well with this basic Gnostic view of the Risen Jesus as the one who passed on true knowledge and the true meaning of what the "earthly" Jesus had said. Life-giving knowledge lies hidden in the sayings which go to make up the gospel, sayings which are considered to originate from the "earthly" Jesus. There is even a hint that the "heavenly" Jesus is not only the Revealer, but also the "Interpreter" of truth—an idea common among Gnostics. In *Jesu Christi Sophia*, referring to Jesus, we read: "At that time the Light of this Power showed himself to be the first immortal male-female human, so that men might win salvation through this immortal, and awaken out of their unknowing to knowledge through the Interpreter, who is sent out and who is with you, even to the end of the robbers' poverty . . ." 94. The Interpreter who is Christ is in Papyrus Berolinensis called ⲣⲉϥⲃⲟⲗ, while CGI (Nag-Hamadi Library) reads ἑρμηνευτής.[1] Christ is thus the one who is sent, the one who can save by "interpreting" the secret knowledge. Farther on in the same document we read that the Saviour explained his teaching to the mature, and liberated them from the bonds of their ignorance, in which the "robbers"—the powers of the material world—had imprisoned them. "And I have explained the immortal man to you, and have loosed the robbers' bonds from him." 121.13ff.[2]

As a further example of this Gnostic concept, Jesus as "Interpreter," we may mention a few lines from a fragment of a conversation between Jesus and John. "Behold, I (Jesus) have expounded, ἑρμηνεύειν, to you, O John, all that has to do with Adam and Paradise and the five trees in comprehensible symbols . . ."[3] Jesus' main task is here to interpret revelation,

[1] W. Till, Die gnostischen Schriften des koptischen Papyrus Berolinensis 8502, Texte und Untersuchungen z. Gesch. d. altchr. Lit. 60 (1955), p. 16. For treatment of the term "robbers," see below, p. 177ff.

[2] Cf. The *Gospel of Truth* 27.7 "He (the Father) revealed of himself what was hidden, and *explained* it."

[3] See further P. Kahle, Bala'izah I (1954), p. 473ff., and Puech in Neutest. Apokryphen, p. 244f.

ἑρμηνεύειν, particularly as it is given in the Bible, and to give the spiritual meaning of the "superficial" Bible text. In the prologue to the *Gospel of Thomas*, the reader or listener had to win the "interpretation," of these sayings of Jesus, which interpretation can in point of fact only be given by Jesus himself. The term "interpretation" is also the same special expression as in Gnostic literature in general, standing for the secret gnosis which is expounded. Thus in the *Second Book of Jeû* the term "interpretation" is the permanent expression denoting the most secret doctrine, explaining "signs and secrets." The same applies to *Pistis Sophia*.[1]

This principle, of deep, secret knowledge hidden in the Holy Scripture, is known both from Judaism and from the New Testament; the fact of these ideas having been used by the Gnostics gives authoritative support to their declarations as to the revelation which they hold. In the teaching parables of Mk. 4, Jesus shows that the parables have a meaning which cannot be comprehended by anyone who does not possess the key to their understanding, namely, that Jesus is the Messiah and that the Kingdom of God is at hand. "To you has been given the secret of the Kingdom of God, but for those outside everything is in parables; so that they may indeed see but not perceive . . ." v.11f. In Luke 24.27 there is laid down the principle that there is a deeper meaning to the Messianic promises in the Old Testament, but that this meaning cannot be grasped without explanation. Here we also encounter the term ἑρμηνεύειν, meaning "expound," which is extremely rare in the New Testament, though the same term appears on several occasions in Clement of Alexandria precisely when it is the actual meaning of the Scriptures which is in question.[2] But what makes it possible to place the *Gospel of Thomas*

[1] The *Second Book of Jeû* 45 and 49, and *Pistis Sophia* 62. Cf. The *Manichæan Kephalaia*, where the "interpretation" also plays an important role, e.g. 6.20; 16.36; 17.3ff.

[2] W. Völker, Der wahre Gnostiker nach Clemens Alexandrinus, Texte und Untersuchungen z.Gesch.d.altchr.Lit. 57 (1952), p. 354ff.; M. Hermaniuk, La parabole évangélique (1947), p. 421ff.

in the Gnostic stream of tradition which we have sketched above is the context in which we encounter the concept of "interpretation," and the combination of terms vital to the Gnostics.

The knowledge gained by means of the correct "interpretation" makes it possible for man to avoid tasting death, as we read at the beginning of the *Gospel of Thomas.* Salvation means to obtain knowledge; knowledge, through the Saviour's mediation, gives life. This principle is not limited to Logion 1, but is uttered in other sayings, e.g.

> Jesus said:
> Blessed is he, who was
> Before he came into being.
> If you become my disciples,
> And hear my words,
> These stones shall serve you.
> For you have five trees in Paradise
> Which are not changed in summer (nor) in winter,
> And their leaves do not fall.
> He who knows them shall not taste death.
>
> Logion 19

A number of the expressions in this logion are obscure, and it is not possible to say precisely what they refer to; what is important in this context is, however, that knowledge gives life. To be a disciple of Jesus means to hear his word of knowledge, which gives a secret power over "these stones," whatever that may mean. (Some part of the material world?) Knowledge of the five eternal and immovable trees of Paradise gives eternal life: "He who knows them shall not taste death." The five trees probably have to do with the five æons in the light-world, mentioned e.g. in the *Apocryphon of John* and in *Pistis Sophia.*[1]

[1] Doresse, Les livres des gnostiques d'Egypte, p. 124, 22; idem, L'Evangile selon Thomas, p. 149ff. and Puech in Neutest. Apokryphen, p. 244f.

This should then imply that knowledge of the five mysteries in the heavenly world is something mediated by Jesus (" and you hear my words ") which enables the true Gnostic to " avoid " death.

We catch a glimpse of a similar concept in Logion 111.

> Jesus said:
> The heavens shall be rolled up, and the earth, before you,
> And he who may live through the Living One
> Shall not behold death nor <terror>. . . .

Over against the transitory world, which is a work of the Creator and is to perish, stands that life which is mediated by the Living One, seemingly Jesus. Those who have been entrusted with knowledge shall themselves not be subject to decay, since knowledge is the life-giving factor, liberating the heavenly life from its bondage to material things. The fact of this implication in Logion 111 places it in line with Logion 1: " He who finds the interpretation of these words shall not taste death."

A further expression in the prologue to the *Gospel of Thomas* which is important for the character of the Gospel as a whole is ⲛ̄ϣⲁϫⲉ ⲉⲑⲏⲡ, " those words which are secret," " These are the secret words spoken by the living Jesus." In the above quotations, taken from various Gnostic writings, Jesus' *secret* doctrine has played a considerable role, and it can be seen how this ties up with the Christological view of Jesus as the Living and the Risen, the one who bestows life-giving knowledge. However, if we investigate the Gnostic textual material more closely, we discover that the very term ϩⲱⲡ, " to hide," " to be secret," which is also important in the *Gospel of Thomas*, must almost be considered to be a technical term for the Divine revelation.[1] Furthermore, " the secret thing " often stands as an adjunct of

[1] Cf. The *Book of Thomas the Athlete*, the introduction of which reads, " The secret words spoken by the Saviour to Judas Thomas. . . ."

μυστήριον, " the secret," these being the two most usual terms with which to describe the content of the deepest knowledge.[1] In the *Gospel of Mary*, Peter requests on behalf of the disciples to be told what were the depths of knowledge entrusted to her by Jesus. She answers, " I shall tell you what is hidden," 10.7, after which follows a description of various central points in the revelation. In the *Apocryphon of John* the gnosis passed on to John by Jesus is characterised as the " mysterion," which may only be spread *in secret*. " But I am telling you (John) this in order that you may write it down and pass it on in secret to your kindred spirits. For this mystery belongs to that family which does not waver." 75.15ff. The mystery is the hidden knowledge of the heavenly secrets, the saving gnosis which is linked in particular with the true nature of the Saviour and with man's share in the light-world.[2]

Similarly in the *Gospel of Truth* it is a central thought, repeated several times, that salvation is linked with Jesus; this is characterised as " the hidden mystery," ⲡⲓⲙⲩⲥⲧⲏⲣⲓⲟⲛ ⲉⲑⲏⲡ ⲓⲏ̅ⲥ̅ ⲡⲉⲭ̅ⲣ̅ⲥ̅, 18.15ff. That which is " secret " is that which belongs to the life-giving knowledge, 20.16ff. In this document ϩⲱⲡ appears almost without exception as a designation of gnosis, or of the one who reveals it, i.e. the Son. " He (the Father) reveals his *secret*—His *secret* is His Son—in order that they through the Father's sympathy may know him and suffer no more: they, the æons, in that they seek the Father and rest in Him, in that they know that this is rest." 24.12ff.[3]

Another document with a close theological affinity to the *Gospel of Thomas* is the *Acts of Thomas*; in the Greek version of this collection of traditions are used different forms of ἀπόκρυφος, which corresponds to the Coptic ϩⲱⲡ, a word which is very

[1] Cf. The *Manichæan Kephalaia* 15.1.

[2] Cf. 76.15ff. and *Jesu Christi Sophia* 78.9f. See also Charlotte A. Baynes, A Coptic Gnostic Treatise Contained in the Codex Brucianus (1933), under the word " Hidden " in the index.

[3] Cf. 37.37f., 40.28f.

closely connected to the expression for revelation, also said to be hidden. It is a secret mystery. Of Jesus it is said, "Thou art he that revealeth secret mysteries and discloseth words that are secret." Ch. 10. And "Thou (Jesus) art the heavenly word of the Father: thou art the hidden light of the understanding." Ch. 80. The Apostle is thus the one who is specially trusted, the one who is "initiate in the hidden word of Christ, who receivest his secret oracles." Ch. 38.[1] "The secret," *τὰ ἀπόκρυφα λόγια*, is here also primarily a technical term used to describe the mysteries, and all that belongs to gnosis.[2]

The Prologue and its Relation to the Gospel of Thomas as a whole

The teaching on Jesus' relatively long stay with the disciples after the Resurrection, which was common among the Gnostics and which can also be traced in the prologue to the *Gospel of Thomas*, gave the Gnostics an excellent opportunity of referring large numbers of secret sayings to Jesus, and of building up collections of sayings and mystical expositions purporting to come from Jesus. In this way, the literary "epigones" were at liberty to compose freely, and to substantiate their speculations by giving them the appearance of being built upon those scarcely verifiable secret doctrines mediated by the Risen Jesus to his little circle of disciples, or to some individual disciple. Closely connected with these concepts was the Christological idea which gave this period in the life of the Risen Christ enormous importance for the Gnostics. For them—speaking generally—it was not the "earthly" Jesus, the one who walked this earth as a man, and whose life ended on Golgotha, who was the real Saviour, but the heavenly Christ who came down to earth from "the unutterable," through the æons, to liberate souls fettered in *hylē*. And the way of

[1] Cf. Ch. 39, 47 and 78.
[2] See also the introduction to the *Apocryphon of James*, Puech in Neutest. Apokryphen, p. 247.

salvation which he showed is the way of gnosis: knowledge of one's own situation, of the heavenly origin of one's soul, of the æons and of the Father. The " earthly " Jesus was a manifest being with whom the heavenly combined. Not until after the Resurrection does Jesus appear as the pure light; and not until then does he carry out his great work of mediating knowledge undisguised.

It may be thought that this is a far too advanced Gnostic concept-world to be applicable to the *Gospel of Thomas* in its present form, since the latter contains only sayings, and gives no spiritual commentary on them. But a survey of the most important terms in the prologue and Logion 1 shows that the " Compiler " of these sayings of Jesus considered them to be the true revelation—also referred to in other texts as " the secret." Thus the prologue points out the path we are to follow if we would understand the Gospel. " It is esoteric—or is considered to be so—and contains secret utterances hidden from the profane, but the understanding of which ensures eternal life for the one who is able to apprehend it."[1]

But there is one difficulty with this view of the *Gospel of Thomas*, namely, that it is not like other Gnostic gospels or tracts which claim to contain " secret doctrine." This Gospel in fact consists for the most part of well-known sayings of Jesus, without any direct commentary. The " Compiler " has evidently not wanted to present any commentary on the logia, but a collection of sayings of Jesus, taken from various traditions, and which seem to reflect the theological demands of the " Compiler," or demands made by the circle to which he belonged. We have in a sense, therefore, to admit that the prologue's view of the material does not agree particularly well with the material itself, if we follow our principle—of " superficial " sayings and their deeper understanding—strictly. The prologue indeed speaks in

[1] Puech in Neutest. Apokryphen, p. 205.

Gnostic fashion about " secret words," mediated by the Risen Lord, although the majority of these are identical with what the " earthly " Jesus had said; then the first logion presents the view that the sayings of Jesus contain life-giving knowledge, though in a hidden form, and that this must be deduced, as it is not explicit. In this context it may be possible to interpret the new combinations of sayings, the new compositions, the additions and the alterations which we find in the Gospel as an attempt to express the real meaning of the sayings. There are no logia which are absolutely identical with the New Testament, and those which have been altered may be an expression of the " secret doctrine."

This possible discrepancy between the introduction to the *Gospel of Thomas* and the following logia may be evidence that the prologue has been subsequently added on to an already complete collection of sayings. But so many of these sayings witness to the " Compiler " having had an overall Gnostic view of the material that it can scarcely have been the case that the gospel came into existence and was then given a Gnostic introduction. Instead, the " Compiler " appears to have brought together different traditions upon a definite basis, expressed *inter alia* in the prologue and in Logion 1. The discrepancy seems to be more apparent than real.

Are there then any logia in the Gospel which prove that the concepts which we encounter in the introduction agree with the basis of the subsequent sayings? In the prologue, Jesus is called " the Living," an expression which recurs in a few instances: ". . . then you shall become children of the Living One and shall not be afraid." (37). " You have forsaken the Living One who is before you, and have spoken of the dead." (52). " Behold the Living One as long as you live, lest you should die . . ." (59). " He who may live through the Living One shall not behold death nor <terror>." (111). It is difficult in these cases to know whether " the Living One " refers to the Father or to Jesus. In other Gnostic texts the epithet " the living " can be accorded to both, and it also appears in the *Gospel of Thomas* as an expression qualifying " the Father," as in Logion 50, where we read "... we are his children and the chosen of the living Father." In Logion 52 it seems to be quite clear that the term refers to Jesus;[1] similarly in 59. In the three other sayings, it may be Jesus who is referred to, though this is difficult to prove. We may also recall the transference of epithet from the Father to Jesus which we have previously mentioned in connection with the " levelling-out " of the distinction between the two in certain of the apocryphal Acts. It is in any case noteworthy that all five sayings belong to the category of " Gnostic logia," and that the term " the Living One " fits in very well with the Gnostic Saviour-concept of the prologue.

In the prologue it is stressed that the following sayings of Jesus form part of the " secret doctrine." There is a logion which expresses the same concept, and with which is also linked the Gnostic idea that the " secret doctrine " can only be given to those who are worthy to receive it, to those few who are trusted.

> Jesus said.
> I reveal my secrets, *μυστήριον*,
> To those [who are worthy of my] secrets.
> That which your right (hand) shall do,
> Allow not your left to know what it does.
>
> Logion 62

Here is the same view of the mystery as we have encountered earlier in Gnostic texts. " The mystery " is the normal way of alluding to the " secret doctrine " which is not to be passed on to all and sundry. We may make a comparison here both with the words of the prologue and with Logion 13, which refers to the

[1] See below, p. 150ff.

inability of Thomas to pass on to others the most secret part of the doctrine. We can also see how the statement according secrets only to the worthy has been linked to part of the saying in Matt. 6.3, "... do not let your left hand know what your right hand is doing," here used as an illustration of how to give alms. It is usual in Gnostic literature to connect the work of the demiurge, the material world, with the left side, and the heavenly world with the right.[1] It is evidently the same idea which lies behind this logion. Man must not allow the material—or for that matter anything belonging to this world—to encroach upon the heavenly. Those who are worthy to receive Jesus' "secret doctrine" are precisely those who have neither given themselves over to the world nor allowed worldly things to corrupt them.

It was important to emphasise, when expounding the prologue, that the Risen Lord spent some considerable time with his disciples, during which time he passed on his secrets to them. It is difficult to find anything in the logia which corresponds directly with this idea. There are, however, two logia which may very well be connected with such a concept—with the idea of Jesus as the Risen Lord. In Logion 38 we read:

> Jesus said:
> Many times have you desired to hear these words,
> Which I am speaking to you,
> And you have none other from whom to hear them.
> (But) the days shall come when you shall seek me
> (And) you shall not find me.

We have reason to parallel this logion with another which occurs in three versions: in Irenæus and Epiphanius, in the *Acts*

[1] See e.g. Baynes, A Coptic Gnostic Treatise, p. 25, " The simile of the Right-hand and the Left-hand—here mentioned for the first time—is used, primarily, in the treatise —as is in Gnosticism generally—to denote the spiritual and material principles"; Irenæus, *Adv.haer.* I, 5, 1; the *Hypostasis of the Archons* 143.32ff. (See the German translation by Schenke, Das Wesen der Archonten, Theol.Lit.Zeit. 10: 1958.); *Excerpta ex Theodoto* 37.

of John and in the *Manichæan Psalm-book*. Irenæus does not place the saying in its situation, and only gives a short commentary,[1] but in the *Acts of John* it occurs in the course of a conversation between Jesus and John on the Mount of Olives. John had gone there when Jesus was crucified, but it was only a body which was crucified and tortured. At the same instant Jesus himself comes and reveals himself to John, saying that he needs him as bearer of the secret doctrines. "John, it is needful that one should hear these things from me, for I have need of one that will hear."

In the *Manichæan Psalm-book*, Mary Magdalene is commissioned by the Risen Lord to go to the banks of the Jordan and try to persuade the disciples once more to leave their fishing and serve Jesus. She is to go up to Peter, and remind him what Jesus once said to him. "Remember what I uttered between thee and me. Remember what I said between thee and me on the Mount of Olives: 'I have something to say, but I have none to whom to say it.'"

It seems to me to be correct to bring together these various forms of one saying of Jesus, since they probably stem from one and the same tradition. It is interesting to see the way in which this logion in two totally different traditions, the *Acts of John* and the *Manichæan Psalm-book*, reports a situation which is closely connected with the Gnostic concept, that the Saviour wishes to give the true gnosis, after having been liberated from his "earthly" body. The fact that both traditions have to do with the Mount of Olives is also evidence that the logion was originally linked with the Risen Jesus, since in Gnostic tradition he showed himself on that hill. As Logion 38 now stands, it states that the disciples longed to receive true gnosis from the only one who could

[1] Irenæus, *Adv.haer.* I, 20, 2, "I have often desired to hear one of these words, but I had no one, who said it to me." The "one word" is then interpreted as the one God, whom they had not learned to know. Cf. Epiphanius, *Panar.haer.* XXXIV, 18, 13. See further in Neutest. Apokryphen, p. 218.

mediate it—of Jesus himself. But he soon leaves them, even as the Risen Lord, and they are left alone.

The other logion which should be considered at this point is 92, which is evidently a variant of the same theme, and is therefore to be expounded from the same background.

> Jesus said:
> Seek and you shall find,
> But those things which you asked me about in those days,
> I did not tell you then.
> Now I wish to say them,
> But you do not ask about them.

Clearly this part of the logion is directed towards a contrast between Jesus' "earthly life" and his life as the Risen Lord. Jesus said nothing during his "earthly life" about those things the disciples wished to know concerning the true gnosis. Not until after the Resurrection can he pass on knowledge about the heavenly world. It is this which is the highest, and this into which Jesus "now" desires to initiate them, but they are dull when it comes to asking about it and understanding it. Other Gnostic texts also witness to this dullness in the disciples.[1]

[1] Cf. *Acts of John* 96, where Jesus says, immediately before his Passion, " Who I am, thou shalt know when I depart, What now I am seen to be, that I am not . . ."

III

THE NATURE OF JESUS

The Secret which Must Not be Disclosed

SO FAR, in our estimation of the prologue and Logion 1, we have established that it is a Gnostic Saviour idea which is presented here. The Saviour is "the living Jesus," the Risen Lord who mediates and "interprets" the secret gnosis which can save men. Certain sayings proved to fit in well with that Gnostic scheme according to which the most important period of Jesus' activity is taken to be the time immediately after the Resurrection, when he instructed his disciples. One wonders now whether there may not be further material in the Gospel which can show us how Jesus was thought of. Is the Christology which runs through this Gospel to all intents and purposes Gnostic in character and presentation, or has it some other character? In order to shed some light on this point it may be of value to analyse a couple of logia which contain direct instruction on the nature of Jesus, the Saviour-idea stamped on the entire Gospel.

In the prologue it was the Apostle Thomas who stood out as the disciple whom Jesus particularly trusted, and who was allowed to receive the true gnosis. Logion 13 speaks about Thomas in the same high terms. But what is also of interest is that the logion in question contains concepts vital for an estimation of the Gospel's view of Jesus' nature. This logion may be split up into two separate logia. It might perhaps have been better to examine the passage as a whole, the theme being in any case the same throughout, but the logion is a long one, and it is simpler to divide it into two halves. Since the first part becomes clearer by referring to the interpretation of the second, we shall analyse the latter half first. It reads:

> And he took him, went on one side,
> Said three words to him.
> When Thomas came back to his friends they asked him,
> " What did Jesus say to you? "
> Thomas said to them,
> " If I tell you one of the words
> Which he said to me,
> You will take up stones and cast them at me,
> And fire will come out of the stones and burn you."
>
> Logion 13

According to this, Jesus has evidently in these "three words" given Thomas the key to the understanding of his true nature. The threat concerning the other disciples' reaction, as well as the words about fire coming from the stones if the secret revelation were to be divulged, witness to its being extremely sacrosanct. An explanatory parallel to this logion is to be found in the apocryphal *Acts of Thomas*, according to which it is the Risen Lord who sends the Apostle as a missionary to India. In connection with the narrative of the woman possessed by a demon, and Thomas's conversation with her, Thomas sends up a prayer, the introductory words of which provide a parallel to Logion 13b.

> Jesus, the hidden mystery that hath been revealed unto us, thou art he that hast shown unto us many mysteries; thou that didst call me apart from all my fellows spakest unto me three (Syr. one) words wherewith I am inflamed, and am not able to speak them unto others.
>
> *Acts of Thomas*, Ch. 47

It is probable that the *Acts of Thomas* and Logion 13 are built upon one and the same tradition, though expressed somewhat differently. The main point of divergence concerns the threat of punishment. Here it is the Apostle who is inflamed by the deep secret he has received; there is no mention of devouring fire, nor of stoning, but only that he is not allowed to repeat the words to anyone. Logion 13b is in a more extended form: " If I tell you one of the words which he said to me, you will take up stones and cast them at me, and fire will come out of the stones and burn you." It is typical of Old Testament and Jewish teaching that God punishes with fire anyone who violates his name and his glory,[1] and this motif is also suited to Gnostic doctrine. Disclosure of the secret words implies that Thomas should be stoned—the Jewish reaction to anyone who pollutes the name of God by pronouncing it; but a punishing fire also comes out of the weapons used, the stones, to destroy the person who attacked the true Gnostic. The deepest mystery was indeed not to be dealt out to the unworthy. We may also observe that the same motif is found in the narrative of the demon and the woman, immediately before the passage from Thomas's prayer which we have quoted above. There, in Ch. 47, we read that the evil spirit found out far too much about the mysteries, and therefore had to be destroyed by fire. " This devil hath shown naught that is alien or strange to him, but his own nature, wherein also he shall be consumed, for verily the fire shall destroy him utterly and the smoke of it shall be scattered abroad."

Furthermore, the theme of Logion 13b is typical of Gnostic texts, or more recent legendary material which has been influenced by Gnosticism. It is not only of Thomas that it is related how he is taken on one side and initiated into the secrets; the same applies e.g. to Peter, James and Bartholemew. " Leave James and Peter to me, that I may fill them with fullness. And when he had called them both, he drew them aside, at the same time command-

[1] E.g. Lev. 10. 2, Num. 16. 35, Judg. 6. 21.

ing the others to attend to their tasks." (*Apocryphon of James.*) In the same document we read that James said to Peter, " Nevertheless, since you are a servant of holy salvation, control yourself, and beware of conveying this book to many persons, for the Saviour does not want us to entrust it to all us his disciples, without distinction."[1]

The concept of the secret which must not be disclosed, not even to the Apostles, can also be found in the *Gospel of Bartholemew*. Mary, the mother of Jesus, who had carried Jesus in her womb, gives this answer to the Apostles' question: " Ask me not concerning this mystery. If I should begin to tell you, fire would issue forth out of my mouth and consume all the world." The idea that the disclosure of the deepest secrets is dangerous to the whole cosmos is here expressed with great clarity. Further on in the narrative of Mary and the Apostles, however, it is said that despite this Mary began to relate what happened in the Temple at the Annunciation. At once the punishment struck. " And as she was saying this, fire issued out of her mouth; and the world was on the point of coming to an end. But Jesus appeared quickly and said unto Mary: Utter not this mystery, or this day my whole creation will come to an end."[2] From these examples it is clear that in Logion 13b we encounter a concept which was fairly widespread in Gnostic circles, that certain trusted Apostles received teaching of such secrecy that its disclosure would have fatal consequences for the whole world.

The Three Secret Words

What kind of a concept can it be which lies behind the expression "the three words," which Jesus, according to Logion 13b, entrusted only to Thomas? To judge from the version

[1] Cf. Puech in Neutest. Apokryphen, p. 247f. For the role of Bartholemew, see e.g. James, p. 167ff.
[2] James, p.172.

given us in the *Acts of Thomas*, the three words must have to do with the most secret of all secrets, connected with the nature of Jesus. The deepest secret in Jesus' nature is often linked with his name, a name which cannot be bestowed indiscriminately. Further material illustrating the idea that the Saviour's nature lies hidden in his name is to be found in the *Martyrdom of Thomas.* Among the many questions asked by the Indian King Misdeus of the imprisoned Thomas is one which is particularly interesting in this context. "And Misdeus said: Who is thy Lord? and what is his name? and of what country is he? And Thomas said: My Lord is thy master, and he is Lord of heaven and earth. And Misdeus saith: What is his name? Thomas saith: Thou canst not hear his true name, *τὸ ἀληθινὸν ὄνομα,* at this time; but the name that was given unto him is Jesus Christ." Here we have a new example of the way in which Thomas refuses to disclose the hidden mystery, the Saviour's actual name, since the name would reveal the secrets of his innermost nature.[1] In addition, this connection between Jesus' name and the deepest secrets of his nature occurs as an important element in other Nag-Hamadi scriptures. The *Gospel of Philip* on more than one occasion speaks of the mysterious name which Jesus bears, a name which is not to be pronounced. "One single name in the world is not to be spoken, the name which the Father gave to the Son, which is exalted over all things, which is the Father's name. For the Son would not be the Father if the name of the Father were not ascribed to him. Those who have that name surely know it, but do not speak about it." 102.5ff.[2]

The *Gospel of Truth* contains similar texts, which say that the name which the Son bears is the unspeakable name, the most secret name, linked with the nature and origin of the Son. "But the Father's Name is the Son. He was that which first named

[1] Cf. the *Martyrdom of Matthew* 15. (Lipsius-Bonnet, Acta apostolorum apocrypha II, 1,236).

[2] 104.4ff. and 110.7ff. also reproduce mystical expositions of the name of Jesus.

that which proceeded from himself, which was himself and (which) he bore as Son. He gave him his name, which he had. . . . He has the Name—he has the Son. It is possible to see him (the Son), but the Name is invisible, for it is alone the mystery of the invisible . . ." 38.6ff.—" For that Name does not belong to (the normal) words, λέξις, and his Name is not among denominations, but is invisible." 39.4f.[1]

It seems probable that behind " the three words " in Logion 13b lie these or similar speculations about Jesus' unspeakable name, and it is particularly in Gnostic circles that this atmosphere of secrecy surrounds it.[2] It is conceivable that this motif may have emanated from Jewish speculation on the name of God, " I am that I am, אהיה אשר אהיה." Ex. 3, 14, but in that case we must reckon with the fact that the logion, as it now stands and in the context in which it is now placed, has been coloured by Gnostic interpretation. We may refer at this point to a speculation on three words—or three letters—in *Pistis Sophia*, to which is connected just such a secret " interpretation." " And Jesus cried out; being with his disciples, who were dressed in linen clothes, he turned to the four corners of the world, and said: *ϊαω· ϊαω· ϊαω*. Its interpretation is: Iota, because the all has proceeded; Alpha, because it shall return; Omega, because the consummation of all consummations shall take place." Ch. 136.

This tradition of the three secret words in the *Gospel of Thomas* recurs in the *Manichæan Kephalaia*, in which "the three words," **ⲡϣⲟⲙⲧ ⲛϣⲉϫⲉ**, stands as a special term in the introduction, denoting the innermost heart of the revelation. Unfortunately this entire passage is fragmentary, and thus we do not find the explanation we would have wished for. But from that part of the text which is preserved, we gain the impression that

[1] 40.1ff. interprets the name by " the Son," and his revelation of gnosis is said to be connected with his name. Cf. *Excerpta ex Theodoto* 26.1.

[2] See e.g. Irenæus, *Adv.haer.* I, 14 and II, 24. Cf. H. Leisegang, Die Gnosis (1955), p. 327ff.

the passage contains in broad outline the main points of the subsequent long doctrinal exposition. " The teacher " evidently means that he has written down this doctrine under the name of " the three words " in his longer writings, " The Great Gospel," " The Treasure of Life," etc. " For [these three] words are the measure of all wisdom. All that has [happened] and all that is to [happen] is written in them . . . [The] scribe [who revealed] these three great words [is the true scribe]. Furthermore, the teacher who teaches and preaches from these [three words is] the true teacher. Behold I, I also, [have revealed] these three great words and given them to you . . ."[1] It is most probable that this tradition about " the three words " was taken over from the *Gospel of Thomas*, and then won acceptance in the Manichæan scriptures—a way followed by several other traditions from the same gospel.

We may also observe that the unutterable "name" is in other Gnostic writings connected with the number three, and that in the *Gospel of Thomas* we are therefore dealing with a common Gnostic tradition. Hence in *Excerpta ex Theodoto* 31.1f. an account is given of a Valentinian speculation in which "the Name" is identical with the Son, identical with Form, *μορφή*, identical with Knowledge, *γνῶσις*. The Name is here an expression of unity, but is nevertheless divided up into three " functions," as a word is divided into letters.[2]

This fear lest the hidden name should be disclosed to those who are still immature, or unworthy, is based on the belief that the one who knows a name exercises a certain degree of power over the thing which the name describes, a power which can be misused. Thus it is also common in Gnostic circles to find warnings being issued against sharing gnosis with the unworthy.[3] In the *Apocryphon of John*, Jesus warns against just such a practice

[1] The *Manichæan Kephalaia* 5.26ff.
[2] Cf. F. Sagnard, Extraits de Théodote (Sources chrétiennes 23, 1948), p. 127.
[3] See e.g. the *Gospel of Truth* 21.3ff.

with these words: "Cursed is everyone who communicates it for the sake of a gift, or for the sake of food, or for the sake of drink, or for the sake of clothes, or for the sake of anything similar."[1] Nothing belonging to this world can be given in exchange for knowledge, gnosis. The same principle is uttered in the *Gospel of Thomas*, Logion 62: "I reveal my secrets to those [who are worthy of my] secrets."

The Unutterable Nature of Jesus

If we now turn to the first half of Logion 13, which deals with the same theme as that we have already described, we find a concept of Jesus' mysterious and unutterable nature which fits in well with the above-mentioned Gnostic Saviour-idea.

> Jesus said to his disciples:
> "Liken me (to something), and tell me whom I am like."
> Simon Peter said to him:
> "You are like a righteous angel."
> Matthew said to him:
> "You are like a wise philosopher."
> Thomas said to him:
> "Master, my mouth is not at all able to bear
> That I say whom you are like."
> Jesus said:
> "I am not your master.
> Since you have drunk, you have become drunk
> With that sparkling source which I have measured out."

This logion is evidently an edited and expanded form of Mk. 8.29, "And he asked them, 'But who do you say that I am?' Peter answered him, 'You are the Christ.'" It is probable that the "Composer" of the logion has reminded himself of the

[1] The same tradition in the *Second Book of Jeû*, Ch. 43.

three alternatives in the previous verse of the Markan text, where Jesus asked the question, " Who do men say that I am? " and received the answers, " John the Baptist . . . Elijah and . . . one of the prophets." The Markan text is a central Christological text, as is Logion 13a. There is no need to make any further comment on Thomas's unwillingness to answer the question which was put to him. It is quite consistent with what has been said above on Thomas's refusal to pronounce the unutterable name of God, when he now says, " My mouth is not at all able to bear that I say whom you are like."

One question which it is worthy pursuing further concerns the reasons for the re-expression of the synoptic text's " But who do you say that I am? " as " Liken me (to something), and tell me whom I am like." It is only natural that a Gnostic, according to the teaching of the *Gospel of Thomas*, had no particular interest in attempting to identify the Saviour with any kind of Messiah in Old Testament—Jewish meaning. The Old Testament background is indeed conspicuous by its absence, and the task of the Saviour, and his conduct in the world have totally different dimensions from anything we see in Christian or Jewish-Christian traditions. It is for this reason that the re-expression is of such interest. On the other hand, what could be of interest to the Gnostic would be to find support for the relation of the nature of Jesus to the created world. It is important in Gnostic theology to present that which belongs to the eternal, heavenly mystery as something so far exalted above the world that it is by and large impossible to compare it with anything belonging to this world. It is therefore meaningful to allow Jesus to ask his disciples if there is anything with which he can be compared, for it is clear from the answers which are given that the Saviour cannot be compared with anything created, whether angel or the wisest of men.

It is well that we remember an important principle among

the Gnostics, namely, that knowledge of the heavenly things is in general impossible to express in words which men can grasp. Thomas says that his mouth cannot bear to pronounce anything which has to do with the nature of Jesus and the heavenly world. The expression occurs again, in the *Hypostasis of the Archons*, 141.13ff., where the "author" of this document speaks of the angel of the Holy Spirit in the following terms: "I should, however, be unable to describe this angel's power. His form was like pure gold and his garments were like snow. For my mouth will not be able to bear that I describe his power and the appearance of his face." In general, it can be said of the Gnostic idea of God that knowledge of the real nature of God can only be reached when the outer bodily senses are ignored, for God can only be comprehended by the spiritual, and adored with "the voice of silence" with which the Spirit speaks.[1] It was for this reason that the Saviour had to appear in a form foreign to him—in the dress of this world—so that men could see and hear him.

The *Apocryphon of John* is in this respect typical in its long description of the nature of God, a description the object of which is to demonstrate that human expressions are useless when it comes to dressing the deepest gnosis in words, 22ff. Christ, in his conversation with John, finally gives up his attempt to explain the secrets which contain his knowledge, saying, "What shall I tell you about him, the Incomprehensible—the appearance of light—corresponding to what I shall be able to understand—for who shall ever understand him—in the way in which I shall be able to speak to you?" 26.1ff. The only ones who can grasp anything of this are those who have lived in the heavenly world, "head over the æons." "For none of us came to know how it is with the Unfathomable, except the one who has lived in it." 26.11ff. In *Pistis Sophia*, Jesus makes a statement on this principle,

[1] The *Martyrdom of Peter* 10 (Lipsius-Bonnet I, 96, 12ff.)

after Mary had asked what "the 24 invisible ones" in the thirteenth æon were like. "What is there in this world which resembles them, or rather, what place is there in this world which is comparable with them? And now, with what shall I compare them, or rather, what shall I say concerning them? For nothing exists in this world with which I might compare them, and no kind exists in it which might be compared to them. And now, nothing exists in this world which is of the character of heaven . . ." Ch. 84. We can thus say, in line with this, that when in Logion 13a we read that the Apostles cannot compare Jesus with anything whatever, we are dealing with an essential Christological statement. Everything which has to do with this creation shall perish, and hence it is impracticable to compare any part of the kingdom of light with the things of this world.[1]

The Intoxication of Knowledge

In this logion, Jesus answers Thomas in words which throw further light upon the ideas which are connected with the Saviour-idea in this gospel. "Since you have drunk, you have become drunk with that sparkling source which I have measured out."

Thomas is the only one who has understood anything of the secret nature of Jesus, and he can therefore be said to be "drunk" with the knowledge of this secret. As a background to this part of Logion 13 it would seem that we must reckon with John 4.14, or with some Jewish or Jewish-Christian tradition having similar contents. The motif is a common one;[2] in Jesus' conversation with the woman of Samaria he says, ". . . but whoever drinks of the water that I shall give him will never thirst; the water that I shall give him will become in him a spring of water welling up

[1] Cf. the *Acts of Thomas* 34.
[2] See J. Daniélou, Le symbolisme de l'eau vive, Revue des sciences religieuses 32 (1958), p. 335ff.

to eternal life." In the Johannine milieu, this "spring" refers to the Holy Spirit; it also refers to the knowledge which comes through the Spirit (Cf. John 7.37ff.), and a mass of material comparative to this can be found in Jewish texts.[1] A combination of the Spirit, the spring of water and Christ is found e.g. in the syncretistic Jewish-Christian *Gospel according to the Hebrews*, in which is described how the Spirit is united with Jesus at his baptism. " And it came to pass when the Lord was come up out of the water, the whole fount of the Holy Spirit descended and rested upon him . . ."

But this description of the Spirit as a "spring" does not help us in our attempt to be more precise about the contents of this part of Logion 13a. Nor does there appear to be anything more than a general resemblance to the *Acts of Thomas*, where the theme of "drinking from the fountain" occurs on a couple of occasions, e.g. in Thomas's prayer to Jesus for King Gundaphorus and his brother, who had been "converted": "And give them drink out of thine immortal fountain which is neither fouled nor drieth up, Ch. 25.[2] In purely Gnostic texts, " fountain," πηγή, often refers to the Father. The Father is described in the *Apocryphon of John* in these words: " He has told us that, he who comprehends himself in his own light which surrounds him, he who is indeed the fountain of the water of life, the light full of purity. The fountain of the Spirit streamed forth from the living water of light . . ." 26.14ff. The " Fountain " which is the Father is here associated in the Gnostic manner with light, life and the Spirit, all expressive of that which gives life, proceeding from the one who is above the æons, the indescribable one.[3] But these and similar texts give us no more than a general idea that in Logion

[1] H. Odeberg, The Fourth Gospel (1929), p. 154ff. Cf. Strecker, Das Judenchristentum in den Pseudoklementinen, p. 202f., and *Ox.Pap.* 840 the last lines (see Grenfell-Hunt, Fragment of an Uncanonical Gospel from Oxyrhynchus, 1908, and Jeremias, Unbekannte Jesusworte, p. 39ff.).

[2] Cf. Puech in Neutest. Apokryphen, p. 206.

[3] Cf. *Jesu Christi Sophia* 87.3; Baynes, A Coptic Gnostic Treatise, p. 42ff. and the *Manichæan Kephalaia* 90.18f.; R. Reitzenstein, Poimandres, p. 337.7ff.

13a it is a circle of Gnostic motives in which we find ourselves, and a very wide circle at that.

But what may contribute to a more precise expression of the meaning of the second part of Logion 13a is the important item of information that Thomas drank from the source and became intoxicated. " Since you have drunk, you have become drunk with that sparkling source which I have measured out." " To be drunk " (or intoxicated) is a standard phrase in Gnostic texts, denoting the state of the ignorant man in the world without saving knowledge. Thus in the *Apocryphon of John* 59.20 we find, in connection with Jaldabaoth's difficulties at the creation of Adam, that Adam was overcome by ἀναισθησία; he was "incapable of perception," i.e. he was in that state in which man is unable to understand his situation—that in him there is a spark of light belonging to the heavenly world. Adam was drunk with ignorance, but was later made sober again, after suffering from " the intoxication of darkness."[1]

Intoxication as a sign of ignorance and captivity in the material is also encountered in the *Gospel of Truth* 22.17f. " He who gains insight, he knows whence he has come and whither he is going. He knows in the same way as one who, after having been intoxicated, returns from his intoxication and, when he comes to himself, retrieves that which is his." We also have examples in the *Gospel of Thomas* of this common usage of the term "drunkenness" when Jesus says, according to Logion 28, "... I found them all drunk. I found none among them who was thirsty, and my soul was full of pain for the children of men. For they are blind in their hearts, and do not see that they have come empty into the world (and that) they seek to go empty out of the world. But now they are drunk. When they have shaken off their wine, then they will repent."[2]

[1] See H. Jonas, Gnosis und spätantiker Geist (1934), p. 115ff., on "intoxication" in Hermetism, Mandæism, etc. Cf. the *Manichæan Psalm-book* 56.16 and 32.

[2] R. Reitzenstein, Das iranische Erlösungsmysterium (1921), p. 136ff.

Logion 13a is, however, contradictory, since a positive evaluation is placed upon intoxication, an intoxication from the Saviour's fountain. Logion 108 is similar in content: there, "drinking from the mouth of Christ" means becoming like him, having the possibility of true knowledge through the revelation of the hidden mystery.

> Jesus said:
> He who drinks from my mouth
> Shall become as I am,
> And I myself shall become him,
> And that which is hidden
> Shall be revealed to him.

The concept which we have in this logion, of the mysterious knowledge which is only to be offered to the initiated, is a further piece of evidence in support of what we have hitherto said, that it is the Gnostic teaching on the Risen Lord which is determinative for the *Gospel of Thomas*. Logion 108 states, as a condition for initiation into gnosis, that man must receive the secret from Jesus and that in this way a unity is created, so that there is a form of identity between the particle of light in man and the light which is the nature of Jesus. To drink from the mouth of Jesus is thus nothing more or less than an equivalent expression for " intoxication " in its good meaning.

Thus the concept of "drunkenness" is used in the *Gospel of Thomas* in two senses, one positive and one negative, of which the positive is the more interesting, because the more unusual. In order to find a parallel to this positive evaluation we have to turn e.g. to the *Manichæan Psalm-book*, where we can read how intoxication comes from the new wine which is bestowed by Jesus. " They that drink thy wine, their heart rejoices in it. They are drunk with thy love and gladness is spread over their . . ." 151.14f. Or we may turn to another type of writing, the *Odes of Solomon*, the origins of which are much disputed but which contain a large amount of syncretistic material: Christian, Jewish and Gnostic. In this document the expression " the mouth of the Lord " occurs on a couple of occasions, referring to the Logos (the incarnate Son ?). " Because the mouth of the Lord is the true Word and the door of his light." 12.3. And: " For the mouth of the Most High spoke to them; and the interpretation of himself had its course by him." The divine Logos is the mouth of the Lord, and this expression refers to the Logos and its mediation of gnosis—an idea which resembles Logion 108 very closely. This "mouth"—Logos speculation is also linked with the concept of "good intoxication." In the mysterious phraseology of Ode 30, we find, " Fill ye water for yourselves from the living fountain of the Lord, for it has been opened to you. And come all ye thirsty and take a draught; and rest by the fountain of the Lord. For fair it is and pure. And it gives rest to the soul. Much sweeter is its water than honey. And the honeycomb of bees is not to be compared with it. For it flows from the lips of the Lord. And from the heart of the Lord is its name. And it came unlimited and invisible. And until it was set in the midst they did not know it. Blessed are they who have drunk therefrom. And rested thereby. Hallelujah."

Here the fountain and its water are interpreted as being the Spirit whose gifts are to reveal mysteries.[1] This is expressed clearly in Ode 11, where it is described how the " initiated person "(?) is circumcised by the Holy Spirit and treads the path of knowledge. We then read, " And speaking waters drew near my lips from the fountain of the Lord plenteously. And I drank and was inebriated with the living water that doth not die, and my inebriation was not one without knowledge. . . ." This Ode then goes on to describe how the initiate then turns aside from

[1] Harris-Mingana, p. 368, " This would mean that the water is the knowledge of the Lord . . ." Cf. Ode VI.

the vanity of this world. It seems to me that it is in these texts which we have quoted that we have the best parallels to the latter part of Logion 13a, and Logion 108.[1] It is just this combination of " the mouth of the Lord," the fountain of living water, the water of the Spirit which gives knowledge and salvation, the intoxication of knowledge, and other elements which bears witness to the fact that these logia belong together theologically, and that in this respect the *Gospel of Thomas* has taken material from a syncretistic milieu. We could also point to many other details in which there is a distinct resemblance between the *Odes of Solomon* and the *Gospel of Thomas*: e.g. the part played by "rest" as well as "knowledge," the spiritual circumcision, reminiscent of Logion 53, the work of salvation, etc. It has already been pointed out that the *Odes of Solomon* stand in close relationship to another of the "gospels" from Nag-Hamadi.[2]

There are also other texts of Gnostic character which can be brought together with these concepts in the *Gospel of Thomas*; this is a further indication of the Gnostic milieu in which we are working. We can exemplify by comparing Logion 108 and the *Acts of John*. In the logion in question it is stated that there was a certain identity between Christ and the true Gnostic, an identity having to do with knowledge and revelation. " He who drinks from my mouth shall become as I am, and I myself shall become him, and that which is hidden shall be revealed to him." A passage from the *Acts of John*, dealing with Jesus' teaching on suffering and the identity between his suffering and the suffering of the faithful, reads: " But when the human nature (or the upper nature) is taken up, and the race which draweth near unto me and obeyeth my voice, he that now heareth me shall be united therewith, and shall no more be that which he now is, but above

[1] We may also compare with Eph. 5. 18, and the "pun" which we have there, concerning the "drunkenness" caused by strong drink and the state of being " filled with the Spirit " which is to characterise the Christian. See also Ignatius, Rom. 7.2.

[2] F. M. Braun, L'énigme des Odes de Salomon, Revue Thomiste 57 (1957), p. 609ff. Schenke, Die Herkunft des sogenannten Evangelium Veritatis (1959), p. 26ff.

them, as I also now am. For so long as thou callest not thyself mine, I am not that which I am (or was): but if thou hear me, thou, hearing, shalt be as I am, and I shall be that which I was, when I <have> thee as I am with myself." Ch. 100. The true nature of Jesus can be understood only by that soul which by nature belongs to him, is a part of him, and therefore can win knowledge concerning him. There seems to me to be a distinct resemblance between Logion 108 and this passage from the *Acts of John.*

The Heavenly Nature and Earthly Appearance of Jesus

Comparison with Gnostic texts or with "later Jewish-Christian" texts influenced by Gnostic ideas has so far shown that the Christology of the *Gospel of Thomas* exhibits characteristics distinctly resembling the Gnostic concept of Jesus. The "Compiler" of the gospel has evidently brought together material which represented or pre-supposed the Saviour as having descended from the Highest Being, the Incomprehensible, to this world and its ignorant men. Saving gnosis has come within the grasp of men through the action of the Risen Christ in revealing the mysteries to his disciples—and to Thomas in particular. He who allows himself to be illuminated by the Spirit or "intoxicated" by knowledge wins salvation. We shall now, in order to determine even more closely what was the main concept of Jesus' nature in the Christology of the *Gospel of Thomas*, examine a few further logia which express this theme.

In Logion 61b[1] the nature of Christ is expressed in a way which further helps to support the contention that it is a basically Gnostic attitude to Jesus which governs the *Gospel of Thomas.*

[1] It is a moot point whether there should be two logia or one here. It seems to me that Logion 61 is an independent logion, included here on account of its contents. Note the connection with what follows.

Salome said:
" Who are you, man, as one (who comes) from what?
You have sat upon my bench
And you have eaten at my table."
Jesus said to her:
" I am the one who came into existence out of that which is the same.
To me has been given from that which is my Father's."
<Salome said:>
" I am your disciple."
<Jesus said to her:>
" I say therefore,
When he is united, he shall be filled with light,
But when he is divided, he shall be filled with darkness."

Salome is evidently inquiring here after Jesus' true nature. She is bewildered that this Jesus, who sat down on her bench, who ate, and who appeared as a man in every respect, can have any pretentions to being a Saviour. " Who are you? Where have you come from? " she asks. Jesus' answer begins with the words ⲁⲛⲟⲕ ⲡⲉ, corresponding to the Greek epiphany formula ἐγώ εἰμι, " I am"; implying that Jesus is identifying himself with the divine world, and that he is the Revealer who can utter these words. The two statements, " I am the one who came into existence out of that which is the same," and " To me has been given from that which is my Father's," in Jesus' answer are expressive of the same thing. To have proceeded from that which is the same, leads on to the thought that the heavenly world is that which is "the same" through and through, the ultimate "unity."

The "division" named farther on in the logion belongs to this world, which is "darkness"; "unity," which is the same throughout, is of the heavenly world. Thus according to this logion Jesus has said what the Gnostics considered him to be, the heavenly Saviour who proceeded from the incomprehensible, from the Father, the " Unutterable ": " To me has been given from that which is my Father's."[1] Jesus' point of departure is thus the heavenly world which in Gnostic terminology is called the "same part."[2]

When Jesus says, according to Logion 61b, that he belongs by nature to the divine sphere and has received "of that which is the Father's," he is expressing the concept that there is a resemblance in nature between Jesus and the Father. This is also the theme of Logion 15.

> Jesus said,
> When you see him who was not born of woman,
> Fall down on your faces and worship him.
> He is your Father.

This logion may refer only to the Father, who is to be worshipped in self-abasement; the expression " him who was not born of woman " may then be understood as an explanation of the Father's nature, in line with what is said in *Jesu Christi Sophia*: " He (God) is indeed immortal and eternal; he is an Eternal One who was not born. For he who is born shall (also) perish. He who is not born has indeed no beginning. For he who has a beginning (also) has an end." 84.1ff. " Being born" is no part of the nature of the Highest, since birth implies a limitation. This is the simplest interpretation of the logion. The difficulty with this interpretation is, however, connected with the expression, "when you see him who was not born of woman," and with the command to worship him. The Father of course cannot be seen by man; nor is it possible in the normal meaning of the term to fall down and adore him. It is then more probable

[1] Cf. *Jesu Christi Sophia* 102.1ff.
[2] See below on the interpretation of the " Unity," p. 221ff.

that we are here dealing with an idea related to the one we have encountered earlier in certain of the apocryphal Acts, in which Jesus and the Father are interpreted as being a unity. According to this view everything which is said of the Father may be said of the Son, since they are in their heavenly nature identical. This implies that here in Logion 15 we have an expression of the concept that Jesus, present among men, represents the Father, that he shares his nature and reveals his secrets, and that he who understands this—sees this—will worship Jesus.

Certain expressions in Logion 15 are capable of further clarification. When we see the expression "him who was not born of woman," we easily associate this with another logion in which Jesus speaks of his birth and his "mother," Logion 101. This logion is, however, damaged and it is as well to exercise caution in its interpretation, though its main idea is quite accessible.

> <Jesus said:>
> He who does not hate his father and mother in my way
> Cannot become my [disciple].
> And he who does [not] love [his father] and mother in my way
> Cannot become my [disciple],
> For my mother [ ]
> But [my] true [mother] gave me life.

The basis of this logion is probably two sayings of Jesus from the New Testament: Matt. 10.37, "He who loves father or mother more than me is not worthy of me ..." and Luke 14.26, "If any one comes to me and does not hate his own father and mother ..." A similar combination of these two sayings comes in Logion 55, though without the commentary which follows in 101. The contradiction in Logion 101 between the "hate" of the first sentence and the "love" of the second, due to the combination of sayings, would seem to have to do with the antithesis between earthly parents and " spiritual " parents. Since the exposition at the end of the logion sets his " true mother " in relief over against another mother, who is presumably mentioned in the lacuna of the previous line, we may conclude that the same principle of antithesis applies to the first sentences. The disciple is to hate this world and its " parents," but love those who gave him life. The same applies to Jesus. It is Jesus' heavenly mother (the Spirit, Sophia ?) who " bore " him, and no earthly woman.[1] The nature of Jesus excludes any share in anything belonging to the world.

When it is mentioned in the exposition of Logion 15 that Jesus reveals the nature of the Father in himself, we may comment that this is by no means an unusual idea among Gnostics. The *Gospel of Philip* from Nag-Hamadi expresses the same idea: " The Father was in the Son and the Son in the Father. This is the Kingdom of Heaven."[2] 122.23f. The *Manichæan Psalm-book*, too, has the words, " I hear that thou art in thy Father, thy Father is hidden in thee." 121.25. The concept recurs in the opening scene of the *Apocryphon of John*. There is described how John hid himself in distress, after a Pharisee had claimed that Jesus had deceived him. But Christ comes down to him in a revelation, in a threefold form, and the form which is the heavenly Christ says to him, " Do not be timid. (For) I am he who is with you always. I am the Father, I am the Mother, I am the Son." 21.17ff. We may also mention an expression in *Excerpta ex Theodoto* 31.1, which, referring to the Saviour, reads: ". . . in him was the whole pleroma in flesh, σωματικῶς."[3]

[1] There may possibly be an element of criticism here against the NT assertion that Christ was born of an earthly woman, a thought abhorrent to some Gnostics. This may also be behind Logion 105, with its mention of "parents," "Jesus said: He who knows his father and mother shall be called the child of a harlot." A comparison may also be made with the criticism made particularly by Jews that Jesus was an illegitimate child. Cf. E. Stauffer, Jesus, Gestalt und Geschichte (1957), p. 22f.

[2] Cf. 104.15f.

[3] Epiphanius, *Panar.haer.* LXII, 2, 4f., says of the Sabellians that they used the " Egyptian Gospel," according to which the Saviour is said to have shown the disciples "that the same person was Father, Son, and Holy Spirit."

The meaning of Logion 15 would therefore seem to be that when man sees and understands the real nature of the Saviour—that he is not a human being, not born, and of a heavenly nature—then he worships in all humility the Highest Being which is revealed in him. This fits in very well with another form of expression in some of the logia in the *Gospel of Thomas*, where Jesus appears as the Revealer, and where understanding of his nature brings with it access to saving gnosis. Thus Logion 5 reads:

> Jesus said:
> Know that which is before you,
> ⲡⲉⲧⲙ̄ⲡⲙ̄ⲧⲟ ⲙ̄ⲡⲉⲕϩⲟ ⲉⲃⲟⲗ,
> And that which is hidden unto you
> Shall be revealed unto you;
> For there is nothing hidden
> Which shall not be revealed.

" That which is before you " must refer to Jesus himself who is speaking these words: he who is, and reveals, the heavenly mystery. The same expression comes again in Logion 52, with the same meaning, "... you have forsaken the Living One who is before you, ⲙ̄ⲡⲉⲧⲛ̄ⲙ̄ⲧⲟ ⲉⲃⲟⲗ, and have spoken about the dead." The Living One who is " before " the disciples is Jesus, the Revealer. Similarly in Logion 91, which is introduced with a direct question about the person of Jesus, the answer referring in turn to the questioner's inability to apprehend Jesus' nature.

> They said to him:
> " Tell us who you are, so that we may believe in you."
> He said to them:
> " You try the face of heaven and earth,
> But he who stands before you
> Have you not learned to know,

And you do not understand how to try this opportunity (this time).

The logion has borrowed part of Luke 12.56 (rather Luke than Matt. 16.3), but the New Testament saying used has as usual been altered. A typical addition is the phrase "and earth," whilst the focus has been shifted to " learned to know," the element of knowledge. In addition the background situation of the saying has changed. In Matthew, the saying has to do with the question of signs: the demand on the part of the Jewish leaders for a Messianic sign to substantiate Jesus' Messianic claims. Jesus' answer to this demand is a judgment upon the Jews' " superficial " way of asking questions, when they are now in point of fact in the period of the Kingdom of Heaven. In Luke the saying is to some extent free of situation, but even such indications of context as it still possessed in Luke have disappeared in the *Gospel of Thomas*. The main point in the *Gospel of Thomas* is the question of the person and nature of Jesus, and the way in which it becomes possible for man to gain an insight into the secret knowledge, which is hidden, but which is revealed in Christ. We do not know whether or not it is the opponents of Jesus who are lurking behind the introductory " they "—" They said to him,"—but it is most probable. We can, however, see in other traditions that Jesus can turn against his disciples because of their slowness to understand. There is, for instance, an apocryphal saying of Jesus which reads, " *Qui mecum sunt, non me intellexerunt.*"[1] Here the disciples are reprimanded for not seeing and understanding what lies so near at hand, namely, that Jesus is the Son of God. This same idea is found in a further logion in the *Gospel of Thomas*, one which closely resembles Logion 91.

[1] The *Acts of Peter* (The *Vercelli Acts*) 10, (James, p. 314).

His disciples said to him:
" Who are you, that you tell us this? "
<Jesus said:>
" From what I tell you, you do not know who I am.
But you have become like the Jews,
For they love the tree (and) hate its fruit,
And they love the fruit (but) hate the tree."

Logion 43

The metaphor of the fruit and the tree may very well be a " genuine " saying of Jesus, but it seems to me to have been provided with a "new" introduction, which pushes a Gnostic problem into the foreground, namely, the question of the nature of Jesus and its connection with the mediation of knowledge—the decisive question for Gnostic theology.

Closely related to the words " that which is before you " as an expression for the heavenly revelation found in Jesus are the first lines of Logion 28, where we notice in particular the term *sarx*. This is one of the most important Christological statements in the *Gospel of Thomas*.

Jesus said:
I stood up in the midst of the world,
And I revealed myself to them in flesh, *σάρξ*.

Ox. Pap. I reads:

ἔ[σ]την ἐν μέσω̣ τοῦ κόσμου καὶ ἐν σαρκὶ ὤφθην αὐτοῖς.

There is a great similarity between these and various New Testament texts: texts which say that Jesus was manifested in the flesh, *ὃς ἐφανερώθη ἐν σαρκί*, I Tim. 3.16, or that Jesus Christ has come in the flesh, *ἐν σαρκὶ ἐληλυθότα*, I John 4.2, or refer to the coming of Christ in the flesh, *ἐρχόμενος ἐν σαρκί*, II John 7. But there are a number of details in the words of Logion 28 which are evidence that the saying as we now have it expresses a Gnostic view of Jesus. The strange fact has been pointed out that this important statement is made by Jesus himself, and not by another, referring to him; he speaks as a divine being, on the basis of his pre-existence.[1] But we must point out a striking discrepancy between this logion and the New Testament texts. *Ox. Pap.* has the text *ὤφθην ἐν σαρκί*, a form of expression impossible in the New Testament, which says that Jesus " became flesh," John 1.14, or " came in the flesh," or " was manifested, *φανεροῦν*, in the flesh." Forms of *ὤφθην*, the word used in Logion 28, are on each occasion—numbering more than twenty—they occur, used to express the revelation of someone or something belonging to the supernatural sphere. Moses and Elijah revealed themselves on the Mount of Transfiguration, Mk. 9.4 par., the angels revealed themselves, Lk. 1.11, 22.43, Christ revealed himself as the Risen One, Lk. 24.34, Acts 9.17, 13.31, 26.16, I Cor. 15.5ff., etc.[2] This seems to me to be evidence that there had been a little displacement in the forms of expression used in Logion 28, over against the New Testament; a displacement in line with the Gnostic concept that the heavenly Christ came to dwell in another being, Jesus, who was *sarx*. Nor is it necessary to deduce from the words " revealed himself in flesh " an incarnation in the New Testament sense. This is supported by the term *ὤφθην*, as well as the Gnostics' use of the word *sarx*.

This can also be illustrated from other texts. In the *Gospel of Truth* there is a form of expression highly reminiscent of Pauline phraseology, but which nevertheless proves to be a description in Docetic categories of the Son's entry into the world. " For he came in a similitude of flesh, **ⲛⲟⲩⲥⲁⲣⲝ ⲛⲥⲙⲁⲧ**, although

[1] Harnack, Über die jüngst entdeckten Sprüche Jesu (1897), p. 14; Jeremias, Unbekannte Jesusworte, p. 67.

[2] The verb has to do with the concept of resurrection also in LXX. See W. Michaelis, art. *ὁράω*, Theol. Wörterb. V, p. 324ff. and 359.

nothing could obstruct its course, because it was incorruptible and uncoercible." 31.4f. This is extremely suggestive of the phraseology of Rom. 8.3, "God . . . sending his own Son in the likeness of sinful flesh, *ἐν ὁμοιώματι σαρκὸς ἁμαρτίας*," and of Phil. 2.7, "He . . . emptied himself, taking the form of a servant, *μορφή*, being born in the likeness of men, *ἐν ὁμοιώματι ἀνθρώπων*. And being in human form, *σχῆμα*, he humbled himself . . ."[1] Jesus appears in the world, revealing the heavenly Christ in the image of *sarx*. In the *Gospel of Truth*, the Saviour is also called the Logos, the Word which proceeds from the Father. What is characteristic for this Word is that it is given a body, *soma*, which causes confusion among ignorant men, 26.5f.: ". . . when the Word appeared, which is in their hearts, which pronounces it—it was not only a voice, but took a body—a great confusion arose among the vessels . . ." Here the Saviour appears as a man, but it is only an apparent body, in the Docetic sense, which he possesses.[2] We encounter the same idea, of an apparent body, in the *Gospel of Philip*. "Jesus bore them in all secrecy. He, in fact, revealed himself not as he [really] was, but revealed himself in such a way that [they could] see him . . . He [revealed] himself to the great as great. He revealed [himself to the] little as little. He [revealed himself] to the angels as an angel, to men as a man. For that reason his Logos was hidden from all. Some certainly saw him, in that they believed that they saw themselves. But when he revealed himself in glory to his disciples on the mountain, he was not small, but great. But he made the disciples great so that they could see him, when he was great." 105.28ff.[3] In the light of these texts, the fact that Jesus revealed himself in *sarx* means that he took on a guise which could be apprehended by men, though the guise he took was not his own, but only an apparent body.

[1] Cf. The *Manichæan Kephalaia* 12.22ff.; *Psalm-book* 194.1ff.; *Epistula apostolorum* 19.
[2] A similar idea is to be found in Marcion. See Harnack, Marcion, p. 109ff. and 164f.
[3] Cf. the *Hypostasis of the Archons* 144.33ff.

Jesus as the Light and the All

According to the *Gospel of Thomas*, when Jesus appears in the world he does so claiming to be the heavenly being who stands over all created beings and penetrates all creation.

> Jesus said:
> I am that light which is over them all.
> I am the All. The All has proceeded from me
> And the All has come to me.
> Cleave a tree, and I am there.
> Lift a stone, and you shall find me there.
>
> Logion 77

The first sentence closely resembles John 8.12, "I am the light of the world," but goes beyond the Johannine saying of Jesus; it is more pointed, in that Jesus says, "I am that light which is over them all." In John, Jesus is the divine Revealer, illuminating the true path for a world which has fallen into sin and death. Logion 77 assumes a different situation, since in the first sentence Jesus claims his superiority over other light, and in its parallel sentence speaks of his identity with the All. It may, however, be difficult to identify the correct background to this saying about the light and the All. We may think about advanced Gnostic doctrinal edifices in which the Son is stated to be the best, the one who is created from the best of the æons. It is more probable, however, that the concept of Jesus as the light which is "over them all"—superior to all men—refers to the fact that Jesus, having proceeded from the Father is of the world of light, and that he is leader and "Lord" over all the sparks of light which are imprisoned in enlightened men. This might be compared with a similar idea in Logion 83,[1] in which case we should

[1] See below, p. 190f.

have a doctrine comparable to the one presented in the *Gospel of Truth*, where " light," **ⲟⲩⲟⲉⲓⲛ**, stands for that which emanated from the Father and is revealed by the Son. This " light " is connected with the saving knowledge, gnosis; we therefore read that he who allows himself to be illuminated by the Son's message receives " the light," and that " the light " dwells in him: " In you dwells the light which does not yield." 32.34. " The light " therefore refers to the revelation mediated through the Son, and to the particles of light in man. This appears to be a good background for the words of the logion, " I am the light which is over them all."[1] In Gnostic texts it is indeed often the Father himself who is referred to as " the light," but the expression can also stand for Jesus; this is a further manifestation of the tendency we have met before in the *Gospel of Thomas*, that Jesus, as the one who reveals the Father, is of the same nature as the Father, and that anything which can be said about the Father can equally well be said about Jesus. Thus in the *Acts of Philip*, Jesus is called " the holy Light " or " the true Light," and in *Excerpta ex Theodoto* Jesus is " the light," the one who revealed himself in our world as " the light."[2]

The concept that Jesus comes as a being of light to the imprisoned sparks of light in man is in line with the second sentence in Logion 77, " I am the All. The All has proceeded from me and the All has come to me." If we illustrate this statement from the *Gospel of Truth* 24.1ff., we have an excellent possibility of understanding the background to the words, and of observing the close connection between the two statements on the light and the All. In this passage we have in fact a description of the relationship between the Word—the Son—and the All. " The Word of the Father goes forth into the All thus, in that it is a fruit of his heart and a form of the revelation of his will. It bears up the All, it

[1] Cf. 30.33ff. and 43.12ff.; the *Acts of Thomas* 27 and 153. See also Odeberg, The Fourth Gospel, p. 287.

[2] The *Acts of Philip* 10 and 53; *Excerpta ex Theodoto* 34.1, 35.1, 41.1, etc.

makes a choice there, and further, it takes (clothes itself in) the form of the All, it purifies it, it causes it to return to the Father (and) to the Mother (the Word, which is), Jesus of unlimited sweetness." Special attention should be paid in this context to the statement in Logion 77 that " the All " has proceeded from " Jesus " and that it will return thence; this is precisely an expression of the Gnostic view of salvation which recurs in the *Gospel of Truth*. The Father causes the world—the " All "—to come into being through the Word, the Son, but there are fragments of the heavenly world imprisoned in matter, sparks of light in man, and it is their return which means salvation and the restoration of unity.[1]

When, according to Logion 77, Jesus says, " I am the All. The All has proceeded from me and the All has come to me," we once more hear tones which sound like an echo of a statement on the essence of the Father. The Father is the point from which all proceeds, and the point to which all eventually returns. In *Excerpta ex Theodoto* this relationship between the Son and the Father is so constructed that the Son, when he appears here on earth, does not leave one place and proceed to another, since he is simultaneously with the Father (he who is everywhere, *τὸ πάντῃ Ὂν*), an expression decidedly pantheistic in tone, 4.2. It may be some such basically " pantheistic " view of the Son—as the one who is in all places—which caused the typically pantheistic statement, " Cleave a tree, and I am there. Lift a stone, and you shall find me there," to be coupled to Logion 77. This statement has in fact a different position in *Ox. Pap.*, possibly for reasons of content. We should also remember here the pantheistic estimation of the nature of Jesus which we find expressed not only in Valentinian gnosis but also in documents influenced thereby. As Jesus in Logion 77 says, " I am the All,"

[1] For the " All " and Christ as ruler over the " All," see e.g. the *Apocryphon of John* 32.9ff., 68.14f. and *Jesu Christi Sophia* 78.3f.

so in the *Acts of Peter* 39 (The *Vercelli Acts*), Peter says about Jesus Christ, " Thou art the All and the All is in thee, *σὺ τὸ πᾶν καὶ τὸ πᾶν ἐν σοί*." Once more we can see how Gnostic or gnosticising texts illustrate and clarify the meaning of expressions in the *Gospel of Thomas*.[1]

Thus according to this logion and to others which we have mentioned earlier, Jesus appears as revealer of the heavenly world, which has nothng whatever in common with the material world. Jesus is the Alli and the light. The content of the revelation, connected with Jesus' heavenly nature, must then be something high above all human comprehension. This is explicitly said in the context of the previous quotation from the *Acts of Peter*, where we read that " the word of life " in Jesus Christ cannot be heard by the earthly ear, or be apprehended by anything belonging to the material world. Only that which is of the Spirit of Jesus can comprehend him. It is the Spirit, says Peter, which enables him to love Jesus, talk with him, see him and pray to him: " Thou art perceived of the Spirit only." This is also approximately the same as Logion 17 in the *Gospel of Thomas*.

> Jesus said:
> I shall give you that
> Which eye has not seen
> And which ear has not heard
> And which hand has not touched
> And (which) has not arisen in the heart of man.

Jesus' gift of salvation, knowledge of the heavenly world, is of the same character as his true nature, and cannot be grasped by the human intelligence. It is probable that behind Logion 17 lies the same apocryphal text, built upon Is. 64.3, as that which the Apostle Paul quotes in I Cor. 2.9, when he talks about God's secret decree of salvation in Jesus Christ, hidden from the begin-

[1] Cf. Irenæus, *Adv.haer.* I, 2, 6 and 3, 4; II, 12, 7.

ning of time. " As it is written, ' What no eye has seen, nor ear heard, nor the heart of man conceived, what God has prepared for those who love him.' "[1]

In Logion 17 a further clause has been added, " and which hand has not touched," in order to stress even more strongly that the nature of the heavenly world is to be grasped by no unaided human sense. Not until Jesus, who is one with its nature, grants the revelation, can they understand. This same quotation from Isaiah crops up in other Gnostic texts, witnessing to the important role it played. In the *Acts of Thomas* Ch. 36, the Apostle teaches about the heavenly things, which are invisible and far surpass anything on this earth, where all things are subject to corruption. " But we speak of the world which is above, of God and angels, of watchers and holy ones, of the immortal (ambrosial) food and the drink of the true wine, of raiment that endureth and groweth not old, of things which eye hath not seen nor ear heard, neither have they entered into the heart of sinful men, the things which God hath prepared for them that love him."[2] This reference to the text from Isaiah does not, however, contain the addition from Logion 17, " and which hand has not touched," though it does occur in that part of the *Gospel of Mani* which was discovered in the Turfan Fragment, " I shall give you what eye has not seen, ear has not heard, and has not been touched by hand." The last clause, " and what has not arisen in the heart of man, " is, however missing.[3] We can thus see that the sayings in Logion 17 have been used in different writings and traditions, and that they were made either to represent the content of the heavenly nature of revelation,[4] or to express Jesus' incomprehensible nature. We have also observed that the additional clauses in the version of

[1] Is. 64. 4, " From of old no one has heard or perceived by the ear, no eye has seen a God besides thee, who works for those who wait for him."

[2] Cf. *Two Epistles concerning Virginity* I, 1, 9 (The Ante-Nicene Fathers VII, p. 58) and Resch, *Agrapha*,[1] p. 154ff.

[3] See Puech in Neutest. Apokryphen, p. 217 and 263.

[4] Cf. *Pistis Sophia* 114; *Excerpta ex Theodoto* 10.5.

the text in the *Gospel of Thomas* recur in Mani, which supports the contention that Mani had access to gospel traditions which recur in the *Gospel of Thomas*, or indicates purely and simply that he made use of the gospel itself.

The additional phrase, " and which hand has not touched," in Logion 17 must be treated, on the basis of its special use in Gnostic texts, as a typical Gnostic supplement, connected with the role played by the five senses in their doctrinal system. We encounter the idea of " touching with the hand," e.g. in the *Gospel of Truth* 30.25ff., in a description of the way in which revelation brought men to knowledge of the Son. " When they had seen him and heard him, he allowed them to taste him and smell him and touch the beloved Son." The same is true of the Manichæan texts.[1] We encounter the concept of " touching " Jesus in the New Testament too, but there it expresses the reality of Jesus' appearance in earthly categories, with the intention of proving the true, corporeal existence of Jesus. " That which was from the beginning, which we have heard, which we have seen with our eyes, which we have looked upon and touched with our hands . . . that which we have seen and heard we proclaim . . ." I John 1.1, Cf. Lk. 24.39.

The fact that we have this additional clause, " and which hand has not touched," in Logion 17 in all probability has to do with a development within Gnostic circles of the thought that there is no physical way for man to win knowledge of the heavenly world; this was done by linking up with the doctrine of the five senses. The Jesus who is the All and the light is, in common with the gift he mediates, incapable of being grasped by anything human.

[1]E.g. the *Manichæan Kephalaia* 140.10ff.

" *The Living Jesus* " *contra the Old Testament Messiah*

A striking characteristic of the *Gospel of Thomas* is its lack of interest in the Old Testament. In direct contrast to the canonical Gospels, and even to most of the apocryphal gospels, it carries no reference to the Old Testament prophecies and Messianic promises, which otherwise are necessary constituents of similar expositions. This may appear strange when we remember that there are so many New Testament sayings in the *Gospel of Thomas*, but it is evident that the " Compiler " of the gospel has had some definite end in view in not wanting to use such references. The main background to this attitude can perhaps best be illustrated by reference to Logion 52. This is in fact probably the only one which considers this question of the Old Testament prophecies, their Messianic pronouncements, and their relation to Jesus.

> His disciples said to him:
> " Twenty-four prophets spoke in Israel,
> And all spoke in (before, about?) you, ϩⲣⲁϊ ⲛ̄ϩⲏⲧⲕ."
> He said to them:
> " You have forsaken the Living One who is before you,
> And have spoken about the dead."

This logion is not particularly easy to interpret directly, partly because the expression ϩⲣⲁϊ ⲛ̄ϩⲏⲧⲕ is ambiguous, and partly because the contrast between the disciples' words and Jesus' answer is not immediately obvious. The best way of getting at its meaning would, however, seem to be to begin with an apocryphal saying of Jesus, to which Augustine refers in his writing *Contra adversarium Legis et Prophetarum*.[1] Augustine probably came across this saying in some Marcionite tract, and

[1] Migne PL XLII, 647.

refers to it in the course of his polemic against the heresy he has detected there.

" *Sed apostolis, inquit, Dominus noster interrogantibus de Iudæorum prophetis quid sentiri deberet, qui de adventu eius aliquid cecinisse in præteritum putabantur, commotus talia eos etiam nunc sentire, respondit: Dimisistis vivum qui ante vos est, et de mortuis fabulamini.*"

" But when the Apostles (he said) had asked how they should regard the prophets of the Jews, who are thought to have prophesied (proclaimed) in the past about his coming, he answered, surprised (or annoyed) that they still harboured such an idea: you have forsaken the Living One who is before you, and speak about the dead."[1]

The saying of Jesus, " you have forsaken the Living One who is before you, and speak (have spoken) about the dead," is identical in the *Gospel of Thomas* and in the writing quoted by Augustine. A further noteworthy point is that the framework which in these two traditions surrounds the sayings themselves is similar, Augustine's report of the conversation between the disciples and Jesus shows that their respective views on what the Old Testament prophets have to say about the Messiah do not coincide. Jesus is surprised—or annoyed—that they still consider the prophetic words to be of any importance, now that they have the Revealer in their midst.

We must now examine more closely, in order better to understand the two points of view, an idea which occurs particularly in a Jewish-Christian milieu and which may be important for the framework of the saying, particularly the version in the *Gospel of Thomas*: " Twenty-four prophets spoke in Israel, and all spoke in (before, about?) you . . ."

[1] The translation advanced by Jeremias in his book, Unbekannte Jesusworte, p. 70, seems to me to make its meaning more obscure than that previously given by, *inter alia*, James, p. 20, Santos, p. 72. It is easier to understand the expression *in praeteritum* as an accusative, closely related to the ablative, and which may here mean " formerly," " in the past " (not, as Jeremias, " etwas in Bezug auf die Vergangenheit "). Cf. e.g. Dictys Cretensis 4.15, *quo fortiorem ne optasse quidem quemquam existere nunc vel in praeteritum excepto uno illo Hercule*. See further Stolz-Schmalz, Lateinische Grammatik (1928), p. 558.

There was among the Jews an expectation that in the last days there would be a return of the prophetic age, when the true, the eschatological prophet would arise.[1] This thought was often linked to two other ideas. They considered that this prophet would sum up in himself the proclamation of all the earlier prophets, and in his own person sum up all the prophets of Israel. To this was added the other concept, that all the prophets proclaimed the same message, and could thus be said to be one and the same prophet, although appearing in different forms at different times. This view of the prophets and their message is partly reflected in 1 Peter 1.10f. "The prophets who prophesied of the grace that was to be yours searched and inquired about this salvation; they inquired what person or time was indicated by the Spirit of Christ within them when predicting the sufferings of Christ and the subsequent glory." Here we have an expression of the idea that it is the same "person" who proclaimed the same message through the old prophets, a thought which is hinted at in other passages of the New Testament, and recurs in certain of the Church Fathers.[2]

The concept of the true prophet in the prophets recurs particularly in theology influenced by later Jewish Christianity, where it is said that Christ was in the prophets of the Old Covenant. A fragment of the *Gospel according to the Hebrews*, which has been preserved in Hieronymus's *Commentary on Isaiah* (Is. 11.2) reads, "And it came to pass when the Lord was come up out of the water, the whole fount of the Holy Spirit descended and rested upon him, and said unto him: My son, in all the prophets was I waiting for thee that thou shouldst come, and I might rest in thee. For thou art my rest, thou art my first-begotten son, that reignest for ever." Thus the whole fount of the Spirit comes

[1] Cf. O. Cullmann, Die Christologie des Neuen Testaments (1957), p. 12ff.; P. Volz, Die Eschatologie der jüdischen Gemeinde im neutestamentlichen Zeitalter (1934), p. 193ff.
[2] Cf. J. Daniélou, Sacramentum futuri (1950).

upon Jesus at the time of his baptism in Jordan; this is interpreted so, that the Spirit who spoke in the prophets of the Old Covenant and who has hitherto waited in vain for Jesus' appearance, can now find his peace in the true Revealer. It is, however, difficult to decide whether the text means that it is the pre-existent Son for whose appearance the Spirit was waiting, or whether there is some question of " adoption " in the Docetic sense.[1] The important point here, though, is the " continual " appearance of the Spirit, through the Old Covenant and on to his final " indwelling" of Jesus.

We find a similar idea in the *Pseudo-Clementines*, where very little is said about the eschatological prophet who is to appear in the last days, but a good deal about " the true prophet," ὁ ἀληθὴς προφήτης, the possessor of the full truth, the one whom the other prophets referred to, and prophesied about. This true prophet is Christ, who has been " incarnated " in the earlier prophets, and who finally rested in Jesus, after having been through all generations. Adam, the first man, already had the Spirit of the true prophet. Adam was in fact a higher being, free from sin, and since he was the first-born, and had been anointed with oil from the tree of life, he was the Messiah. Hence there is a certain identity between Adam and Christ:[2] Adam was the first prophet and Christ the last. The last appearance of the true prophet was in Jesus, who was anointed as prophet and Messiah at his baptism. Since then Christ, the true prophet, has " changed his forms and names from the beginning of the world, until coming upon his own times and being anointed with mercy for the works of God, he shall enjoy rest for ever."

In this context we may refer to an apocryphal saying of Jesus which Epiphanius reproduces no less than four times, ὁ λαλῶν ἐν τοῖς προφήταις, ἰδοὺ πάρειμι, " Behold, I who speak in the

[1] Vielhauer in Neutest. Apokryphen, p. 106.
[2] Strecker, Das Judenchristentum in den Pseudoklementinen, p. 145ff.

prophets am here (present)."[1] Epiphanius uses this *agraphon* in order to emphasise the identity between the Old Testament and New Testament revelations, as against those Gnostics (such as Cerdo and his school) who claimed the opposite, maintaining that the God who spoke in the Law and the Prophets is different from the one who spoke in the Gospels, and was born of Mary.[2]

If we now proceed to inquire what, according to our quotation from Augustine, was the point of view held by the disciples, we may well turn first to the concept of the prophets who spoke through the Spirit of Christ in the age of the Old Covenant, and secondly, to the Christ who passed through the various prophetic figures before finally being revealed in Jesus. It is not improbable that the disciples' words to Jesus in Logion 52, " Twenty-four prophets spoke in Israel, and all spoke in (before, about?) you," reflect this idea. There is, it is true, a certain amount of difficulty in the translation of the Coptic expression for " in, before or through you," as it is impossible to be absolutely certain which is the correct preposition. But a perfectly admissible translation would be: " and all spoke in you,"[3] meaning that all the statements made about Jesus by the Old Testament prophets had been made in his Spirit. This fits in well with the basic view of Christ in the Old Testament which we have mentioned above. If it means simply " about you," then the disciples' words refer to the prophecies concerning the Messiah, without thinking about the common Spirit which spoke through them in Jesus. The twenty-four prophets who spoke in Israel are probably the twenty-four books of the Old Testament. Reference has been made with good reason to the *Ezra-Apocalypse* 14.44ff., where five men are said to have been given the task of copying out the holy traditions. " So in forty days were written ninety-four books. And it came

[1] Cf. Resch, *Agrapha*,[2] p. 207f.
[2] Epiphanius, *Panar.haer.* LXVI, 42, 8 and XLI, 1, 7.
[3] J. M. Plumley, An Introductory Coptic Grammar (1948), § 271; G. Steindorff, Lehrbuch der koptischen Grammatik (1951), § 183.

to pass when the forty days were fulfilled, that the Most High spoke unto me, saying: The twenty-four books that thou hast written publish, that the worthy and unworthy may read (therein). But the seventy last thou shalt keep, to deliver them to the wise among thy people. For in them is the spring of understanding, the fountain of wisdom, and the stream of knowledge." The twenty-four books are those which were read in the synagogue and which were accessible to all. In the Talmud and the Midrash, twenty-four is the normal total of the books of the Old Testament. In this passage we also read that the twenty-four books in the Old Testament were for the unworthy as well, whilst the seventy books of the secret doctrine were only for "the worthy." I consider the resemblance between the *Ezra-Apocalypse* and Logion 52 to be considerable; it is this background which illustrates the form in which the logion is expressed, and marks it out as being a direct polemic against the Old Testament.

Irrespective of which translation—" in you " or " about you " —is preferred, it is nevertheless clear that Jesus' answer to the disciples' statement is a rejection of the doctrine claiming an identity in revelation between the Old and New Testaments, and also of the doctrine that the prophets spoke in the Spirit of Christ. This seems to me to be supported by the context in which the saying of Jesus appears in Augustine, as well as by the pointedly polemical character of the saying concerning Christ in the prophets, as we find it in Epiphanius. This latter saying—" Behold, I who speak in the prophets am here "—is clearly an expression of the identity between the Spirit in which the prophets spoke and the true Revealer as he now appears: " Behold, I am here." The point is directed against the Gnostics' negative attitude to the Old Testament revelation, and in Augustine's reference to the apocryphal saying, the polemic is aimed at the same mark. The heretics turn against the revelations in the Old Testament, and so Augustine refers to Lk. 24.27, where Jesus explains for the two disciples on the road to Emmaus everything the Scriptures say about him. The anti-Marcionite tendency in the *Pseudo-Clementines* is often remarked upon, and the important role played by the concept of " the prophet in the prophets " must be seen in the light of an anti-Gnostic polemic. According to these traditions Peter attacks Simon Magus vigorously when the latter tries to say that there are several gods, the one who appears in Creation and in the Old Testament being an evil god; in this context the Christological concept of the true prophet is important as an argument in favour of the identity of the divine revelation in the Old and New Testaments.

It is in this polemical situation that we have to see Jesus' answer to the disciples in Logion 52. " You have forsaken the Living One who is before you, and have spoken about the dead." " The living Jesus," the true Revealer, stands over against the " dead " prophets, who did not understand. One ought to remember here Marcion's negative attitude to the Old Testament, expressed *inter alia* in his interpretation of Lk. 9.35, the Transfiguration text, " This is my Son, my Chosen; listen to him! " over against 16.29, Abraham's word to the rich man in Hades, " They have Moses and the prophets; let them hear them." Marcion says, according to Tertullian, " *Immo, inquit, nostri dei monela de cælo non Moysen et prophetas jussit audire, sed Christum: hunc audite.*"[1] The fact that the dead man in Hades is told that Moses and the prophets are to be read means for Marcion that the one who listens to them will never reach true life, but is dead, whether evil or good (Lazarus). Life is only for those who listen to Christ. In addition, Marcion claimed that Christ suddenly came down from heaven and revealed himself in the fifteenth year of the reign of the Emperor Tiberius: "*Anno XV. Principatus Tiberii proponit Christum descendisse in civitatem Galilææ Capernaum,*

[1] Tertullian, *Adv. Marcionem*, IV, 34.

utique de cælo creatoris, in quod de suo ante descenderat."[1] Therefore he is not mentioned by any prophet and his works are not spoken of in any prophecy. Logion 52 should be treated in accordance with this.

It is sometimes possible to discover a certain affinity between logia in the *Gospel of Thomas*, either on the " key-word principle " or on a basis of common theological content. We should therefore note that this logion, with its polemic against the Old Testament revelation and possibly against the doctrine of Christ and the Spirit of prophecy, is followed by another, also polemical in content, directed against Jewish-Christian ideas. This time it is circumcision which is rejected.

> His disciples said to him:
> " Circumcision, is it of value or not? "
> He said to them:
> " If it were of value,
> Their Father would have created them circumcised from their mother's womb.
> But the real circumcision in the Spirit has become of full value."

If the negative attitude of the *Gospel of Thomas* to the Old Testament has to do with tendencies such as those for which Marcion in particular was spokesman, it is not surprising that it contains an attack on circumcision. Marcion of course made the most of every opportunity for pouring scorn on the God of the Old Testament, who had been capable of commanding such a practice as circumcision.[2] His criticism of the Old Testament and of circumcision went hand in hand. The fact of the close proximity of logia 52 and 53 can also be taken as evidence that No. 52 is directly polemical against the Old Testament.[3]

[1] Tertullian, *Adv. Marcionem* IV, 7. Cf. Harnack, Marcion, p. 108f.
[2] Origen, *Comm. in epist. Rom.* II, 13.
[3] See above, p. 59.

The Old Testament was not, however, dispensed with altogether from the Gnostic side; it was believed that it contained glimpses of the truth, though in such a distorted form that the reader was compelled to interpret the actual meaning as being diametrically opposed to the apparent meaning. Then we can also see how ideas from later Jewish Christianity were absorbed into the highly syncretistic Gnostic blood-stream, where they were transformed even more. This means that the concept of " the prophet in the prophets " is to be encountered in a Gnostic context, though expressed differently. Hence in *Pistis Sophia* we encounter on a couple of occasions a doctrine which evidently resembles that of the Spirit, or incarnation, of Christ in the prophets. There is given an account of how the soul of Elijah was in one of the æons, but that Jesus took it and brought it to Elizabeth, the mother of John the Baptist. So " the power of the little Jao " which comes from " the midst " and the soul of Elijah were bound together in John the Baptist.[1] Similarly it is said that the prophet Isaiah possessed a power which enabled him to speak in his proclamation about Jesus.[2] Furthermore, all the prophets were to be found in the æons, though they lacked the true knowledge until Jesus passed on his way through the æons, and enlightened them. It might be said that we have here a reminiscence of the doctrine of the Spirit of Christ and the prophets, though more developed, and adapted to another system of thought. The soul of Elijah, or a power set in motion by Jesus, has spoken in the prophets. But the form of this doctrine is so adjusted that it fails to coincide with the concept of identity between Old and New Testaments. *Pistis Sophia* even teaches that all the patriarchs and prophets of the Old Testament had to do penance and " be born again " before being admitted into the kingdom of light.[3]

[1] *Pistis Sophia* 7. [2] *Pistis Sophia* 18. [3] *Pistis Sophia* 135.

IV

THE WORLD AND MAN IN THE WORLD

Corpse, Lion, Life and Death

IN THE Gnostic system, statements about the heavenly nature of the Saviour-figure have their necessary background in a negative view of matter, that which belongs to the created world. The basic view of the world is governed by fear of matter, *hylē*, which imprisons the sparks of heavenly light, preventing them from being united with the heavenly world. The Saviour has no part in the material world, and his task is therefore to open a way of knowledge and enlightenment back to heaven. This negative estimation of the world naturally forms part of the theological system of the *Gospel of Thomas*. We encounter in several logia the concept of the world as something evil, which imprisons the souls of men. For instance, Logion 56 reads:

> Jesus said:
> He who learned to know the world found a corpse, πτῶμα,
> And of him who found a corpse is the world not worthy.

Scorn for the world is here expressed by using the image of a corpse.[1] All things which are in the power of death and corruption are useless, and only smother the true life. None but the man who values the world as he would value a corpse, and recognises that it stifles the heavenly life, is worthy to arise from the world to the highest æons. Thus the world is " a corpse,"

[1] The Naassenes compared the body to a grave and a corpse, according to Hippolytus, *Refut.* V, 8, 22f.; similarly in the *Apocryphon of John*, 55.9ff., 126.6f. Cf. Doresse, L'Evangile selon Thomas, p. 177.

πτῶμα, but is referred to in the otherwise identical words of Logion 80 as " a body," σῶμα.

> Jesus said:
> He who learned to know the world found the body, σῶμα.
> But of him who found the body is the world not worthy.

The question here is whether the different forms of these logia, with the terms πτῶμα and σῶμα, are due purely to chance. It would appear to be so if we compare them, e.g. with the word-exchange which has presumably taken place in the two sayings of Jesus: " Wherever the body, πτῶμα, is, there the eagles will be gathered together," Matt. 24.28, and Lk. 17.37, " Where the body, σῶμα, is, there the eagles will be gathered together." But this may also be due to the fact that in certain Gnostic ideas about the " upper worlds " and " the lower," πτῶμα and σῶμα were mentioned; the material element in the human body was also referred to in the same terms. " The upper worlds became ψυχικοί and πνευματικοί, but [the worlds] which are below became σωματικοί and πνευμ[ατικοί . . .] " *Manichæan Kephalaia* 120.31ff. Similarly we can read about the heavenly " elements " which come to " their σώματα and πνεύματα on earth," 121.2ff.

The first condition for the man who would make any progress whatever along the way of salvation, liberation from the death-grip of *hylē*, is that he should recognise the character of the world; once this has been done, he is freed from its power, " of him . . . is the world not worthy," Logion 56. The world, then, is something best described by a term such as " death " or " corpse," or, as we read in one of *Thomas's Psalms*, " I have tried the world and known it, that there is not a tittle of life in it." 17.16f.[1] In addition, those who live in the world without

[1] Cf. 12.19ff., 63.22f. " The world is nothing, there is no gain in it at all," and 135.23f. " None shall be able to glory while he has yet an hour in this prison."

knowledge of the heavenly life above, or of its heavenly particles imprisoned here below, are " the dead." " The living " are those who are illuminated through knowledge of the Saviour. The beginning of Logion 11 reads:

> Jesus said:
> This heaven shall perish,
> And the one above it shall perish;
> And the dead are not alive,
> And the living shall not die. . . .

By " heaven " is meant here the " higher " part of the material world, and not the eternal heaven. The Creator-God, Jaldabaoth, the Demiurge, also created a heaven for himself and his highest angels, and since everything created is to perish, that heaven shall also be destroyed. The text of the Logion, that heaven and " the one above it " are to perish, may refer to two superimposed heavens, but it is more probable that it refers to the " created heaven " and its ruler, i.e., the ruler of this world, Jaldabaoth, the Demiurge. All those who belong to his world, and have not part in the heavenly light-world, are " the dead " and have never really possessed life. Only those who have the spark of light within themselves, and have been illuminated thereby, are " the living," who never die.

A similar thought is encountered in Logion 111, where it is said that " the living " shall not die, since they have won life through knowledge of the Living One.

> Jesus said:
> The heavens shall be rolled up, and the earth before you,
> And he who may live through the Living One
> Shall not behold death or <terror>. . .

Here also is expressed the idea that the created world, with its earth and its heaven, shall perish, and he who does not wish to be involved in its disintegration must win the knowledge of salvation through the Risen and Living One.

The peculiar saying about the lion should be placed in the same conceptual scheme; though at first sight it seems to have nothing to do with "the world and man in the world," it nevertheless contains direct teaching on this subject.

> Jesus said:
> Blessed is the lion
> Whom the man devours,
> And thus the lion becomes a man;
> And cursed is the man whom the lion devours,
> And thus the lion becomes a man.
>
> Logion 7

In order to understand this saying we must first of all be clear as to what "the lion" symbolises. This expression does not occur elsewhere in the *Gospel of Thomas*, but is found on several occasions in other Gnostic texts. In the *Hypostasis of the Archons*, another document from the Nag-Hamadi library, Samael, the Creator-God, is said to be characterised by a shadowy existence below the limits of the æons. He became a wilful animal in the form of a lion, and is both male and female, since he came into existence from matter, *hylē*.[1]

The highest in the created world, and he who came into existence from matter, bear the symbol of the lion; this connection between the material world, which is evil, and the lion-symbol is to be found in other Gnostic texts, such as the *Mandæan Ginza*, in which the body is referred to as a lion. Here it is the material side of man which bears the lion-symbol. The guiltless soul is told, "O soul, stand up, go forth, enter the body and

[1] 142.10ff. In Origen, *Contra Celsum* VI, 30, it is said of the same archon, the highest, that his appearance was that of a lion. Cf. VI, 33. See also the *Apocryphon of John* 123, which speaks about "Jaoth with the face of a lion." Cf. 37. *Pistis Sophia* also has this lion-symbolism (Index: "Löwe" and "Löwengesicht" in Schmidt-Till, Koptisch-gnostische Schriften).

become imprisoned in the palace. The fierce lion shall through you be taken prisoner, the fierce raging lion."[1] The Valentinian material of *Excerpta ex Theodoto* also contains a saying which couples together the cosmos and the lion: "The soul shall be saved from the world and from the jaws of the lion." 84. The *Manichæan Psalm-book* likewise uses the lion-symbol, for instance in that passage in which it stands for physical desire: "What shall I do with this lion that roars at all times? What shall I do with this seven-headed serpent? Take unto thyself fasting that thou mayest strangle this lion: lo, (take) virginity and kill this serpent." 149.22ff.

Behind this saying on the lion in the *Gospel of Thomas* there would appear to be the thought that when man conquers the material side of existence—the body which is of matter—he is then saved; but if he is seduced by the material world, he is without knowledge and under the curse of oblivion. There is, however, a further metaphor which witnesses to the transforming power of the heavenly life. If "the lion," the material in or around man, can be "absorbed" by his higher nature, then it is no longer in control. But if the lower, the material, in man absorbs the higher, he is cursed and lost. This interpretation of the "lion-saying" gives us the key to the interpretation of another, otherwise obscure, part of Logion 11.

> On that day when you ate the dead
> You brought it to life.
> When you come into the light,
> What shall you do then?

Here it is probably once more a question of the true Gnostic who, through the living and the eternal in him, is able to "bring

[1] Lidzbarski, Ginza, p. 430 and 507. Cf. the *Psalms of Thomas* 11.1ff., where "the lion" stands for the power of evil in the world. Similarly in 14.5, "How shall I heal thee, o *hyle*, the Lioness (?), the Mother of this world?" Reading, "Lioness" in A. Adam, Die Psalmen des Thomas und das Perlenlied als Zeugnisse vorchristlicher Gnosis (1959), p. 21.

to life" his own material existence. This saying of Jesus is also to be found in Hippolytus, *Refutatio* V, 8, 32, though it is there formulated somewhat differently. "You who have eaten of dead things and have brought (them) to life, what will you do if you eat living things?" The context of this saying in Hippolytus does not make clear how it was understood, but it was most probably interpreted on the same principle as Logia 7 and 11. The same concept, dealing with the way in which to the Gnostic the physical in man was capable of being absorbed by the heavenly, is also expressed in the *Gospel of Truth*, 25.10ff. "Through the Unity shall every one find himself. Through Gnosis shall he be purified from a manifold creature to a unity, in that like a fire he absorbs the material in himself, darkness with light, death with life." Thus the body, because it belongs to the physical, is in itself useless, but the heavenly life is able, by virtue of its enormous power, to sanctify even its "container." The body, the flesh, can never rise from the dead, but as long as it harbours the spark of light it can be "purified" by it. This may possibly be what is meant by this passage from the *Gospel of Philip*: "The holy man is entirely holy, even in his body, σῶμα. For if he took the bread he would make it pure, or the cup, or any other thing he takes, in that he purifies (sanctifies) it. And how (can that be) if he does not also purify (sanctify) the body?" 125.2ff. It is a risky undertaking to try and interpret these words, but it is most probable that the "holy" refers both to Christ and to the Christian—the Christian, the anointed Gnostic, has in fact according to this gospel become a Christ. 115.26f. He who is "holy" is capable of making everything "holy"; he makes use of the material world without allowing himself to be corrupted by it.

The actual expression "eat the dead" in Logion 11, in common with "eat the lion" in Logion 7, does not appear to be uncommon in Gnostic texts. We have a typical example of this in the *Gospel of Philip*: " This world, means to eat a corpse. Everything which is eaten of it is also hateful. Truth, means to eat that which is living. Therefore none of those who are sustained by it are among [those who] die. Jesus has come from that place and has brought with him sustenance from thence. And to them who are willing gave he the living [in order that] they should not die." 121.19ff.

Another passage in the *Gospel of Thomas* which expresses itself in the same conceptual categories, though is considerably more obscure, comprises Logia 59 and 60. The extent to which these logia belong together has been discussed, since they are two independent logia, brought together on the " key-word " principle.[1] I consider it most likely that they were originally two distinct logia which have been brought together on account of their common theme, but that they were already combined in the source which the " Compiler " used. The two sections are so closely bound together that it is difficult to draw a clear distinction between them; this difficulty is not lessened by the fact that a haplography in the Coptic text occurs right on the place where they are assumed to join. However, this has little effect on the interpretation of the words, and it is unnecessary to examine the difficult sentence in detail at this point.

> Jesus said:
> " Behold the Living One, as long as you live,
> Lest you should die,
> And try to see him and not be able to see."[2]
> (60) <They saw> a Samaritan
> Who carried a lamb
> (And) was on his way into Judæa.

[1] Cf. Leipoldt, Ein neues Evangelium ?, col. 488, which makes them into one logion, while the English edition counts them as two. See the discussion given by Giversen, Thomasevangeliet, p. 101f.

[2] Or ". . . And try to see him.—And you cannot see a Samaritan . . ."

He said to his disciples:
" This person beside the lamb?"
They said to him:
" In order to kill and eat it."
He said to them:
" As long as it is alive he shall not eat it,
But (only) if he kills it
And it becomes a corpse (then he will eat it)."
They said:
" Otherwise he would not be able to do it."
He said to them:
" You yourselves seek a place of rest,
Lest you become a corpse
And be eaten."

Logia 59 and 60

The first section, Logion 59, is in full accordance with the logia we have quoted previously on the subject of the way from death to life. It is a matter of beholding the Saviour and holding on to the true gnosis as long as one lives, for there is no other way in which to win true life. But if, through dullness and unwillingness to be enlightened, the Saviour is not seen, then the person in question is already dead in this life and there is no possibility for him to seek and find the Saviour. Or do the words on death refer to physical death, the implication being that there is no chance of seeing the Saviour after death? In either case it can be said that this logion also plays upon the idea of becoming " a corpse." The same is true of Logion 60, where the central thoughts are " the corpse " and the danger of being eaten.

Even though the image of the Samaritan carrying a lamb into Judæa has no known parallels, and is thus new in both form and content, it should nevertheless be possible to understand its meaning. We grasp its basic viewpoint most simply if we start with the final summary, in which Jesus warns his disciples by pointing to the contrast between death (the corpse), which is this material world, and life, which is won through the Saviour.[1] If man does not find rest, salvation, he becomes like this world, a corpse, and is consumed by " the dead." This is a genuine Gnostic concept, which is further strengthened by a passage in *Pistis Sophia*, where one of the *Psalms of Solomon* is expounded. " And that word which your power has said is (quoting from *Ps. Sol.*), ' you have liberated her from the tombs and brought her out from the midst of the corpse.' This is the same word which Pistis Sophia has said: And you have liberated me from chaos and brought me forth out of the material darkness, that is out of the dark emanations, those which are in chaos, from which you have taken their light." Ch. 71. This is the thought-world to which Logion 60 belongs.

But we may approach the image of the Samaritan and the lamb more closely if we start from the thought that the Samaritan was to kill and eat the lamb. The actual image of a Samaritan on his way into Judæa with a lamb is unknown to us, and seems rather strange, remembering the prevailing enmity between Jews and Samaritans. A Samaritan could not come to Judæa and sacrifice a lamb. We are therefore tempted to regard this image as a *reductio ad absurdum*, a picture of something which could not possibly happen. But we have the explanation of what the saying meant—in the context in which it was used in the *Gospel of Thomas*—in Jesus' question at the beginning of the conversation between himself and the disciples, " This person beside the lamb? " Jesus asks this in order to draw attention to the key figure. The disciples' answer does not, however, make it clear

[1] The same view occurs several times in the *Gospel of Philip*, e.g. 100.15ff. " A heathen does not die. For he has never lived, to be able to die. He who has come to believe in the truth, he has found life. And he is in danger of dying, because he is alive." Cf. 100.6ff.

who this man beside the lamb is, but only says that he is the one who is to kill and eat it. There is, though, a passage in the *Manichæan Psalm-book* which is reminiscent of Logion 60, although its imagery is entirely different.[1] The image here is that of a lamb tied to a tree, and while its shepherd looks for it, another eats it. "We also, my beloved—let us separate the word 'Who is this that eats?' [and] 'Who is this that is eaten?' Thou dost not. Who is this that seeks? Who is this that is sought? The sheep that is bound to the tree for which its shepherd searches. Thou dost not. There is a sheep bound to the tree: There is another [that] ate the sheep ..." 172.15ff. An explanation is then given: "The sheep bound to the tree is the Love that died: the Wisdom that reveals is the shepherd that seeks after it. He that ate the sheep is the devouring fire, the God of this Æon that led the whole world astray ..."[2]

The aspect of this image which is of value for the interpretation of Logion 60 is the question of who it is that eats and what the lamb is. The eater is the Lord of this world, the Creator-God, the Demiurge. If Logion 60 has the same meaning, then the one who carries the lamb into Judæa is the Demiurge, intent on destroying man and his particle of light. The lamb is man, and this is why it reads (in accordance with what is said in Logion 59), "As long as it is alive he shall not eat it." But if he succeeds in killing it, in ruining man so that he is no longer among the children of light, then he destroys it altogether. The disciples' answer, "otherwise he would not be able to do it," fits in well with this interpretation. What according to the image is a ridiculous truism, that the man has to kill the lamb before he can eat it, is by no means ridiculous to the Gnostic, because it has a deep meaning; the Gnostic knows that the ruler of this world is intent on preventing his salvation by binding him fast in the

[1] Doresse, L'Evangile selon Thomas, p. 180, refers to this passage, without giving any commentary.

[2] In the Manichæan text, Jesus is evidently the lamb which was bound.

corruption of material things, and that the only salvation is to become—and remain—"living," for then the Demiurge can do nothing. The Gnostic is nevertheless constantly threatened, "lest you become a corpse and be eaten."

It is, however, important to remember that the antithesis between life and death, "the living" and "the dead," does not only occur in Gnostic texts. Jesus calls the Jews who do not heed his message "the dead," according to the well-known text in Matt. 8.22 (Lk. 9.60). "Another of the disciples said to him, 'Lord, let me first go and bury my father.' But Jesus said to him, 'Follow me, and leave the dead to bury their own dead.'" The same form of expression recurs in John, e.g. in 5.24f., where "death" is a symbol for life without Christ and "the dead" are those men who have still not heard the voice of Jesus. Paul also cries in desperation, "who will deliver me from this body, of death?" Rom. 7.24, expressing the deepest pessimism when faced with the body's captivity to sin.[1] In the Letter to the Ephesians which, of all the Pauline letters, stands nearest to Gnostic terminology and a Gnostic concept-world, the Gentiles who have not come to know Jesus are called "the dead," 2.1, 5, "And you he made alive, when you were dead through the trespasses and sins in which you once walked . . ." One also wonders whether the little hymn in 5.14 may not reflect a terminology which later became current in a Gnostic milieu. "Awake, O sleeper, and arise from the dead, and Christ shall give you light." In Gnostic texts, these terms dealing with "the living" and "the dead" have become general, and have taken their absolute contents from the decisive antithesis between the material world and the world of the æons. Such an antithesis does not play such an important part in the New Testament. "The dead" are those who have no faith in Christ, and thus cannot reach eternal life in the new existence. "The living" are those

[1] Cf. the *Manichæan Psalm-book* 56.29, 57.17 and 75.25.

who have been baptised and believe, and have thus been incorporated into living fellowship with Christ. The "new birth" which has come to pass in this way stands in relation to the power which will eventually bring about the resurrection to new life. This new life in Christ creates no antithesis between creation and salvation. But the Gnostic system is orientated differently. The Gnostics did not accept the resurrection of the body, and their baptism marked a step which they took when they rejected all created things, determining only to kill all material things which hold the sparks of light imprisoned in them. We notice therefore a shift in the direction of replacing the "resurrection" by the "enlivening" of man, i.e. liberation of the particles of light in matter. Death is everything which is in the power of matter; life is everything belonging to the heavenly world of light. This shift, away from the New Testament and towards Gnosticism, is to some extent illustrated by the logion which follows the above-quoted No. 60, on the Samaritan and the lamb, in which the antithesis was between life and death. Logion 61, which is probably an independent logion, begins:

> Jesus said:
> Two shall go to rest on a bed.
> One shall die,
> The other shall live.

In its Lukan version this saying of Jesus reads, "I tell you, in that night there will be two men in one bed; one will be taken and the other left." Lk. 17.34. This saying speaks of the last day, when the Son of Man returns on the clouds of heaven, and takes the faithful up to himself, whilst those that do not believe shall be left in the doomed world. But this background has no meaning in the Gnostic version, since there was no place in their system for such an expectation of a returning Saviour. The logion has therefore been given a different appearance; the terms "die" and " live " have become the main concepts, and there is no longer any need to look at the logion from an eschatological point of view. Thus the verb " be taken " has been exchanged for " live," and " be left " for " die." In this new milieu the death of one and the life of another comprise an act of salvation which happens here and now: liberation from the grip of matter, or destruction in *hylē*, and not something belonging to the last day. Within the New Testament, our closest comparative material is provided by the Gospel of John and its view of life and death in the present situation, e.g. 5.24 and 8.51, but this view is still linked with the Resurrection of the dead and—as against Gnostic teaching—had a definite relation to the last days.

The House, the Robbers and the Field

There is another term in the *Gospel of Thomas* which ought to be taken into consideration in connection with this theme, of the world and man in the world, and that is " the house." The question is whether the word has been used to denote this world, the " house " in which mankind dwells or—seen individually—the " house " in which the individual dwells, namely, the body. Metaphors for the world and the body are in fact frequently identical in Gnostic texts, as we have already observed. As a background to this use of the word " house " in the *Gospel of Thomas* we may refer to a passage in the *Pseudo-Clementines*, where the cosmos is described in the following way: " In the beginning, when God had made the heaven and the earth, as one house, the shadow which was cast by the mundane bodies involved in darkness those things which were enclosed in it . . ."[1]

[1] *Rec.* I, 27, 1. Cf. *Hom.* I, 18, where the Saviour's coming into the world is described thus: " One living outside the house which is filled with smoke may approach and open the door, so that the light of the sun which is without may be admitted into the house, and the smoke of the fire which is within may be driven out."

In Mandæan texts, " the house " is also a common expression for this world, " the mortal house," " the dark dwelling." The world is like a locked house, within which is imprisonment and which man must leave if he would find liberty.[1]

But if the world is a " house " for man, the body is also a " house " for the soul. To be unenlightened as a man " in the body " is to be in the dark house. " Many are the labours that I suffered while I was in this dark house."[2] Scorn for the body means that in this context the concept " house " has a negative sound—" the stinking body," " the dark house."[3] Or as the *Ginza* says, when describing how Adam was to be saved, ". . . brought forth from the body, from this world, from the bonds, the fetters, the snares and bands, in order to take him away from the earth built by Ptahil and the seven planets, to which they then brought him and in which they have made him to dwell and to sit, in order to save him and bring him forth from the dirty, stinking, devouring, pernicious body, the raging lion . . ."[4] The same concept of the body as a " house " is also to be found in Jewish texts, e.g. Wisd. 9.15, and in the New Testament, II Cor. 5.1, but the metaphor there does not have such negative implications as it does among the Gnostics, where it is naturally due to their utter scorn for the things of this world.

The first logion in the *Gospel of Thomas* which can be associated to the complex of ideas surrounding the term " house " is:

> Jesus said:
> I shall tear [down this] house
> And none shall be able to build it up [again].
>
> Logion 71

[1] Lidzbarski, Ginza, p. 25. Cf. Jonas, Gnosis und spätantiker Geist I, p. 100ff.
[2] The *Manichæan Psalm-book* 152.14ff. Cf. the *Gospel of Truth* 25.21f.
[3] Lidzbarski, Mandäische Liturgien (1920), p. 102.
[4] Lidzbarski, Ginza, p. 430. Cf. Jonas, op. cit., p. 130ff.

This saying of Jesus is probably based on Mk. 14.58, where the accusation against Jesus—presumably a theme from his teaching—has to do with the Temple: " I will destroy this temple that is made with hands, and in three days I will build another, not made with hands." John interprets this saying with direct reference to Jesus' body, broken in death and raised up again in the Resurrection, 2.19—an idea which the Markan saying may also be hinting at.[1] In its present form in the *Gospel of Thomas*, the saying can scarcely be interpreted other than as a polemic against the canonical saying of Jesus and its content—Jesus' bodily resurrection. Since the focus of the New Testament text lies in Jesus' promise to build up the temple-body once more, the word " temple " was exchanged for " house " and Jesus was made to say that " none shall be able to build it up again." The meaning would then be that the Gnostic Jesus despised the body, since it was in any case only an apparent body, which shall be destroyed and has no value while it exists. Jesus has in fact come in order to condemn the material world to which the body belongs, as being the most dangerous enemy of the particle of heavenly light—the soul. Furthermore, in the *Gospel of Mary* the soul is called a " murderess of man "; the reason for this is that when a man dies, his soul is permanently divorced from his body, being freed from matter, and hence the soul kills the body, 16.14ff. This thought also fits in with the " lion-saying," Logion 7. A resurrection of the body is quite out of the question,[2] and it is therefore of profound importance when Jesus says that he will destroy " the house " and none shall be able to build it up again. The word " house " may naturally also refer to this world, but the meaning remains virtually the same. Jesus' task is, in the last resort, that of breaking apart the material world, by cutting a path to freedom in the heavenly world for all the " particles of

[1] Gärtner, The Areopagus Speech and Natural Revelation (1955), 209ff.

[2] See e.g. the *Gospel of Mary* 7.1; *Jesu Christi Sophia* 79.1ff. Cf. Harnack, Marcion, p. 118 and 177.

light" imprisoned in this world, leading to their eventual reunion.

It is sometimes difficult in the continuous text of this gospel to decide where the boundaries lie between logia, and to decide whether from the point of view of content various logia belong together or not. After Logion 71 there follows another which may belong together with it; one part of the logion seems to support this. If this were the case, then it would mean that the two logia had a common theme, and that the word about the "house" could be interpreted on a basis of the following one, on inheritance, and vice versa. Logion 72 reads:

> [A man said] to him:
> "Tell my brethren
> That they should share my father's goods with me."
> He said to him:
> "O, man, who made me a divider?"
> He turned to his disciples (and) said to them:
> "Am I indeed a divider?"

The scene is the same as in Lk. 12.13-14. The difference between Luke and Logion 72 is, apart from some minor details, that the latter adds the word "father"—"my father's goods"—and omits the word "judge" in Jesus' answer. "One of the multitude said to him, 'Teacher, bid my brother divide the inheritance with me.' But he said to him, 'Man, who made me a judge or divider over you?'" Luke then adds to these words a warning against covetousness. The purpose of the saying in Logion 72 is evidently different, and therefore the word "judge" is omitted and Jesus' rejection of the role of "divider" is emphasised by causing him to repeat the statement. It is conceivable that the logion was given this form so that it might fit in better with some Gnostic item of doctrine. The addition of the word "father" *can* be evidence of gnosticising, since the idea of the heavenly Father's "goods" plays some part in the Gnostic thought-world. In the same way the omission of "judge" *can* have its background in a concept similar to that which Marcion defended, that the true God judges no one: Marcion therefore removed all the texts in which God was presented as judge.[1]

What is the idea behind Jesus' pointed denial that he is a "divider"?[2] The term used in this logion to express "sharing," "dividing out" is the verb "to divide," **πωϣε**; and the person who does the dividing, "the divider," **ρεϥπωϣε**. This verb is used in the Bohairic translation of Lk. 12.14 for the Greek *μεριστής*, "divider." One would really have expected to find the verb **πωρϫ**, since this is the word used in the Sahidic translation of this text, and the *Gospel of Thomas* is written in Sahidic. Perhaps the choice of **πωϣε** may be connected with the fact that **πωρϫ** is often used in a positive sense, referring to the activity of Jesus. The "division" which Jesus justly carries out according to Gnostic ideas is a work of separation, i.e. the separation of the two natures, light and darkness, the heavenly and the material, good and evil, etc.[3] It is out of the question to interpret "division" in this positive sense in Logion 72.

On the other hand, the verb **πωϣε** is often used to describe "division" in the sense of that dissolution which leads to destruction and death. Such is the case in the *Gospel of Truth*, where man is spoken of, in a common Gnostic metaphor, as a "vessel," which is either sanctified and filled, or empty and broken, **πωϣε**. 26.15. Or in the description of this world, which "was a terror and confusion and uncertainty and doubt and division, **πωϣε** ..." Logion 61 also uses this verb to express

[1] Harnack, Marcion, p. 176f.

[2] D. Gershenson and G. Quispel, "Meristae," Vig, Christ. 2 (1958), p. 19-26, interpret "divider" as being almost a "sectarian," "one who introduces dissenting opinions."

[3] The *Manichæan Psalm-book* 26.29, 30.26, 56.21, etc. Cf. *Pistis Sophia*, ed. C. Schmidt in Coptica II (1925), p. 300f. The use of these two terms varies in *Pistis Sophia*, but a differentiated use can still to some extent be discerned.—The positive division is also mentioned in *Excerpta ex Theodoto* 36.1f., where it is said that Jesus came to "divide up" man, to unite his best part with the heavenly element, and thus to create "unity."

the division of evil, "... when he is united, he shall be filled with light, but when he is divided, he shall be filled with darkness." It seems thus to be the case that behind these terms, as used here, there lie two distinct ideas. On the one hand, there is the dividing of a unity—negative meaning—and on the other, the distinguishing between different unities, between good and evil—positive meaning.

In Logion 72, Jesus' denial that he is a " divider " is to be understood on the basis of the important position of " division " within the Gnostic world of ideas. Jesus' task is in fact that of bringing division to an end. It is as unthinkable that he could do the work of dividing, according to Logion 72, as that he should rebuild the " house " that he tears down in Logion 71. Both logia seem to me to be in line, and to have a certain polemical character.

This interpretation of Logia 71 and 72 can also throw light on to Logion 21.

(*a*) Mary said to Jesus:
" Who are your disciples like? "
He said:
" They are like little children, living in a field which is not theirs.
When the owners of the field come, they say,
' Leave our field to us.'
They strip themselves before them
That they might leave it to them and give them back their field.

(*b*) " Therefore I say:
' If the owner of the house knows that the thief is coming,
He will watch before he comes,
And will not let him break into the house of his kingdom in order to carry away his goods.

Be watchful against the world.
Gird your loins with great power,
So that the robbers do not find (a) way to reach you.
When they find the adversity you look out of,
May there be a learned man in your midst.
When the fruit was ripe, he came quickly with the sickle
In his hand and cut the grain.
He who has ears to hear with, let him hear!' "

The two sections, consisting of quite different " metaphor-groups," the children in the field and the thief who breaks in, (*a*) and (*b*) have been coupled together in one edition. This seems from the point of view of content to be correct, since the second section seems to be an explanation of " the children in the field," introduced by the words, " therefore I say . . ." The two sections can nevertheless be understood as being independent logia, but in either case the interpretation is the same. In order to link up with the term " the house " it may be most suitable to begin with section *b*.

This consists of a number of sayings of Jesus from the canonical Gospels, all having the theme of watchfulness in face of Jesus' second coming and judgment. As to its composition, the first part of this logion seems to have been constructed from material from Matt. 24.43-44: " But know this, that if the householder had known in what part of the night the thief was coming, he would have watched and would not have let his house be broken into. Therefore you also must be ready . . ." This text has later been combined with part of Matt. 12.29, " Or how can one enter a strong man's house and plunder his goods . . ." and possibly with part of Lk. 12.35 also, "Let your loins be girded . . ." There follow some typically Gnostic phrases in which the main terms are " power " and " the robbers." The logion is rounded off with some clauses dealing with the harvest of the ripe fruit, connected possibly with Mk. 4.29. One has the impression that the existence of this part of the logion is due to a combination from memory of phrases dealing with one and the same theme; further interference with the New Testament sayings has been resulted in their being recast in such a way as to make it impossible to ignore their theological purpose.

As we have already said, there is a quite natural shift of meaning in the term " house," between " this world " and " the body "; the world is man's house, just as the body is the individual's house. On the basis of those ideas which we have mentioned as being connected to the " house," the world and the human body, we might interpret the logion as follows: " the owner of the house " is man, and " the house " is his body ; in this house are preserved " his goods," the most important thing he possesses—a share in the kingdom of light. This is the part which the evil powers are bent upon destroying. It is described in the *Apocryphon of John* how the stupid Creator-God Jaldabaoth, son of Sophia, blew a spark of his light into his creation, man, where it remained imprisoned. Jaldabaoth wants on no account to lose this power which he has implanted in man, for it is his own property. He therefore attempts, with the help of his wicked angels, to prevent the liberation of the soul from the material world, the body, and stop it launching out on its ascension. If the particle of light once quits man, then Jaldabaoth has lost it for ever.

To return to Logion 21, it may be said that the moment of the expected " break-in " which the owner of the house knows is coming, is the moment of death.[1] The " break-in " is the moment when the soul leaves the body, and the soul must rescue the particle of light. The exhortation to watchfulness is an exhortation " against the world," the material world which will not release the particle of light. When faced with death one

[1] A comparison may be made here with the *Manichæan Psalm-book* 188.17, where " the thief " represents the element of Darkness in the body, " Bind me to thy guard because of the thief that is in the house with me."

must be on one's guard; here we notice a most important alteration in the New Testament text, from ". . . if the householder had known in what part of the night the thief was coming, he would have watched . . ." to "If the owner of the house knows that the thief *is* coming, he will watch *before* he comes, and will not let him break into the house of his kingdom . . ." This alteration turns the logion very decidedly towards Gnosticism, which can be very well illustrated from a passage in *Pistis Sophia*, where this interpretation of "the coming of the thief" is supported by quotations from exactly the same New Testament text, Matt. 24.42, though as always in this document, in its canonical form. The man who is enlightened through the mystery, and who has obtained gnosis, cannot sin "consciously."[1] Heimarmene can however compel anyone who has not reached the highest mysteries to sin, because he has a body of *hylē*, but these sins may be repented of and cleansed, and the person in question may thus preserve his "state of salvation." But if death strikes *before* repentance and cleansing have taken place, then the soul is cast out into the farthest sphere. Thus man must watch, "so that you may not pile evil upon evil and leave the body without repentance having taken place, and so become eternally estranged from the kingdom of light." It is in this context that the alteration of the New Testament text, exhorting the householder to watch *before* the thief comes, is of real importance.

The logion goes on to say that the "owner of the house" must watch and gird himself with "great power, δύναμις," so that the robbers find no way in. With this clause is introduced into the logion a passage which has no direct connection with any New Testament texts, but which is made up of Gnostic formulæ. It is therefore of considerable interest to see to what extent this section agrees with the above interpretation of the first half of the logion. The same expression, "great power" occurs in

[1] *Pistis Sophia* 120.

Acts 8.10 as a name given to the "great father of the Gnostics," Simon Magus: "they all gave heed to him, from the least to the greatest, saying, 'This man is that power of God which is called Great.'" Then the term "power," appears continually in Gnostic literature as denoting the heavenly power of light which is active here below;[1] it sometimes parallels closely "the Spirit," as active in Jesus, or as a gift of the living Jesus.[2] Thus according to the *Gospel of Bartholemew*, Bartholemew himself receives "a spirit of power" from Jesus enabling him to endure the sight of the devil.[3]

As far as the term "robber" is concerned, this also has its special use in Gnostic literature. Thus the human body is sometimes called a "robber's grave," i.e. the place where the robbers, the material powers, have buried the particle of heavenly light. Or the body, the physical side of man, may be called "the robber's bonds" which hold captive the divine particle.[4] The powers, therefore, which control the material world—in particular the body—are called "the robbers," an expression which we also find in the *Gospel of Philip*. "The souls were in the power of the robbers who had imprisoned them. But he (Christ) saved them ..." 101.11ff.[5] The robbers are seeking to reach the divine part of man, the part which has a share in the heavenly world of light. If the interpretation of the English edition is correct, it supports our case, being translated: "because they (the robbers) will find the advantage which you expect."

In the New Testament texts from which this logion is built, "the thief" stands for the sudden and unexpected coming of the Messiah—an image used in this and other contexts with eschato-

[1] The *Hypostasis of the Archons* 136.2, 142.2; *Pistis Sophia* (in the index "*dynamis*").
[2] *Excerpta ex Theodoto* 4.2, 17.3, 24.2, 82.1; the *Acts of Thomas* 10 and 52.
[3] James, p. 174.
[4] *Jesu Christi Sophia* 104 and 121.
[5] Cf. the *Manichæan Psalm-book* 70.1f. "... the habitation of the robbers which is the body of death, for which every man has wept"; *Excerpta ex Theodoto* 72.2; *Corpus Hermeticum* 7.2.

logical implications.[1] But it is not a metaphor for death. It is, however, easy to understand how the eschatological image came to be applied to death when it entered a Gnostic world of ideas. The concepts of the last day and the second coming of the Messiah have receded into the background, and the judgment and separation which according to the New Testament are to happen on that day are transferred to the sphere of man's decision during his lifetime. It is therefore not surprising to find eschatological imagery applied in Gnostic circles to death. The same can be said about the logion's concluding words, on the ripe fruit and the harvest. This is in the New Testament an expression for the coming day, and coming judgment—its meaning is eschatological. But for the true Gnostic, it can apply equally well to death and its decisive test, for the meaning of death is that the soul is liberated from the body and sent out upon the last difficult steps of its journey to the boundaries of heaven.[2] There is no question of waiting for the resurrection of the body on the last day. We should also pay attention to this shift in meaning, in the direction of a judgment in this life, here and now: this is typical of the Gospel of John, a tendency which may well be due in this case to the front-line position occupied by John's Gospel in the struggle with gnosticising tendencies.[3]

This interpretation of Logion 21b is supported not only by its own composition and way of expression, but also by the *Gospel of Thomas* as a whole, with its dominant concept of man. In addition, it is to some extent supported by Logion 103, the

[1] Cf. H. Preisker, art. κλέπτης in Theol. Wörterb. III, p. 753ff.

[2] "The harvest" is mentioned on two further occasions in the *Gospel of Thomas*, Logia 58 and 73. In the former logion, which is a shortened and altered version of the Parable of the Tares, Matt. 13. 24-30, the same shift may have taken place, even if it is not altogether obvious. In the latter logion, which is an almost word-for-word reproduction of the saying on the workers and the harvest, Matt. 9. 37, it is not a question of the last day, but a picture of the emergence of the kingdom of God "in the fullness of time." Cf. a Gnostic exposition of the latter logion, in the *Acts of Philip* (Lipsius-Bonnet II: 2, p. 66, 9ff.).

[3] There is a concept of "resurrection" in Gnostic doctrine, but this does not refer to the resurrection of the body, but rather to that day on which all the sparks of light will have been brought in to the highest.

content of which is similar. Unfortunately, on this occasion the text is damaged, and it is consequently difficult to know how the gaps are to be filled in. On the basis of the parallelism between Logia 103 and 21b, it is however possible to interpret the text as a whole.

> Jesus said:
> Blessed is the man who knows at [what] time robbers are coming in (*or* that wild robbers are coming in),
> So that [he] may raise himself and gather his [strength] and gird his loins, before they come in.

The typical elements from Logion 21b are also to be found here. The blessed man is he who is aware that the robbers are coming, or knows at what time they are coming, and prepares his defences—" gathers his strength "—*before* they come in. The enlightened man must make himself impregnable to the material powers before death comes, and must keep his spark of light inviolate. Here again there has been a shift away from the New Testament meaning; there it was a matter of stopping the thief from getting in: here it is recognised that the thief will get in, and it is a matter of gathering one's strength in order to preserve oneself from the material world and keep one's fragment of light.

It is possible that another logion may be placed in this context, even though the logion in question contains no direct Gnostic additions which prove that it is to be interpreted in this way.

> Jesus said:
> It is impossible
> For anyone to enter a strong (man's) house
> And take him (*or* something) by violence,

If he has not bound his hands.
Then can he rob his house.

Logion 35

The logion follows Mk. 3.27 closely, diverging only in small details. In the New Testament (all the Synoptic Gospels) this saying refers to the struggle with the devil, who is the "strong man," but whose power can be broken. In the *Gospel of Thomas*, it is an independent and disconnected saying. But since, as we have shown, the metaphor of the house and the entry of the thieves has probably been given its particular interpretation on the basis of the idea of the body as a house, whose treasure—the divine spark of light—is the object of the evil power's attentions, it is reasonable to interpret Logion 35 in the same way. A similar interpretation of this saying of Jesus is to be found in the Gnostic *Excerpta ex Theodoto*, which to some extent supports our view of Logion 35. In *Excerpta* 51 is mentioned the "psychic" man who, it is true, has no "pneumatic" divine soul but who has a "psychic" one which, given the correct assistance, can reach saving knowledge. The enemy of this "psychic" soul is the flesh, the "hylic."[1] This hylic part "the Saviour called an 'adversary' and Paul said a 'law warring against the law of my mind' and the Saviour advises us 'to bind it' and 'to seize its possessions' as those of 'a strong man' who was warring against the heavenly soul, and he also advises us to be 'reconciled with him on the way lest we fall into prison' and 'be kind to it' and not to nourish and strengthen it by the power of sin but to put it to death here and now . . ." 52.1f. Here the "strong man" and his house stand for the body, the hylic, which must be vanquished; otherwise the application of the image is somewhat different from that in Logia 21b and 103. It is evident, though,

[1] See Sagnard, Extraits de Théodote, p. 167.

that this is the kind of thought-world which must be understood as applying here.

If we now turn to the first part of the long Logion 21—the little children living in a field which is not theirs—we find it gains in clarity when we observe how the latter part of the logion has to do with man and death; there can be no doubt that death is also the theme of this image of the children and the field. It is difficult to come to an immediate decision as to the correct translation of this passage, but we get the highest degree of coherence if we interpret it as follows: Jesus' disciples are like " little children, living in a field which is not theirs. When the owners of the field come, they say, ' Leave our field to us.' They (the children) strip themselves before them (the owners), that they might leave it (the field) to them (the owners) and give them (the owners) back their field." It is possible to interpret it as being the owners of the field who strip themselves, presumably meaning that they would be better able to chase out the children in that way, but this interpretation seems to me to make the logion even more difficult than it already is.

If we now proceed to inquire after the meaning of this logion in the " milieu " provided by the *Gospel of Thomas*, it is reasonable to interpret the " little children " as being the disciples, the enlightened Gnostics, following upon Mary's introductory question, " Who are your disciples like? " " The little ones " is in fact a common Gnostic term for " the spiritual ones," the pneumatics. For instance, in the *Gospel of Truth* mention is made of the Father's " children who are perfect and worthy of his name, for children of that kind are what he, the Father, loves." 49.19ff., and " the little children, to whom belongs gnosis of the Father." 19.29f. These " little children," the disciples, live in a field which is not theirs, says Logion 21a, but the owner comes, demanding his field.

A form of imagery is occasionally used in the New Testament

which approximates very closely to the words of this logion, concerning the field. In Gal. 6.8, the Apostle Paul refers to the flesh as it were to a field, "... he who sows to his own flesh will from the flesh reap corruption." In Col. 2.11 is used the expression "putting off the body of flesh" and II Cor. 5.4 expresses the Apostle's sense of estrangement while in the body. In this context he speaks of death as putting off the body, and putting on the heavenly body; he who is able to put this on "may not be found naked." Nakedness is here, as in Judaism, an image expressing the condition of the dead man's soul when he has been unfaithful. Such is also the case in Rev. 16.15, "Lo, I am coming like a thief! Blessed is he who is awake, keeping his garments that he may not go naked ..."

This logion should be interpreted in accordance with such ideas and images as are used in Gnostic texts to express their concept of man. The logion is Gnostic in its attitude, as we see e.g. in its extremely negative view of the world, and its thought of nakedness as the natural condition of all the dead. "The field" must therefore be taken to be the world.[1] This world in which the "little children" are living. "The owner of the field" represents the powers of this world;[2] "to leave the field" is to die and let the powers of this world keep what is theirs, i.e. the physical body. Then the statement that the children strip themselves would appear to have the same implication: that they die and put off their bodies. According to a common Gnostic idea the soul of man is naked after death, and must tread the difficult path up to the heavenly world in constant exposure to the attacks of the evil powers. Only those who possess knowledge of the watchword are able to reach the goal.

If we interpret this logion in this way, we find that it fits in remarkably well with the Gnostic concept-world, and has a clear

[1] So in the *Gospel of Philip* 127.18.
[2] Schenke in Theol. Lit. Zeit., col. 485.

meaning. A quotation from the *Manichæan Psalm-book* to some extent illustrates this basic view of death and the body-soul relationship, the same view as appears to lie behind the logion. "I will pass up into the skies and leave this body on this earth. The trumpet sounds, I hear, they are calling me up to the immortals. I will cast away my body upon the earth from which it was assembled. . . . The enemy of my soul is the world, its riches and its deceit. All life hates godliness: what am I doing in the place of my enemies? . . ."[1]

[1] The *Manichæan Psalm-book* 75.13ff. Cf. the *Apocryphon of John* 69.6.

V

THE NATURE OF MAN

The Captive Spark

THE negative view of the world and the body which we find expressed in several logia in the *Gospel of Thomas* has characteristics which are evidence of a Gnostic-type view of the world and of man. Some of these expressions and motives have their place in the New Testament, but their interpretation in the context of the *Gospel of Thomas* illustrates a process of development which took place beyond the bounds of the New Testament; they agree with the governing basis of the Gnostic doctrinal system, and its sharp dualism between the heavenly world and the created. If we now attempt to continue our analysis of those logia in the gospel which have to do with the concept of man and his nature, we soon find how strange this concept is, compared with the New Testament. It is, however, difficult to bring out this concept of man with all its details, clearly and succinctly; this is very largely on account of the limited material at our disposal. Furthermore, a number of important logia are so obscure and so vaguely formulated that their expressions are almost incomprehensible.

Nevertheless, if we attempt to deduce from the *Gospel of Thomas* what are the characteristics of its doctrine of man, a suitable point of departure is provided by a typically Gnostic document which otherwise has a certain affinity with this gospel, namely, the *Apocryphon of John*. This does not mean that we assume an identical doctrine of man in both writings, but only that we are in search of that background without which the short statements in the *Gospel of Thomas* would be most obscure. It may similarly be possible to find distinguishing features which increase our understanding of the logia. What makes the *Apocryphon of John* such good comparative material is that it is an extremely ancient document, probably dating from the first half of the 2nd century. It is commonly said to represent a " pre-Valentinian " Gnosticism, with an archaic and relatively undeveloped mythology. It also had a very high reputation, was widely circulated, and may conceivably have originated in Upper Egypt.[1]

A brief sketch of the myths surrounding the creation of the world and of man according to the *Apocryphon of John* reveals the following main points.[2] The supreme being is the Father, perfect and indescribable. From him were produced a number of divine beings of light, who together form a system. The last of these beings to appear was Sophia, who caused a new being to emerge out of herself, though without the Father's permission. This being, because of its irregular creation, was degenerate, detestable and stupid. Sophia, ashamed of it, expelled it from the kingdom of light. This being was Jaldabaoth, the creator of the world according to the Old Testament, who created for himself servant-spirits and angels, and then the whole world—the material world. Jaldabaoth's powers in their turn created a man after the image of the Father, who appeared upon the waters which surrounded him, " the pure water of light." 27.3. But this act of creation provided man with no more than a "psychic" body, and he was thus useless and incapable of moving. Encouraged by Sophia, Jaldabaoth then proceeded to blow into man that spark of light which he possessed as a result of his

[1] Puech in Neutest. Apokryphen, p. 242f.

[2] See further, Till, Die gnostischen Schriften des koptischen Papyrus Berolinensis 8502, p.35ff.; Puech in Neutest. Apokryphen, p.236ff.; R. McL. Wilson, The Gnostic Problem (1958), p.149ff.

creation by a being of light, Sophia. Man, having received Jaldabaoth's particle of light, now became superior to him in intelligence; he therefore imprisoned the " psychic " man in a physical body " of coarse *hylē*," in order not to lose the particle which he had deposited in man. Since then, Jaldabaoth has kept a close watch on man and his particle of light, lest it should be liberated, break away from his created world and return to heaven. Thus all men, being descended from the first man, bear a spark of light within themselves, a spark which is imprisoned in matter, in the body.

But the world of light is attempting to win back the imprisoned, alienated spark of light; thus Christ was raised up in order to go down to men and enlighten them concerning the particle of light in them, thereby encouraging them to seek their home in the kingdom of heaven. But Jaldabaoth and his powers resist this attempted liberation, and fight to keep the particles of light. He creates an *Antimimon Pneuma*, ἀντίμιμον πνεῦμα, a mind bent on earthly things, in order to bind man more tightly than ever to this world and the body; this results in man's fall into sin and his consequent unwillingness to seek the kingdom of light above. If the sparks of light gain control of a man through saving gnosis, he can turn from the material world to the kingdom of light, and return thence. The body, on the other hand, has no part in the kingdom, and must submit to corruption. The resurrection of the body is not taught. Man is from the beginning ignorant concerning his particles of light, and his attentions are concentrated on the material world, captive as he is in a body misled by the *Antimimon Pneuma*. More or less the same basic view of the origins of the world and of man is presented in the *Hypostasis of the Archons*, a tract which, in common with the *Apocryphon of John*, belongs to the Nag-Hamadi Library, and which seeks to explain exactly these things; it is clear from this that the point of view in question was widespread, and that it may therefore be useful for an interpretation of the logia in the *Gospel of Thomas.* There is no direct reference in any of the logia to the myths we have described, but the statements dealing with man and his share in the kingdom of light which do exist would seem to presuppose a teaching not far removed from that of the *Apocryphon of John* and the *Hypostasis of the Archons.*[1]

The condition of man prior to his attaining of knowledge is in the *Gospel of Thomas* interpreted with the help of a number of expressions which recur continually in Gnostic literature. Thus in Logion 28 we can read of Jesus' experience of men.

> Jesus said:
> I stood up in the midst of the world,
> And I revealed myself to them in flesh.
> I found them all drunk.
> I found none among them who was thirsty,
> And my soul was full of pain for the children of men.
> For they are blind in their hearts, and do not see
> That they have come empty into the world
> (And that) they seek to go empty out of the world.
> But now they are drunk.
> When they have shaken off their wine, then they will repent.

We have earlier had occasion to quote examples of how " intoxication," " being drunk " in Gnostic usage stands for ignorant man, who is drunk with " the wine of ignorance," *Corpus Hermeticum* 7.1; " becoming sober " refers to the first stages on the way to salvation, learning about the heavenly origin of the soul. " He who gains insight, he knows whence he has come and whither he is going. He knows in the same way as one who, after having been intoxicated, returns from his intoxica-

[1] Cf. *Excerpta ex Theodoto* 2.1f.

tion and, when he comes to himself, retrieves that which is his." *Gospel of Truth* 22.14ff.[1]

According to Logion 28, Jesus also calls men " empty " in their ignorance of salvation; when they fail to understand that they must seek for the place of their heavenly origin, ". . . they seek to go empty out of the world." " Emptiness " is also a common Gnostic expression for describing man's ignorance. In the *Gospel of Truth* also we have a description of how Jesus appeared as a teacher among such as were wise only in their own estimation, and how he laid bare their ignorance. 19.9ff. " But he showed them, to their shame, that they were empty. They hated him, for they were not wise in truth."[2] In the *Manichæan Psalm-book* 217.24ff., we read how three ships (representing different kinds of men) " voyage in the river of testing " which flows through the world. One of them was laden, one half-freighted, the third was empty, " there being nothing in it." Referring to the last ship, we read: " That which is empty is left behind. Woe to it, the empty one, that comes empty to the place of the customs: it shall be asked, having nothing to give. Woe to it, for it has nothing aboard: it shall be despoiled evilly as it deserves and sent back to the μεταγγισμός. It shall suffer what the corpses suffer, for they called into his ear, he did not hear."

We might be able to record Logion 28 as being a genuine saying of Jesus, since it says nothing which contradicts the New Testament, nor is it directly Gnostic in character.[3] There are, however, two reasons for not holding this view: first, the introduction, referring to the coming of Jesus in flesh, the Christology of which seems to be better suited to a Gnostic circle than to the New Testament and related literature; and secondly, the expressions " drunk " and " empty " are far from being typical

[1] Cf. Lidzbarski, Ginza, p. 123.
[2] Cf. 20.34f.
[3] Cf. Jeremias, Unbekannte Jesusworte, p. 66ff.

New Testament words. There is scarcely a single passage in the New Testament which can be advanced in support of the usage of the term " drunk " as symbolising the state of the un-saved. On those occasions when the term does occur it has its literal meaning—the vice of drunkenness. The same applies to the word " empty," κενός, which actually occurs only once in the New Testament to characterise a vain and empty person, viz. James 2.20, where the R.S.V. translates the word as " foolish." Later Christian writings, such as the *Shepherd of Hermas*, do, however, use the term " empty " in a context which is reminiscent of the *Gospel of Thomas*.[1] On the other hand, both these terms, "drunk" and "empty" are typically Gnostic, and the combination of them seems to me to be evidence of the Gnostic character of the logion. Naturally, there may have been behind the logion a saying of Jesus, which has been clothed in Gnostic language, but any attempt to get behind such a logion as this, in order to reach an older, " more genuine tradition " is virtually impossible.

Another term which occurs in Logion 28, and which denotes the condition of the un-saved, is " blind." It goes without saying that it is used in a figurative sense in most religious texts; it may, however, be worth pointing out its close connection with the words " drunk " and " empty," and that it occurs frequently in Gnostic expositions. For instance, the *Hypostasis of the Archons* speaks of salvation from the hope of the ignorant as " a laying aside of blind thought," 145.6.[2] The Creator-God Samael (otherwise Jaldabaoth) is called " the God of the blind." He himself is blind in his confused notion that he alone is God, and his whole creation is " blind." Passages illustrating the meaning of " blindness " are also to be found in the *Gospel of Truth*, and these provide us with a good background to Logion 28. That

[1] Cf. Doresse, L'Evangile selon Thomas, p. 164, with examples from Clement of Alexandria.

[2] Cf. 134.28, 135.3, 142.26.

which is most worthy of mention describes the progress of the ignorant towards salvation in terms of an awakening from bad dreams. " Thus did every one, in that he slept whilst he was ignorant, and thus he arose, as when he awoke. And happy is the man who was converted and awoke, and blessed is he who opened the eyes of the blind . . ." 30.7ff. According to this passage Jesus came to release the blind, or, as we have it in *Jesu Christi Sophia*, " But I have come to lead them out of their blindness, so that I might show unto all the God who is over the All . . ." 125.19ff.[1]

One wonders constantly, when faced with logia which contain passages from the New Testament, or which comprise variants of New Testament sayings, why these particular ones should have been chosen by the " Compiler," when he certainly had an extensive material from which to choose. This is a question which one asks when dealing with Logion 34.

> Jesus said:
> If a blind man leads a blind man,
> Both fall into a pit.

This logion stands closest to Matthew 15.14, except that it omits the introductory clause linking it up with a polemic against the Pharisees. " Let them alone; they are blind guides . . ." But in Luke the saying appears minus the polemical introduction, being built up instead from two questions: " Can a blind man lead a blind man? Will they not both fall into a pit? " 6.39. The connection with the expression " blind " may be the reason which prompted the " Compiler " to make use of this logion; it fits in well with the concept that the creator and leader of this world is " blind," and those who allow themselves to be led by

[1] Cf. *Pistis Sophia* 141 and the *Gospel of Philip* 112.5ff. " If a blind man and a man who can see are in darkness, they are no different from each other. But when the light comes, then the man who can see shall see the light, and the blind man shall remain in darkness."

him remain in their blindness, in their ignorance, and are lost together with the " blind " world.

The Flesh and the Spirit, Poverty and Wealth

The logion which follows No. 28, which we considered above, seems to have a close affinity with it, as it also has to do with the nature of man. The consecutive placing of the two logia can also be understood as being a result of the " key-word " principle, where *sarx*, the flesh, is the key-word in question.

> Jesus said:
> If the flesh, σάρξ, came into existence for the sake of the spirit, πνεῦμα, it is marvellous.
> But if the Spirit (came into existence) for the sake of the flesh, it is even more marvellous.
> But I marvel at this,
> How this great wealth came to dwell in this poverty.
>
> Logion 29

With the Gnostics' basic view of man, the actual creation of man must be a mystery. How can one ever hope to understand the paradox—that man consists of two such widely differing elements as a heavenly, of light, and an earthly, of matter? Or, as Valentinus taught, a " seed from the higher existence," σπέρμα τῆς ἄνωθεν οὐσίας, is planted in the human body;[1] a higher spirit is breathed into man. These are probably the questions which lie behind the logion, where two seemingly irrational points of doctrine are taken into consideration. If the spirit emanated from the heavenly world, it is indeed remarkable that these lofty things were the cause of the emergence of the flesh and the imprisonment of the spirit therein. Surely this cannot be the meaning of creation. But it would be even more strange if

[1] Clement Alex., *Strom.* II, 36, 2.

it were true that the spirit came into existence for the sake of the body. It is most probable that these two statements are to be understood as doctrines which must be rejected, because totally unreasonable. According to the logion, all that can be done is to marvel at this mystery, avoid the question of its cause, and be satisfied with the statement, "I marvel at this, how this great wealth came to dwell in this poverty."

What is meant by the expressions "the great wealth" and "poverty"? Do they refer to the spirit and the body respectively? In *Jesu Christi Sophia* 87.20f., "the great wealth," refers to the goodness of the "eternal Father," which he caused to appear in order that all spiritual men might share it. Man, through his spark of light, has a share in this "great wealth"; after salvation, all share in "his goodness and the riches of their place of rest." 125.3ff. In this document "poverty" stands for the material world: "the creations of poverty," 95.16 or "the world of poverty."

Thus according to Logion 29, we can marvel at "how" anything belonging to the perfect, heavenly world can possibly be found in this useless, material world. Further support for the thesis that "the great kingdom" refers to the heavenly world is given by Logion 85.

> Jesus said:
> Adam came into being out of a great power and great wealth
> And he was not worthy of you.
> For if he had been worthy
> [He would] not [have tasted] death.

Here "great wealth" represents the heavenly part of Adam. But because Adam sinned, he had to taste death, which the true Gnostic need not do. Adam was not "worthy"—but "worthy" is the term denoting "the saved." Logion 85 has a close affinity with the previous one, 84, which speaks about the nature of man in connection with his creation; this is evidence that we are here dealing with a section of the *Gospel of Thomas* which may have been taken from an exposition of creation-myths.

When considering the final clause of Logion 29, " how this great wealth came to dwell in this poverty," we must also reckon with the fact that this may be a Christological pronouncement on Jesus, and a development of the concept stated by Paul in II Cor. 8.9, " For you know the grace of our Lord Jesus Christ, that though he was rich, yet for your sake he became poor, so that by his poverty you might become rich." Paul interprets the entry of the pre-existent Son into the world as an " emptying " in order to win men who, without him, are in poverty. To judge from the context, the Apostle is here thinking of the coming of Jesus into the world as an example upon which the action of the Christian congregation should be based—a generous collection to help the poverty-stricken Christians in Jerusalem. " Poverty " as a symbol of this world's uselessness and " wealth " as a symbol of the heavenly have, however, no direct analogy in the New Testament. But the question is whether or not Paul's words could " live on " and be developed in another theological milieu. Thus in the *Acts of Philip* are contrasted what Jesus was in reality and how he appeared on this earth for our sake. He was immortal, yet he died for our sake, " he was great, and became small for our sake, until he had caused the small to grow and brought them into his greatness, εἰς τὸ μέγεθος αὐτοῦ." 141.

In line with this latter statement is a question put to the Apostle in the *Manichæan Kephalaia*: " If he is a great God, unchangeable, one who cannot be measured, how can he then come and reveal himself in the insignificance of the body? " 89.32f. Irrespective of how Logion 29 is interpreted, as applying to man in general or the Saviour's coming into the world, it still has to do with the relationship between the spirit which originated in heaven and the body which belongs to useless matter.

The last lines of Logion 3 also speak of man in these categories, and agree very well with what has already been said on the nature of man.

> . . . If you do not learn to know yourselves,
> Then you are in poverty
> And you are poverty.

Inability to break loose from ignorance means that the lost man remains " poor " without the least chance of uniting himself with the heavenly world. And it is precisely this state of affairs which means that he identifies himself with the material world and shares its conditions. In the same way, Logion 112 states that the two parts, body and soul, can never live in peace with each other. If man's higher element is in control, then the flesh is condemned, but if the spirit is dependent upon the flesh, then all is lost, for the spirit has become corrupt.

> Jesus said:
> Woe to that flesh, σάρξ, which depends upon the soul, ψυχή.
> Woe to that soul which depends upon the flesh.
>
> Logion 112[1]

The Heavenly Origin of the Soul of Man

When we attempt to clarify the speculations which may lie behind the description in the *Gospel of Thomas* of the " particle of light " in man, we are faced with what are possibly the most

[1] Cf. Logion 87, "Jesus said: Poor is that body which depends upon a body. And poor is that soul which depends upon both of them."

difficult and obscure logia in the whole gospel. An important basis for the estimation of man in this gospel is, however, the concept of the heavenly origin of the soul of man. Logion 49, which focuses on this theme, therefore comes almost as a Gnostic creed.[1]

> Jesus said:
> Blessed are the solitary and elect,
> For you shall find the kingdom.
> For from it do you come
> (And) to it shall you return.

The energies of saved man are thus concentrated upon his return to his place of origin, the heavenly world. His particle of light emanates from the highest existence; salvation means its liberation from matter and reunion with the light-world. We encounter a similar idea in a passage which we have already quoted from the *Gospel of Truth*. "He who gains insight, he knows whence he has come and whither he is going . . ." 22.14f. The same scripture also speaks repeatedly of "the return" as an expression for salvation. Jesus' task in the world is to awaken men out of their ignorance and oblivion, and to persuade them to return to the Father.[2] Thus in this context, the basis of saving knowledge may be said to be an awareness of the origins of the higher element in man.

It is precisely this theme which is prominent in the wonderful "Song of the Pearl," sung by the Apostle Judas Thomas in India, and preserved in the Syriac and Greek *Acts of Thomas*. "The child" who once lived in the midst of his Father's riches forgets his past in the strange land to which he has been sent. Not until he has brought back to mind the place from which he came, can he start on the return journey. "I remembered forthwith that

[1] Cf. F. Sagnard, La gnose valentinienne et le témoignage de saint Irénée (1947), p. 424.
[2] Cf. 19.5, 22.20, 24.6, 41.7.

I was a son of kings and my freedom sought after its kind." 111.56. The description has to do with the journey of the soul from heaven down to the earth, its imprisonment there in oblivion, and its eventual liberation from the material world and reascension to the Father's dwellings, where the original glory awaits. It is when the soul of man discovers that the "alien" milieu of this world really is "alien" to its innermost being that it is driven to seek its own origins, and is led to remembrance.

The divine pre-existence of the individual soul is of course a concept foreign to the New Testament, in which the only one of whom it can be said that he proceeded from the Father's dwellings, and returned to the Father, is Jesus. We encounter the theme again in Gnostic accounts of the Saviour, e.g. in the *Apocryphon of John* 19.15f., where it is said of him, "He returned to the place from whence he came." But in Logion 49 this applies to all particles of light in man. The same idea is also expressed at the beginning of Logion 19.

> Jesus said:
> Blessed is he, who was
> Before he came into being . . .

This question, of the origin of the soul of man, is extremely common in Gnostic literature. This pronouncement from the *Gospel of Thomas* occurs almost word for word in the *Gospel of Philip*, in one of the few sayings of Jesus we have there: "The Lord said, Blessed is he, who is before he came into being. For he who is, was and shall be." 112.9ff. We may also mention the answer given by the angel to Noria, the wife of Noah, in the tract the *Hypostasis of the Archons*, when she asks whether she—who is one of the enlightened—belongs to the world of matter. "You and your children belong to the Father, to him who has existed from the beginning. Your souls came from above, from the imperishable light. Therefore the powers shall not be able to approach them, on account of the Spirit of Truth who lives in them. But all who have learned to know this way are immortal in the midst of mortal men." 144.19ff.

Image and Likeness

Our search for a more detailed description of the divine origin of the soul in the *Gospel of Thomas* leads us into a realm of images and likenesses, in which it is extremely difficult to follow the trains of thought. Thus in Logion 50 we read:

> Jesus said:
> If they say to you,
> " Where have you come from? "
> Say to them:
> " We have come from the light: that place where the light came into existence of itself.
> It [arose] and revealed itself in their image."
> If they say to you:
> " Are you? "
> Say:
> " We are his children
> And we are the elect of the living Father."
> If they ask you:
> " What is the sign of your Father, which is in you? "
> Say to them:
> " A motion and a rest."

The logion is constructed in accordance with the normal tripartite form, and exhibits characteristics in common with Gnostic creeds. The actual questions are strongly reminiscent of those mentioned in *Excerpta ex Theodoto* 78 in connection with teaching on baptism. " But it is not only the washing that is liberating but also the knowledge (gnosis): Who were we? What have we become? Where were we? [or] Where were we placed? Towards what goal hasten we? From what are we redeemed? What is birth and what rebirth?" The logion also teaches that the saved man has his origin in "light." "Light" is a common term denoting the heavenly world, and also occurs in the above-mentioned *Apocryphon of John*, in which the highest being of light is the Father, he who is "the pure light," 25.12, and is surrounded by the "pure water of light," 27.1ff. The Father's first emanation is "the Image, εἰκών, of the Invisible," or "the likeness of light," and then, little by little, is produced the whole light-world. Therefore when we read in Logion 50 that the true Gnostic has come from the light, it is evidently the light-world which is meant.[1] And the clause which speaks of "that place where the light came into existence of itself" interprets exactly this idea, that the Father himself brought the light-world into being. We then read that this light revealed itself "in their image"—an obscure expression. It *may* mean, if we follow the scheme of the *Apocryphon of John*, that the Father reveals his image in "the reflection in the water," the image after which the Creator-God and his powers then create Adam —after "the image of God." The Father would then reveal himself through his image. We should, however, reach the best interpretation of the logion if we were to translate it, "revealed himself in *an* image" (though this assumes an alteration in the text), since this is precisely what the Father does, according to a number of Gnostic expositions; this is the reason for the creation of man in "the image of God."[2] This statement, that the light is revealed in their image, answers the question: Where has the

[1] Cf. the *Manichæan Psalm-book* 215.1ff. "... it is not possible that the image of the [living] man should [come] to the (?) dwelling-places of the beasts. The Light [shall] go to the Light, the fragrance shall go to [the fragrance], the image of the living man shall go to the living land from which it came. The Light shall return to its place. The Darkness shall fall and not rise again."

[2] The same doctrine is also found in the *Hypostasis of the Archons* 135.11ff.

true Gnostic come from? "Their image" should therefore be connected in some way with the idea that it is the same light-being who is in the Father, in the Father's "image," and in the further image which is man. Or is it possible that "their image" may refer to the place in which the light is revealed: Christ, the Saviour?[1]

We gain a rather closer acquaintance with this "image" speculation in the *Gospel of Thomas* from two other logia, where it is just "the image" which is the main theme, but where the word "image" has rather a different meaning. The first of these is Logion 83, which reads:

> Jesus said:
> The images, εἰκών, are revealed to man, and the light within them is hidden.
> It shall be revealed in the image of the light of the Father
> And his image is hidden by his light.

All men can see the "images," we read, but what they cannot at once see is the light within them. In order to understand these statements we must introduce a new aspect of "the images" into the discussion, an aspect which occurs in a number of scriptures with Gnostic characteristics. As an example of how men thought in certain circles we may give a brief account of a passage in the *Pseudo-Clementines*. First is mentioned the image, εἰκών, which man bears, because of having been created in the image of God. But this is only a "superficial" likeness, which is of no real importance for salvation. It is situated in the body,[2] but has no connection with the concept of the spark of light in man. But then there is another "image," denoted by ὁμοιότης, likeness, which belongs together with νοῦς; together they form

[1] Cf. the *Manichæan Psalm-book* 62.12, 64.12.

[2] See also the *Manichæan Psalm-book* 19.25f. "I bent my knees worshipping him also, that I might divest myself of the image of the flesh and put off the vesture of manhood."

the intelligence without which man would be an irrational animal.[1] It is this latter "likeness" which wins knowledge and leads to a right way of living or, as we read in *Hom.* XI.4, "... the image of God is man. He who wishes to be pious towards God does good to man, because the body of man bears the image, εἰκών, of God. But all do not as yet bear his likeness, ὁμοιότης, but the pure mind, ὁ καθαρὸς νοῦς, of the good soul does ..."[2] This distinction between "image" and "likeness" was also taught by the Valentinians, when they maintained that "hylic" men were also in the image of God,[3] but in its earthly form, ὁ ἄνθρωπος κατ' εἰκόνα, "Likeness," καθ' ὁμοίωσιν is something spiritual which is blown into man by the Creator, and mediated by the angels, *Excerpta ex Theodoto* 50.[4]

This view of the "image" of man also occurs in the *Acts of John*, where we read how Lykomedes, whom the Apostle John raised from the dead, caused a portrait of the Apostle to be painted. When the Apostle saw this, found out that it was meant to represent him and saw his own likeness in a "mirror" (he had never before seen his own image!) he said, "As the Lord Jesus Christ liveth, the portrait is like me: yet not like me, child, but like my fleshly image." 28. The Apostle then teaches his friend that what is of real value is the image of the soul's condition, which is "painted" by faith in God, knowledge, mildness, etc., and whose artist is Jesus Christ. What Lykomedes's artist has done is worthless; "... this that thou hast now done is childish and imperfect: Thou hast drawn a dead Likeness of the dead." 29.

Bearing this background in mind, the first part of Logion 83 might be interpreted in this way: "The images," εἰκών, can be seen by all, though in the earthly man all that is seen is the

[1] *Pseudo-Clementines*, Hom. X, 6ff.
[2] See further, Strecker, Das Judenchristentum in den Pseudoklementinen, p. 207f.
[3] So also Irenæus, *Adv.haer.* I, 5.
[4] Cf. *Excerpta ex Theodoto* 86 and the commentary by Sagnard, Extraits de Théodote, p. 210f. and 233.

outer, the superficial " image." But the " inner light," the higher element, is hidden, and can only be seen by such as have been enlightened through gnosis. In certain Gnostic tendencies, " likeness " represents just that " spiritual " element in man which is the presupposition for the emergence of a perfect light-being. The latter part of the logion is more difficult, but appears to be a statement in which is stressed the exact opposite of what applies to man and his " image " and " light." When it is a question of " the image of the light of the Father," the Father reveals his " image," which has the character of light, but the form in which this " image " is outwardly revealed (or its " outer form ")—is hidden; and that which hides it is the light, which can indeed only be " received " and understood by " those who are of the light." The " image " of the Father is hence something belonging to the kingdom of light, and therefore hidden from man by " the light."[1]

The above distinction between " image " and " likeness " seems to me essential to the understanding of these logia in the *Gospel of Thomas*. The next logion, 84, is also clear evidence of this.

> Jesus said:
> When you see your likeness, you rejoice,
> But when you see your images, *εἰκών*,
> Which came into existence before you
> (And which) do not die, nor are they revealed,
> How much will you endure?

It is apparent that what we have in the first line is not image, but ⲉⲓⲛⲉ, " likeness," the word connected with *ὁμοίωσις*, *ὁμοίησις*, (Cf. Gen. 1.26); this supports the thesis that the logion is referring to the " likeness " which only the enlightened

[1] Cf. I Tim. 6. 16 "... who ... dwells in unapproachable light, whom no man has ever seen or can see."

man possesses, the ignorant having lost his. This gives meaning to the statement that when man can " see his likeness " it is a cause for rejoicing; when he sees his " likeness " develop it means that he is on the way to the winning of salvation, since it implies an imitation of man in the heavenly world.

On the other hand, when we come to consider the second part of the logion—" But when you see your images, which came into existence before you (and which), do not die, nor are they revealed, how much will you endure ? "—it seems that we must bring forward material from another background. The " images "—in this case εἰκών—mentioned subsequent to the " likeness " evidently refer to something belonging to the heavenly world or the world of the æons. It is said that they " came into existence before you " and therefore are situated " in time " prior to the creation of man. Furthermore, these "images" are said neither to die nor to be revealed, by which must be meant that they enjoy a permanent existence in the heavenly world where there is no death—death belonging only to what is created. That they are not " revealed " is a more remarkable expression, but would appear to have to do with the fact that they never penetrate into this world. The expression " to be revealed " in the majority of cases stands for that which enters the created world from the heavenly world, or that which divests itself of something belonging to the higher world. When, in connection with the " images," it is said they are not revealed, it seems to me most reasonable to turn to the Gnostic idea that every true Gnostic has an " angel " or " twin soul " in " the place of life's safekeeping " in the heavenly world, and that the particle of light in man must be united with this heavenly element before salvation can be consummated. The Gnostics are—or reflect—the images of these " angels."[1]

[1] Cf. e.g. the *Manichæan Psalm-book* 203.16f., where it is said that the Father established " the dwellings of life " and placed " images " in them: ". . . and set up living Images in them which never perish." See also the Hymn of the Pearl in the *Acts of Thomas*;

In the *Gospel of Philip* we encounter this concept of the heavenly " angel " and the earthly " image " several times. For instance, in one passage, reminiscent of a liturgical prayer to the Saviour, we read, " Thou who didst unite the perfect, the light, with the Holy Spirit, unite the angels with us, with the images." 106.10ff. The prayer refers to the heavenly reunion between the " image " on earth and the " angel " in heaven.[1] We encounter the same idea once more in a complicated passage which teaches that through baptism an " image " is brought forth, which is to be united with the " bridegroom " in heaven; this represents the final restoration, or consummation, 115.9ff. It is a joy to be able to see one's " likeness " now, but the real goal for the true Gnostic is to be able to see his heavenly image, his " twin soul." The thought of this leads to the question which ends Logion 84, " How much will you endure? "—how much will they need to suffer before they are entirely saved?

The Man of Light and the Hearing Ear

We have already encountered the idea in the *Gospel of Thomas* that there is a " particle of light " in man which belongs to the heavenly world, Logia 50 and 83. This estimate of man is very common, and can be supported by most Gnostic scriptures, as well as by material from other religious writings. Logion 24, referring to this " particle of light " in man, reads:

> His disciples said to him:
> " Teach us about the place where you are,
> For it is necessary for us to seek it."
> He said to them:

---

and the footnote in the *Gospel of Truth* 19.31, Malinine-Puech-Quispel, Evangelium Veritatis (1956), p. 52; and *Excerpta ex Theodoto* 36 and 86.3.

[1] Cf. 105.20f.

"He who has ears, let him hear.
There is a light within a man of light
And it shines over the whole world.
When it does not shine, darkness rules."

That " place " where Jesus is to be found is identical with the " place of life " mentioned in Logion 4. The place about which Jesus speaks in the *Apocryphon of James*—one of the scriptures from Nag-Hamadi which has not yet been published—is none other than the place from which he once set out. " I shall go to that place from which I have come. If you wish to come with me, then come!"[1] Then this heavenly place is linked directly with the kingdom of the Father here on earth. In Logion 24, answering the disciples' request to be instructed concerning the heavenly place which they are compelled to seek, Jesus uses the well-known formula, " He that has ears, let him hear," and then says that there is a light within a man of light. There can be little doubt as to the meaning of this answer, but in order to illustrate it more closely, we must first examine the term " man of light."

" Man of light," is a term which occurs nowhere else in the *Gospel of Thomas*, nor is it particularly common in Gnostic literature (with the exception of *Pistis Sophia*); it is, however, possible to fix its meaning quite closely.[2] There is a passage in the *Apocryphon of John* in which the expression is connected with the first man, Adam, who was created by Jaldabaoth and then further imprisoned on earth through *Antimimon Pneuma*. In this Adam is the " perfect, eternal man of light," 71.12f. But it can scarcely be this " man of light " which is meant in Logion 24, but rather that element in man which is related to him, and to the heavenly light. In *Pistis Sophia*, where the expression is common, it is a

[1] Puech in Neutest. Apokryphen, p. 247.
[2] Cf. the *Manichæan Psalm-book* 22.15, 166.19, 214.13.

recurring epithet for that man who is enlightened through the mysteries. This " man of light " is related to the " power of light " which is found in the Saviour. Thus Mary says to Jesus, referring to the interpretation of some of his words, ". . . concerning these words of yours, my understanding has produced four thoughts within me, and my man of light has led me and rejoiced and welled forth from me, for it would go out of me and go into you . . ." Ch. 113. Or, ". . . concerning the power which has gone forth from the Saviour and makes up the man of light within us to-day." 132.

This seems to be the meaning of " man of light " in Logion 24. But beyond this, what is of particular interest to observe in *Pistis Sophia* is that mention of the " man of light " in the faithful is on several occasions placed together with the phrase, " He that has ears, let him hear," precisely as in Logion 24. According to *Pistis Sophia*, when Jesus gives an abstruse exposition of some point of doctrine which has to do with the higher mysteries, his exposition is often rounded off with this same phrase, " He that has ears, let him hear," to which is then linked the expression " man of light." So, for instance, Mary approaches the Saviour and says, referring to Jesus' teaching, which has just terminated, " My Lord, my man of light has ears, and I hear with my power of light, and your Spirit which is with me has made me sober." Ch. 33. Or again, " My Lord, my man of light has ears, and I have understood all the words which you have said." Ch. 124.[1] The meaning behind the words in *Pistis Sophia* is that the same " light " is in both Jesus and the faithful; none but the one who has received this " light " can comprehend the mysteries and grasp the way of salvation.[2] Seen against this background, Logion 24 becomes much clearer. The answer to the disciples' request for instruction on the " place where Jesus is," is thus that

[1] Cf. 69, 87 and 125.

[2] Cf. *Jesu Christi Sophia* 100.10f. and 107.18f., where the saying, "He who has ears . . ." introduces teaching on the deepest secrets.

the true Gnostic shares the same essential element with Jesus; through it he can understand his teaching, and also recognise Jesus' heavenly origin—his " place "—as well as his own divine element.[1] This combination in *Pistis Sophia*—of Jesus' teaching, ending with the words " let him hear," and its glimpse of the meaning of the mysteries, " I have the ears of the man of light " —also has its counterpart in the *Gospel of Thomas*, which supports the contention that the logion and *Pistis Sophia* share a common basis.

The formal phrase " the hearing ear " returns on five further occasions in the *Gospel of Thomas*, combined with different logia.[2] In each of these five cases the words come as the conclusion of a parable (except here in 24, where the context is one of instruction), and this link between the parables and initiation into the mysteries corresponds most closely to Jesus' instruction in parables, according to Mk. 4.9ff. and Matt. 13.9-16. Those who had grasped who Jesus was could also understand the implications of the parables with which he taught the people. In the New Testament the words " let him hear " follow parables on three occasions, and doctrinal presentations on four. In Gnostic literature the words refer to the idea that only the man who has understood that he has within himself a fragment of light originating in the Father's heavenly kingdom can grasp anything of the mysteries. " The word of God is sweet when it finds ears to hear it."[3] However, the differences in the placing of the " let him hear " statement in the New Testament and the *Gospel of Thomas* are rather remarkable. For example, although it is found in Matt. 13.9, it is missing from Logion 9, which quotes the same text. The same applies to Mk. 4.22 and Logion 5 respectively. But the phrase crops up in logia in the *Gospel of*

[1] *Jesu Christi Sophia* 89.4ff. " He who has ears to hear with, let him hear about the eternal things. I will speak with those who are awake (the Gnostics)."

[2] Logia 8, 21, 63, 65 and 96.

[3] The *Manichæan Psalm-book* 151.17. Cf. 12.16, 14.25, 153.24, 194.26 and the *Gospel of Mary* 7.8f., 8.10f.

Thomas, where the corresponding New Testament text does not have it! The *Gospel of Thomas* is a law unto itself. This can most probably be interpreted as something of a polemic against the New Testament, or an assertion that the persons backing the *Gospel of Thomas* considered themselves to have their own independent traditions.

VI

THE KINGDOM

The Kingdom of the Father is in Man

ACCORDING to the *Gospel of Thomas,* man is in his innermost nature a stranger in this world. He possesses a divine element, a particle of light which unites him with the heavenly world. Thus there are on earth a mass of particles belonging to heaven, which collectively comprise the divine element fettered in man. This basic view of the nature of man, and its orientation according to Gnostic patterns, naturally have direct consequences for the gospel's teaching on the kingdom; its content must be quite different from Jesus' proclamation of the " kingdom of heaven " according to the New Testament. This latter concept is connected in its entirety with the person of Jesus; thus this gospel of the kingdom is the content of his teaching, its manifestation takes place in his appearance on earth, and its final dominion is to be established at his second coming. This special relationship between the kingdom and the person of Jesus is missing from the *Gospel of Thomas,* due to the fact that the kingdom as it exists here on earth is made up of the heavenly particles in man, and its consummation means the reunion of the light-souls, imprisoned here below, with the heavenly world.

In the logia, this kingdom is called for the most part just " the kingdom " (nine times), " the kingdom of the Father " occurring seven times and " the kingdom of heaven " only three times. " The kingdom of the Father " is never used in the New Testament as a definite description; instead " the kingdom of God " is the commonest term. This term is not found at all in the *Gospel of Thomas*. Nor is it usual in the New Testament to refer merely to the " kingdom," as is the case in the *Gospel of Thomas*. It is, however, evident that this gospel seems to use the various terms denoting the kingdom in such a way that they do not coincide with the New Testament. For instance, where Matt. 13.24ff., has " the kingdom of heaven," Logion 57 offers " the kingdom of the Father," an exchange of terms which has several parallels.[1] When the New Testament has " the kingdom of God " or " the kingdom of heaven," the *Gospel of Thomas* has only " the kingdom."[2] And in Logion 107, the parable of " the lost sheep " has as an introduction, " The kingdom is like a shepherd who had a hundred sheep . . ." which is missing in both New Testament versions, Matt. 18.12ff. and Lk. 15.3ff. The versions of the New Testament and the *Gospel of Thomas* agree on this point in only two out of fifteen cases: in the parable of the mustard seed, Logion 20, and in one of the beatitudes, Logion 54, both of which follow the Matthean version, " the kingdom of heaven." These divergences from the New Testament can be explained by the circumstance that the terms " kingdom of heaven " and " kingdom of God " are interchangeable both within the bounds of the New Testament and in subsequent Christian literature.[3] But since there are so many departures from New Testament usage, one wonders whether this may not also be due to a tendency on the part of the *Gospel of Thomas* to want to offer the widest possible range of variant readings, in order to be able to claim " independent " traditions. There is scarcely a single logion which agrees exactly with the New Testament. One difference as against the New Testament which must be due to conscious alteration on the part of the *Gospel of Thomas* is that when " the kingdom " is defined, it is

[1] Logia 76, 96 and 109.
[2] Logia 3, 22, 46 and 113.
[3] K. L. Schmidt, art. *βασιλεία* Theol. Wörterb. I, p. 580ff.

called " the kingdom of the Father " for preference. Behind this form of expression lies the Gnostic predilection, so evident in this gospel, for referring to God as the Father.

A closer definition of what, according to the *Gospel of Thomas*, the kingdom is can be obtained from two logia which contain expressions taken from Lk. 17.20-21, " Being asked by the Pharisees when the kingdom of God was coming, he answered them, ' The kingdom of God is not coming with signs to be observed; nor will they say, " Lo, here it is! " or " There! " for behold, the kingdom of God is in the midst of you (*or* within you).' " The first logion with a theme drawn from this saying is:

> Jesus said:
> If they who persuade (lead) you say to you,
> " Behold, the kingdom is in heaven,"
> Then the birds of heaven will precede you.
> If they say to you,
> " It is in the sea,"
> Then the fishes will precede you.
> But the kingdom is within you and it is outside you.
> When you know yourselves, then shall you be known,
> And you shall know that you are children of the living Father.
> But if you do not learn to know yourselves,
> Then are you in poverty,
> And you are poverty.
>
> Logion 3

We are evidently dealing here with a polemical logion which is directed against various mistaken conceptions of the kingdom, according to the doctrine here represented by the *Gospel of Thomas*. It is more difficult to say what those tendencies are which are being polemised against. But those who teach that the kingdom is " in heaven " or " in the sea " are evidently such as have misunderstood the basic Gnostic idea that the entire creation, including the heaven which belongs to it, is pernicious, the work of a false god. The kingdom has nothing whatever to do with this world, and cannot be localised anywhere within its demesnes. The only place in the created world where this kingdom is to be found is in man. When in Lk. 17.21 we have two possible translations, " in the midst of you " or " within you," it is not surprising to find the *Gospel of Thomas* using " within you," the same interpretation as that of Christian gnosis, as expressed, e.g. in Clement of Alexandria. It is of interest to observe that according to Hippolytus the Naassenes also taught that the kingdom of heaven is within man, and is to be sought there, *Refutatio* V, 7,20. The continuation of the same text in Hippolytus contains reminiscences of Logia 4 and 5, in the same way as we have earlier encountered resemblances to Logion 11[1]; this makes it probable that the Naassenes used the *Gospel of Thomas*, or that the one who compiled the gospel used the same source as that referred to here in Hippolytus.

However, Logion 3 does not merely use the expression " within you," but also a seemingly obscure phrase, " the kingdom is within you and it is outside you." The best parallel to this passage seems to be that given in the *Manichæan Psalm-book*, where this form of expression is found more than once. " The kingdom of the heavens,—behold, it is within us, behold, it is outside us; if we believe in it we shall live in it for ever." 160.20f. This dual existence may allude to the kingdom's existence both within man, and beyond him in the heavenly world. But the question is whether or not this form of expression is intended to represent something of the secrecy of the kingdom, that it belongs to a world which cannot be grasped by human categories. Farther on in the Psalm-book, referring to God, we

[1] See above, p. 161.

read, " One is the God that is hidden, that is revealed . . . silent . . . he it is that speaks also." 161.31f. God is both hidden and revealed, silent and vocal. In the above-mentioned passage from Hippolytus's *Refutatio* it is also said, concerning " the happy nature," the kingdom of heaven, that it is " concealed, and yet at the same time disclosed." This double expression is intended to denote that which stands outside normal human comprehension, over and above this world's contradictions.

Support for this idea—that Logion 3 has to do with one special aspect of the kingdom: the existence of heavenly particles of light in man—is forthcoming in the following clauses: " When you know yourselves, then shall you be known, and you shall know that you are children of the living Father. But if you do not learn to know yourselves, then are you in poverty, and you are poverty." In the Gnostic context, to learn to know oneself meant to discover one's real identity, one's place of origin, and the nature of one's heavenly element. Such self-knowledge results in " recognition " by the Father, and this saving knowledge is the condition for becoming a child of the Father. If this self-knowledge be not attained, then salvation is out of the question; and the only existent reality for such a one is the material world: " you are poverty."

Logion 113 is also expressive of the same view of the kingdom.

> His disciples said to him:
> " On which day will the kingdom come? "
> <Jesus said:>
> " It will not come by expectantly looking.
> They shall not say:
> ' See, here,' or ' See, there,'
> But the kingdom of the Father is spread over the earth,
> And men do not see it."

The disciples' question closely resembles the eschatological expectations found in the early Church.[1] We notice, however, as we have done on several previous occasions, that the eschatological aspect is no concern of the *Gospel of Thomas*. The kingdom of God in the New Testament is indeed powerfully attuned to the coming kingdom, but in Jesus' answer in Logion 113 he says that the kingdom already exists on earth. This has nothing to do with the observations and expectations connected with a coming or a returning Messiah. Nor can the kingdom be localised, as those mentioned in Logion 3 had tried to do. Instead the kingdom of the Father is spread out over all the earth; this would appear to refer to the Father's scattered possessions, his particles of light. This cannot be seen by men, but can only be experienced "introspectively," by learning to know oneself. Logion 113 also reflects Lk. 17.21, in the words, "They shall not say, 'See, here,' or 'See, there,'" but the natural clause on the kingdom being "within you" does not follow; instead there comes the statement that the kingdom of the Father is spread over the earth. A similar exposition of these words out of Lk. 17.21 is also to be found in the *Gospel of Mary*, but with a special interpretation of the words "within you." There we read that the Saviour said, "Peace (be) with you. My peace I bring to you. Be on your guard, so that no one leads you astray with the words: 'See, here!' or 'See, there!' For the Son of man is within you. Follow him. They who seek him shall find him." 8.14-21. Here, it is true, the text does not say that the kingdom is within man, but that the Son of man is, which may be understood as saying that the particles of light in man are of the same nature as the Saviour himself. In any case, the Gnostics must be warned against believing in a kingdom of God which is visible on earth. It is within man, and is to be sought there.

The same shift in treatment from the eschatological to the immanent, which we have seen in Logion 113, recurs to a

[1] Cf. e.g. Matt. 24, Lk. 17. 20, Acts 1. 6.

remarkable degree in another logion, the contents of which cover the same theme.

> His disciples said to him:
> " On which day shall the rest of the dead come
> And on which day shall the new world come? "
> He said to them:
> " That which you expect has come,
> But you do not recognise it."
>
> Logion 51

The disciples' question accords with the New Testament in the sense that it looks forward to the coming of the perfect kingdom. But once again the disciples are on the wrong track, since they have failed to grasp that the kingdom is not something which is to be revealed here. The kingdom and salvation=rest, and the heavenly world is indeed already to be found in this world, since the Saviour has come and demonstrated that the heavenly world of light has elements here below, which only require liberation and union with the light-world to bring perfection into existence. But the disciples fail to see this, since they have still not received knowledge.

Unity and " the Little Ones "

In Logion 3 we encountered a strange expression which led our thoughts to the idea that the kingdom was incomprehensible in human categories: i.e. ". . . the kingdom is within you and it is outside you." That this expression is linked with the kingdom may be explained by the fact that one of the characteristics of the kingdom is " unity," which is over and above all contradictions and is neither the one nor the other. This common Gnostic concept is represented in the *Gospel of Thomas* by Logion 22 in particular.

(*a*) Jesus saw some little ones who were being suckled.
He said to his disciples:
" These little ones who are being suckled are like those
Who enter the kingdom."
They said to him:
" If we are little, shall we then enter the kingdom?"

(*b*) Jesus said to them:
" When you make two into one,
And when you make the inner as the outer,
And the outer as the inner,
And the upper as the lower,
And when you make male and female into a single one,
So that the male shall not be male
And the female (shall not) be female.

(*c*) When you make eyes instead of an eye
And a hand instead of a hand,
And a foot instead of a foot,
An image, *εἰκών,* instead of an image,
Then shall you enter [the kingdom]."

This logion and its individual parts form one of the most complicated passages in the *Gospel of Thomas*, and there are many aspects in which the logion and its details may be considered. We shall, however, limit ourselves to a few, directly related to the kingdom and its character; we cannot deal with the recurrence of the individual sayings in other scriptures. The central theme of the logion has to do with those who may " enter the kingdom," and what is demanded of them. The theme recurs several times in the New Testament Gospels, where on a couple of occasions, as here, it is linked with " the little ones." For instance, we may call to mind Jesus' blessing of the children, Matt. 19.13-15 par. or the dispute about greatness, Matt. 18.1-5 par. Behind the statements paralleling Logion 22b in II Clem. 12.2-6, *Acts of*

Philip 140, *Acts of Thomas* 147, etc., there also lies an apocryphal saying of Jesus touching on the question of the kingdom of God.[1]

The logion is one of the few in the *Gospel of Thomas* having any indication of situation, "Jesus saw some little ones who were being suckled." These "little ones" are meant by Jesus to represent the true Gnostics, who may enter the kingdom. In Gnostic literature, "the little ones" is also a standing term for the saved. In the *Manichæan Kephalaia* 189.21, the Saviour calls the saints "the little believers."[2] The *Gospel of Truth* 19.28f. has the same theme. "After all these there appeared also the little children, those to whom belongs gnosis of the Father." Similarly in many other texts.[3] It is most probable that this indication of situation in Logion 22a has been constructed subsequently, as an excellent introduction to the saying of Jesus which forms the body of the logion, the saying on unity (*b*). This saying is in fact to be found in other traditions in several different forms, but nowhere with this introduction. In II Clem. 12 it refers to the coming of the kingdom of God, "For the Lord himself, being asked by a certain person when his kingdom would come, said, When the two shall be one, and the outside as the inside and the male with the female neither male nor female." v.2. Here we have an introduction which seems much more natural in this context, namely, the question of when the kingdom is to come. The saying itself appears to be a new composition,[4] and its introduction in II Clem. 12 is reminiscent of similar examples in the New Testament, such as Luke 17.20, "Being asked by the Pharisees when the kingdom of God was coming, he answered them . . ." But although this saying of Jesus in II Clem. 12 speaks about *when* the kingdom of God is to come and the conditions

[1] See further, Resch, *Agrapha*,[1] p. 195ff., 287f., 416f.; Puech in Neutest. Apokryphen. p. 217; Doresse, L'Evangile selon Thomas, p. 157ff.

[2] Cf. 201.30.

[3] E.g. *Excerpta ex Theodoto* 11.1; *Pseudo-Clementines*, Hom. XVIII, 15.

[4] Resch, *Agrapha*,[1] p. 196ff. Cf. p. 416f.

for its coming, this eschatological question is replaced in Logion 22 by the conditions for admittance into the kingdom, and nothing more. In consequence, an introduction talking about "*when*" is now quite out of place, and is instead replaced by one dealing with membership in the kingdom, and which is more in line with Mk. 10.14f., "Let the children come to me, do not hinder them; for to such belongs the kingdom of God. Truly, I say to you, whoever does not receive the kingdom of God like a child shall not enter it." The role played in Gnostic circles by the term "the little ones" also favours there having been a new composition.[1]

Logion 22, in its definition of what is meant by "the little ones"—the conditions for entry into the kingdom—has a quite different orientation from that of the question of the children in Mk. 10; instead there is an exposition of "unity" and its relation to the kingdom, 22b. This is where the expression "inner" and "outer" recurs, from Logion 3. "When you make two into one, and when you make the inner as the outer, and the outer as the inner, and the upper as the lower, and when you make male and female into a single one, so that the male shall not be male and the female (shall not) be female . . ." From the examples of this saying of Jesus so far found in other scriptures it is clear that Logion 22b has the most detailed form; but it could be varied in many ways, which is also understandable, remembering the construction of the saying.[2]

It is not particularly easy to fix the detailed meaning of these remarkable words on inner and outer, upper and lower. We can follow the interpretation which we advanced for Logion 3, that the duality in expression expresses the exaltation of the heavenly

[1] Cf. the *Gospel of Philip* 123.7ff.

[2] "For the Lord said to me: Unless ye make that which is beneath to be above, and the left to be the right, ye shall not enter into my kingdom," the *Acts of Philip* 140. (Or: "If you do not change that which is below to that which is above, and the upper to the lower, and the right to the left and the left to the right, you shall not enter into the kingdom of God," Lipsius-Bonnet II: 2, p. 74f.).

world over the categories and divisions of the created world. In this context we may recall some lines from the *Manichæan Psalm-book*: " My God, thou art a marvel to tell. Thou art within, thou art without. Thou art above, thou art below, that are near and far, that are hidden and revealed, that are silent and speakest too; thine is all the glory." 155.32f. The terms of expression here emphasise God's incomprehensibility. Or behind Logion 22b may be the Gnostic doctrine of " unity," as the first words suggest: " When you make two into one . . ."

When we are considering the meaning of this concept of " unity," we may be helped by some clauses from the *Gospel of Truth*, where, as in many other Gnostic scriptures, this world and its conditions of existence are characterised by the words " lack " and " emptiness." The cause of this lack and this emptiness is that the world is not perfect, and that man lacks knowledge of the heavenly world and the origins of his own soul. The only possibility of release from this condition for the imprisoned souls is to win knowledge and be united with the heavenly world. Then the lack is supplied, the emptiness filled and unity is created: a unity between the heavenly element and that element captive in matter. Thus knowledge is the way of salvation. " For in the place where there is envy and strife, there is a lack; but that place which is unity, is perfection. Since the lack is caused because they do not know the Father, from that moment in which they learn to know the Father, shall there be no more lack." 24.25ff. Knowledge leads to perfection, and perfection is described as " unity." Applied to the individual, we read, " Through unity shall each one find himself: through knowledge shall he purify himself from a manifold being to a unity, in that he absorbs matter into himself, like a fire, (and) darkness with light, death with life. If this happened to each of us, it would be best for us to take care that the house (=the body) is pure and quiet for unity." 25.10ff. " Unity " is thus the situation of the saved, which means that in this life the material does not govern man, but vice versa, that everything belonging to the material sphere is absorbed by unity, by perfection. It is more easily understandable in this context that Logion 22b says that unity is a condition for entry into the kingdom.

To " make two into one " may also have its background in what is said in *Jesu Christi Sophia*, where the " two " are the " Spirit " of the heavenly world and the " drops of light " which are imprisoned in men. The task of the Saviour was to lead men out of this ignorance, by means of his enlightening knowledge, and cause them to ascend once more to the Father, where they may find rest. " That is why I have come here, so that they (men and the " drops of light ") may unite themselves with this Spirit and breath, and both become a unity, as it was from the beginning, so that you may bear fruit richly and arise to him who was from the beginning . . ." 122.5ff.

When Logion 22b goes on to say that making " the inner as the outer, and the outer as the inner, and the upper as the lower " belongs among these conditions, this should mean, in accordance with this line of interpretation, that a union between the light in man and the heavenly light takes place. It is possible to see from the *Gospel of Philip* that Gnostic groups—as in Logion 22b—had played with these contradictory pairs and made them mean just this. The union of these antitheses is also spoken about in the passage 115.30–116.17, which is introduced with these words: " [The Lord] said, however: I have come to make [the lower] as the upper [and the outer] as the inner . . ."[1] Unfortunately, the following passage is difficult to reconstruct, but evidently consisted of an exposition of the ideas underlying the phrase " that which is lower " and what there is above it. The text then continues, " Therefore the Lord has called corruption: the darkness which is beyond, and beyond which is nothing. He said: My Father,

[1] Cf. Schenke, Das Evangelium nach Philippus, Theol.Lit.Zeit., col. 15.

who art in the secret place. He said: Go into your room, close the door behind you and pray to your Father, who is in the secret place, i.e. who is within them all. That which is, however, in them all is the Pleroma. According to him there is none other within him. This is that about which it is said: That which is above them." A part of the heavenly world, the Pleroma, exists within man, and its Lord is the Father who is "above."[1] Unity, salvation, consists of the union of the two, and this is what the Saviour says that his task in the world is: "to make [the lower] as the upper [and the outer] as the inner . . ." We may also call to mind the "unity" which results when the particle of light in man is united with its "twin," a unity which characterises the final state of salvation.[2]

These concepts in Logion 22 can also be illustrated from a couple of other passages in the *Gospel of Thomas*, showing that this logion is not an isolated phenomenon. In the first place, the connection between "the little ones" and the kingdom can be illustrated by reference to Logion 46.

> Jesus said:
> From Adam to John the Baptist there is none
> Among those born of women
> Who is greater than John the Baptist,
> So that his eyes shall not break.
> But I have said that the one among you
> Who becomes like a little one (a child)
> Shall know the kingdom,
> And he shall be greater than John.

The logion is clearly a version of Matt. 11.11 (Lk. 7.28), "Truly, I say to you, among those born of women there has risen no one greater than John the Baptist; yet he who is least in

[1] Cf. Schmidt-Till, Koptisch-gnostische Schriften, p. 337, 18; 338, 7, etc.
[2] See e.g. *Excerpta ex Theodoto* 22.3 and 36; Irenæus, *Adv.haer.* I, 21, 3.

the kingdom of heaven is greater than he." But at the same time, the New Testament text has been altered, additions have been made and a certain amount of rearrangement of the contents has taken place. The introduction of Adam in the first sentence has really done nothing other than emphasise that the saying has in view the whole of mankind, from the first man up to and including the Baptist. The clause about the eyes which shall not break is obscure in its context. The other half of the logion, however, contains an important alteration. The categorical statement in Matt. 11.11 has been reshaped so as to state the condition for admittance into the kingdom, "the one among you who becomes like a little one (a child) shall know the kingdom." The resemblance to Logion 22a is striking. Indeed, behind the alteration we may discern a gnosticising tendency which has as its object to emphasise the important term "little," referring to the Gnostic. This tendency is supported by another alteration, the phrase "know the kingdom." The New Testament uses such expressions as "to enter the kingdom of God," or "to receive the kingdom of God," but never "to know the kingdom of God." But in a Gnostic milieu this is a quite natural way in which to express oneself, since it is knowledge—of the light-world above and its fragments here below—which leads to salvation.

Another important Logion in this context is the following:

> Jesus said:
> An old man in his days shall not hesitate
> To ask a little child of seven days about the place of life
> And he shall live.
> For many of the first shall be the last,
> And they shall be a single one.
>
> Logion 4

In this logion we have a number of reminiscences of, and

resemblances to, New Testament texts, but they are less important, and are not essential to the interpretation of the saying. There are, on the other hand, two similar traditions which witness to its Gnostic context. In the *Manichæan Psalm-book* we read, " The grey-haired old men—the little children instruct them. They that are six years old instruct them that are sixty years old." 192.2f. And Hippolytus, commenting on the Naassenes' teaching concerning the heavenly nature of man, writes, " And concerning this (nature) they hand down an explicit passage, occurring in the Gospel inscribed according to Thomas, expressing themselves thus: He who seeks me, will find me in children from seven years old; for there concealed, I shall in the fourteenth age (or æon) be made manifest." *Refutatio* V, 7,20. However, neither of these traditions agrees entirely with Logion 4, but they do reflect an idea which seems to have lain behind it; this idea is not easily fixed in all its detail, but we can determine its main point.

Earlier on, in the passage dealing with the Naassenes, it is said that the kingdom of heaven should be sought within men. In the saying about the children, it is said that he who seeks Jesus will find him in children. " The little ones " or " the children " is of course a common term for the enlightened, the Gnostics, and thus this saying of Jesus would mean that the kingdom, part of the world of light, was to be found within the Gnostics. The Saviour himself (Cf. The *Gospel of Mary* 8.18f.) or, as we read farther on in the same passage from Hippolytus, " the ineffable and mystical Logos " is the one who is in them. In the *Manichæan Psalm-book*, " the child " stands as an expression for the emanation Jesus.[1] The Manichæans can be said to use the word " child " to mean all the heavenly souls or particles of light imprisoned in

[1] The *Manichæan Psalm-book* 233.20ff. " The Little one makes music by night, *Hylē* answered him with a word: ' O Little one that makest music . . . thou it is art not of this world.' [He said: ' I] indeed [am] in this world, but I shall not dwell in it from henceforth.' " Cf. Adam, Die Psalmen der Thomas, p. 43.

man in this world, taken collectively. Therefore it is the " little children " who instruct " the grey-haired old men." A similar motif occurs in the Mandæan literature, where Manda d'Hayye (the Saviour) is said to be a three-year-old child. " I came to him myself, revealed myself to John as a little child, three years and one day old."[1] Once more the Saviour-figure is connected with an appearance in the form of a child.

Where all these traditions disagree is on the question of the age of the " child." The *Gospel of Thomas* gives the youngest age, " a child of seven days." The various figures named are evidently expressive of different interpretations of who or what is hidden behind the " child " or the " children " (probably also æon speculations). From what we have discovered from the previously quoted examples, it would seem that we can expound Logion 4 in the following way. In the little child is the Father's kingdom, as a portion of the light. The child may represent Jesus himself,[2] or the enlightened man, the Gnostic. The fact that it is said to be a baby, only seven days old, may be taken as a symbolic expression that such an enlightened man stands in the closest possible relationship to the heavenly world—in common with the first æon of the Valentinians, which is the Logos, " a child."[3] The " old man " is the man who is deeply anchored in the world of matter, but who can nevertheless still be saved and therefore should not hesitate to ask the " man of light " about the kingdom and its conditions, about the " place of life." If he does this, he will live, despite his nearness to death.

There is probably a further idea behind the expressions " the old man " and " the child," which comes out in the words which end the logion, " for many of the first shall be the last, and they shall be a single one." The logion here reproduces half a sentence

[1] Lidzbarski, Ginza, p. 51, 191ff. and 236.
[2] Cf. the Infancy Gospel, *Gospel of Thomas*, where the child Jesus convinces an old teacher by his wisdom, James, p. 51 and 62.
[3] Cf. Valentinus's Fragment 8 in Hippolytus, *Refut.* VI, 37, 6-8.

which recurs more than once in the New Testament, ". . . the last will be first, and the first last," Matt. 20.16 (19.30 reverses the elements), Mk. 10.31, Lk. 13.30. What is, however, strange, is that the meaning of the words in Logion 4 is the opposite of that of the New Testament text. In the New Testament, the despised and the least of all shall be the first on "that day," whilst the first and the greatest in the world shall be the last. In Logion 4 it is vice versa: the first shall be the last, and as this is the same as the creation of a unity, these are the ones who will be saved, "and they shall be a single one." The question is, though, whether it may not be another passage from the New Testament which is referred to in Logion 4, one which as regards content fits in better with the context, and which also contains Jesus' teaching on the child and the kingdom of God, i.e. Mk. 9.35: "And he sat down and called the twelve; and he said to them, 'If any one would be first, he must be last of all and servant of all.'" This is the only New Testament version of this saying which includes these terms, "first" and "last."[1] This saying fits in better, for Logion 4 would then mean that "the first"—the old and wise, and those who have some position in the world—must become "the last," the smallest and least important in the world, "the suckling babes."[2] But if they become "little," i.e. "Gnostics," they then reach salvation and unity can be created.

What is distinctive of the kingdom is thus that it manifests "unity"; in Logion 4 it was said that the state of salvation is that the faithful become "a single one." We meet the same form of expression in another logion.

> Jesus said:
> Blessed are the solitary and elect

[1] Cf. Matt. 20. 26f., 23. 11, Mk. 10. 43f., Luk. 9. 48, 22. 26.
[2] An idea related to Matt. 11. 25. Cf. *Pseudo-Clementines*, Hom. XVIII, 15.

For you shall find the kingdom.
For from it do you come
(And) to it shall you return.

Logion 49

Here it is said that the kingdom in the heavenly world is identical with the kingdom here below in the souls of men. Those who through saving knowledge find the kingdom discover nothing new, but really only rediscover the home which they once left. Those who are now saved, i.e. the Gnostics, are called " the solitary " and " the elect," μοναχός and **ⲥⲟⲧⲡ**, terms which in Gnostic literature are especially used of the Gnostics, the saved. The latter term is very common among the Manichæans, where it stands for Mani himself and his disciples. The former develops until it finally becomes a technical term for monks and ascetics. " The elect," *οἱ ἐκλεκτοί*, often denotes in Gnostic texts those who have proceeded from the heavenly world, as in Logion 49.[1] We must now ask whether the reason for the prominent place occupied by the term *μοναχός*, " the lonely one, the solitary one " among Gnostics has to do with its close connection with the expression " unity," denoting the condition of salvation. That is the impression given by another logion, which contains the motives " choose " and " a single one."

Jesus said:
I shall choose you, one of a thousand and two of ten thousand,
And they shall stand (there), as they are a single one.

Logion 23

Jesus " chooses " few from among men, and it is only this few who can be saved, and reach true life, unity. The first part

[1] Cf. *Excerpta ex Theodoto* 1.2, and 39; The *Odes of Solomon* XXIII, 2ff.; the *Gospel or Traditions of Matthias* (James, p. 12f.); Till, Die gnostischen Schriften des koptischen Papyrus Berolinensis 8502, p. 37.

of this saying of Jesus can also be found quoted in other Gnostio contexts, and it seems to have existed in such a milieu as this.[1] In Irenæus the saying is used to refer to the few who can possess such a remarkable doctrine and knowledge as do the Basilideans. "Not many can possess this knowledge, but only one of a thousand and two of ten thousand." In *Pistis Sophia*, Ch. 134, Jesus and Mary discuss the possibility of a man being free from sin. Mary is pessimistic on that point, but Jesus says, "There shall be found one among a thousand and two among ten thousand . . ." Some few lines farther on, however, we read that "all are under sin and all lack the gift of the mystery." This could be interpreted so: that the true Gnostics are few in number, that it is true that they live in a material world and are deficient in knowledge, but that thanks to their particle of light they can be so enlightened in the mysteries that they do not sin. As far as Logion 23 is concerned, we really do not know in which context it should be interpreted, since it is not linked to any explanatory clauses. Nevertheless, we can point out that it immediately precedes Logion 24, on which we have commented above, and thus *may* be connected with the predestinatory concept of "the elect," the Gnostics who know that they will be saved. The final clause in Logion 23, "and they shall stand (there), as they are a single one" also demonstrates the connection between the chosen men of light and the unity which is their salvation.

Parables of the Kingdom

The details of some of the most important logia concerning the kingdom are practically impossible to interpret in a way which agrees with the milieu of the *Gospel of Thomas*: the logia

[1] Irenæus, *Adv.haer.* I, 24, 6 and, depending on him, Epiphanius, *Panar.haer.* XXIV, 5 (Die griech.-christl. Schriftsteller, Epiphanius I, p. 262).

in question are the parables of the kingdom. From descriptions in the Church Fathers, of the way in which advanced and emancipated Gnostics interpreted the New Testament "parables of the kingdom of heaven," we can well understand that without a commentary we are not likely to come to terms with the expositions of these parables. For instance, it is not easy to know how the parable of the sower (9) may have been expounded in the milieu of the *Gospel of Thomas*, though we can find a number of main points by referring to certain alterations in the text of the parable. It has been pointed out that a good number of these parables have been displaced, so that their foci—as against the New Testament—have become the localisation and growth of the kingdom within man.[1] This displacement seems to me to connect very well with the concept of the Father's kingdom as being within, a part of the heavenly kingdom of light.

This tendency to stress the immanent perspective may be illustrated by reference to certain of these parables in the *Gospel of Thomas*.

> Jesus [said:]
> The kingdom of the Father is like [a] woman,
> (Who) took a little leaven
> (And) [hid (mixed)] it in meal
> (And) made large loaves of it.
> He who has ears, let him hear.
>
> Logion 96

Compared with the New Testament version, this logion exhibits significant differences. In Matt. 13.33 (Lk. 13.20-21) the parable reads: "The kingdom of heaven is like leaven which a

[1] L. Cerfaux, Les paraboles du royaume dans l'" Evangile de Thomas," Le Muséon 70 (1957), p. 313f.

woman took and hid in three measures of meal, till it was all leavened." We see how "the kingdom of heaven" has been changed to "the kingdom of the Father," how the comparative element in the parable, instead of being "the leaven," is now "the woman" ("The kingdom of the Father is like [a] woman..."), and how the climax of the parable has been altered, so that instead of being the moment when all was leavened, is now the bringing forth of "large loaves." Through these alterations we have now reached the point that the addition of the leaven makes it possible to bake large loaves. Further, we can observe that "large, great" occurs in several other logia in the *Gospel of Thomas*, seeming to stand for what the Gnostic is, or produces—the heavenly element. It is then easy to imagine that on this occasion "the leaven" stands for the heavenly particle of light, or the spiritual element deposited in man, and the "actualisation" of which leads to salvation. Such an interpretation is to some extent supported by other texts. Irenæus quotes a Gnostic exposition which seems to be more developed than that lying behind Logion 96; what is worthy of careful note is that on this occasion "the leaven" is interpreted to mean the Saviour. "The woman means namely Sophia, the three bushels of meal the three kinds of man, the pneumatic, the psychic and the hylic. The leaven stands for the Saviour himself." *Adv. haer.* I, 8, 3. The *Gospel of Thomas* does not, however, reproduce the parable in its New Testament form (the three bushels have disappeared!), although according to Irenæus, the Gnostic did so. A tendency to alter the sayings is, though, typical of the "Compiler" of this gospel. Another example shows that the Gnostics' exposition of "the leaven" was linked up with the Saviour and the spiritual "seed." In *Excerpta ex Theodoto* 2.1f. is said that "an effluence of the angelic seed" came to man, "and this worked as leaven, uniting what seemed to have been divided, soul and flesh, which had also been put forth separately by Wisdom." This form of the parable, as we have it in Logion 96, proves to fit in well with this world of ideas, where the stress is laid on the inner processes in man, and the heavenly element there.

We also read in *Excerpta ex Theodoto* 1.3 that the Valentinians use other, additional similes to describe this doctrine, and the "mustard seed" is mentioned. This suggests the well-known parable of the mustard seed, which also has its place in the *Gospel of Thomas*.

> The disciples said to Jesus:
> "Tell us what the kingdom of heaven is like."
> He said to them:
> "It is like a grain of mustard, smaller than all seeds.
> But when it falls on to tilled ground,
> It sends out a great branch
> And becomes a refuge for <the> birds of heaven."
>
> Logion 20

The logion shows a number of tendentious divergences, when compared with the Synoptic versions, Matt. 13.31-32 par., mainly that the mustard seed falls on to the "tilled" ground and "sends out a great branch." The longer expression "tilled ground" in Logion 20 may naturally be taken to be a harmless variant of the Synoptics' "field," "earth" and "garden," but when we remember the role played by "working" and "labouring" in Gnostic soteriology, it is more probable that the addition reflects a Gnostic interpretation,[1] as is also the case with the statement that the mustard seed sends out "a great branch." Once more it is the term "great" which carries the emphasis, and it is reasonable to interpret the logion in accordance with the parable of the leaven, so that the point is the growth of the "heavenly man."

[1] Cf. Cerfaux, op. cit., p. 319.

In this context, an extremely interesting parable is Logion 8, which once more fits in well with this world of ideas.

> And he said:
> The man is like a wise fisherman
> Who cast his net into the sea,
> (And) drew it up out of the sea
> Filled with small fish.
> Among them he found a large, good fish,
> He, the wise fisherman.
> He cast out all the small fish down into the sea,
> (And) chose the large fish without hesitation.
> He who has ears to hear with, let him hear.

The differences between this parable and its nearest New Testament equivalent, Matt. 13.47-50, are so great that it could be taken to be an independent parable. But at the same time its language[1] and imagery are so closely related to Matt. 13 that it must be treated as a variant of that New Testament text, which reads, " Again, the kingdom of heaven is like a net which was thrown into the sea and gathered fish of every kind; when it was full, men drew it ashore and sat down and sorted the good into vessels but threw away the bad." The main points of the parable are the gathering in and the separation, which in the following verses are interpreted by the judgment at the last day. In Logion 8 the picture has been drastically altered. It is no longer the kingdom which plays the leading role, but " man." Nor is it just any man, but a " wise man," a term which leads our thoughts to the Gnostic possessor of knowledge; he it is who is the " wise man." The point of the parable, as it is now, is that the fisherman, being a wise man, chooses what is most valuable in the catch without hesitation. Among all the small fish there is in fact one " large and good fish," and that is his discovery. Once

[1] Cf. Giversen, Thomasevangeliet, p. 40.

more the emphasis is laid on " large, great "—probably symbolising that which originates in the heavenly world. The terms " wise," " find," and " choose " *may* also be evidence that we are in a Gnostic or gnosticising milieu when dealing with this logion.

It is now possible in the treatment of this logion to refer to another concept, which should reveal rather a different facet. In the Jewish and Christian world of symbols there are in fact a mass of ideas linked to " fish," " the small fish " and " the great fish." Thus the guests at the Messianic banquet, according to Jewish tradition, are said to eat of " the great fish," Leviathan, which is also tasty, " good " to eat, and symbolises something life-giving. " To eat the fishes, or the great fish, was a way of taking into oneself the fluid which embodied the life or being of the Saviour."[1] Christian texts also speak of the " great fish," mainly standing in sacramental usage for the bread, the body of Christ.[2] If we compare this with the fish as a symbol of Christ, and the Messiah as the great fish, we should be able to supply Logion 8 with a background from Jewish-Christian ideas, which might be evidence that the parable could also have been used in an orthodox Christian milieu.

The well-known parable of the lost sheep has also undergone a tendentious alteration in the *Gospel of Thomas*, adapting it to the basic view of man and the kingdom of the Father, which we have sketched.

> Jesus said:
> The kingdom is like a shepherd who had a hundred sheep.
> One of them went astray. It was the large one (the largest one).
> He left the ninety-nine.

[1] E. R. Goodenough, Jewish Symbols in the Greco-Roman Period V (1956), p. 39.
[2] Goodenough, op.cit., p. 40ff., 53.

He sought for that single one until he found it.
When he had tired himself out, he said to the sheep:
I love you more than the ninety-nine.

Logion 107

The first thing we notice when making a comparison with the New Testament parallels, Matt. 18.12-13, Lk. 15.4-6, is that this logion appears as a parable of the kingdom of heaven, but " in Lk. 15 the lost sheep is the sinner and publican over against the righteous man " and " in Matthew the parable concerns the zeal for a brother who has become an apostate."[1] This alteration is vital, since through it the parable gains a different function, one which fits in remarkably well with the Gnostic doctrine of the kingdom. To say that the kingdom is like a shepherd searching for a lost sheep should mean that the kingdom is a whole which has lost something, some part which is particularly valuable. That is the " large " sheep, and the " shepherd " refuses to give up his quest before he has found it, for it is especially loved.[2] Through the finding of the lost one, the whole is restored; the ninety-nine plus " the single one " make up the hundred. There are also other differences, when compared to the New Testament, but they are of less importance.

The Gnostics valued this parable highly, since they considered it to interpret the basis of their soteriology in simple terms. It is retold in the *Gospel of Truth*, where it is coupled with Jesus' saying about the sheep which fell into a pit on the Sabbath, Matt. 12.11. Since this account provides a good background for the understanding of Logion 107, we reproduce its main text.[3] " He is indeed the shepherd, who left the ninety-nine sheep which had not gone astray, and went to seek the one which had gone

[1] K. Stendahl, The School of St. Matthew (1954), p. 27.

[2] Guillaumont, Sémitismes dans les logia de Jésus retrouvés à Nag-Hamadi, Journal Asiatique 246 (1958), p. 120.

[3] Cf. Gärtner, Evangelium Veritatis och Nya testamentet, p. 59f.; Cerfaux, op. cit., p. 324ff.

astray. He rejoiced when he found it, for ninety-nine is a number which can be counted on the left hand, which contains it. But as soon as the single one is found, the entire number goes over to the right hand. In the same way with the person who lacks the single one, that is the entire right hand, who draws to himself what he lacks and takes it from the left side, and causes it to go over to his right hand, and thus the number becomes a hundred." 31.35-32.16. Evidently "the ninety-nine" represents the heavenly world; the missing sheep stands for that part of the light-world which is not "at home," but outside, imprisoned in the material world, in man. It is these lost sparks of light which the Saviour came to save. His love is kindled for the one belonging to the Father's kingdom which has gone astray. The numerical mysticism which follows makes it clear that the rediscovery of the hundredth sheep is the consummation. The number ninety-nine is imperfect, and lacks "the one" which, when found, restores the number to perfection. The number then goes over from the incomplete left to the right, to which belongs fullness.[1] When the Saviour returns the light which has been imprisoned in matter, then the host of light is once more assembled in the æon-world, and perfection is restored. This interpretation of the parable recurs in Irenæus, *Adv. haer.* II, 24,6, where he pays particular attention to the left-hand side in the Gnostics' interpretation as an expression for the material, that which has been lost, and the right-hand side and the number one hundred as a symbol for the state of perfection. The alterations to the parable of the lost sheep in Logion 107 seem to be based upon precisely these ideas about the lost, the "large" sheep, the finding of which means the re-establishment of perfection.

As our last example of the way in which the parables of the kingdom in the *Gospel of Thomas* have undergone tendentious

[1] We encounter a similar idea in the *Manichæan Psalm-book* 170.25ff. "We were numbered in the number of the Right, we passed from the number of the Left. . . . We were numbered in the number of the sheep, we passed from the number of the goat . . ."

alteration so as to fit in with the new attitude to the kingdom of the Father, we may quote Logion 109.

> Jesus said:
> The kingdom is like a man,
> Who had a hid[den] treasure in his field
> Without knowing it.
> And [when] he died, he left it to his [son.]
> The son did not know either.
> He received the field and sold [it].
> And the one who bought it went
> [And] when ploughing [he found] the treasure.
> He began to lend money to whomever he wished.

Alterations to the New Testament text are considerable. The short and pregnant parable in Matt. 13.44 has been built out, and the point altered altogether. " The kingdom of heaven is like treasure hidden in a field, which a man found and covered up; then in his joy he goes and sells all that he has and buys that field." The Matthean version describes the bold venture which the man undertakes in order to obtain the treasure he had so unexpectedly found. Man leaves everything when faced with the kingdom of heaven's boundless immensity and value. In the version we have in the *Gospel of Thomas* the emphasis is transferred to the man's unconscious possession of a treasure, and to the fact that the first person to " work " finds it, and thus becomes enormously rich. It seems to me that this shift should be understood as a conscious focusing of interest on the kingdom within man. The particle of light belonging to the Father's kingdom is to be found there, but most men are ignorant of the origin of their souls, imprisoned as they are in the material world. The fact that it is purposeful labour which is rewarded is entirely in line with Gnostic ideas, in which the search for salvation is " work " and " labour," though salvation itself means " rest." It can also be seen how the verb " to find " in the Matthean version—a man " found " the treasure—has been changed, so that it is the third man who tills the soil and finds the treasure.[1]

How the three stages in the narrative—the father, the son and the buyer—are to be understood, it is hard to say. They can be understood purely and simply as a literary device, belonging to the narrator's technique of building up and embellishing his story.[2] There is, though, a theme from Gnostic texts which might fit in here, if it should be the case—which is far from certain—that there is a deeper meaning behind the three persons in question. There was in fact mention of reincarnation, which meant that such men as possessed a spark of light, but owing to their sins and confinement within the material world " did not learn to know the All," were reincarnated in new individuals, until they reached saving knowledge. The *Apocryphon of John* 69.9ff. states that ignorant souls are imprisoned once more after death in the bonds of bodily existence. We encounter a similar doctrine of the ignorant man's spark of light in *Pistis Sophia*, where it is said after death to be compelled to circle the world as punishment and purification, after which it is once more imprisoned in a body.[3] It is thus possible to understand the three persons in Logion 109 on the basis of a doctrine of reincarnation.[4]

[1] Cf. *Pseudo-Clementines*, Rec. III, 53, which also mentions a serious search for the hidden creature, which is " the possession of the kingdom of heaven, and has laid it up and hidden it as a secret treasure, so that no one can easily attain it by his own power or knowledge." And, in accordance with the two persons who according to Logion 109 did not know about the treasure, there is a mention of those who do not seek for the kingdom, who shall be " deprived of its good things, as lovers of evil things."

[2] Cf. Cerfaux, op. cit., p. 315.

[3] *Pistis Sophia* 122.

[4] Cf. the strange doctrine in the *Hypostasis of the Archons* 144.25ff., about a delay of " three generations " in salvation.

VII

THE NEGATIVE ATTITUDE TO THE WORLD

" *To Deny the World* "

THE kingdom of the Father on earth, according to the *Gospel of Thomas*, comprises the heavenly light-particles in man, and when these are once more liberated and assembled in the heavenly world, the kingdom has attained perfection. With this basic view of the kingdom and of the imprisoned souls, we understand that in this gospel " the Christian life " here on earth has to be painted in dark colours. This world, as well as the human body, is the work of the inferior Creator-God, and is nothing but a stumbling-block to the enlightened man. Man is therefore exhorted to live in as little contact as possible with the created world.

> <Jesus said:>
> If you do not fast from the world
> You shall not find the kingdom.
> If you do not keep the Sabbath as Sabbath
> You shall not see the Father.
>
> Logion 27

The negative attitude to the world is here laid down as a condition for finding the kingdom. To " fast from the world " is an expression which is not found in the New Testament but which in the subsequent history of the Church became the normal expression for asceticism. But such an attitude to the world was far from being a general rule for the Christian, and only applied to " special " Christians. In Gnostic circles, however, this norm could be exalted into a general requirement for salvation, and thus into a criterion separating "the saved" from the world. For instance, there followed in the wake of the Marcionite church a mass of ascetics and martyrs who, drawing the consequences of their master's principles, turned up their noses at the world, "*haec paupertina elementa*," "*haec cellula creatoris*."[1] When the *Manichæan Kephalaia* speaks of the fasting necessary for the saints, it does so on a basis of the same principles, "The holy man mortifies his body by fasting, in order to overcome the whole power of the Archon which is in him." 191.14f.[2] There are a number of parallels to this saying on fasting, but all give the same indication, that this is a logion which came into being in a heretical milieu.[3] When we turn to the latter part of the logion, "to keep the Sabbath as Sabbath," it is more difficult to determine the precise meaning. It has, for example, been interpreted as being purely Gnostic, in which case it would refer to contemplation, which was—together with asceticism—of primary importance for a Gnostic here on earth.[4] But in whatever way this logion should be interpreted, one thing is quite clear: that fasting and keeping of the Sabbath as mentioned in this logion do not correspond to their Jewish and early Jewish-Christian counterparts. The young Church began at a very early date to polemise against a false fasting and a mistaken conception of the commandment to keep the Sabbath, which were not pure Jewish-Christian but belonged rather to syncretistic groups, having gnosticising tendencies, e.g. such as are mentioned in Col. 2.16ff. In the latter passage these commandments have been connected with an asceticism which goes beyond both Judaism and Christianity and approaches a later Gnosticism's entirely negative view of this world.[5]

[1] Tertullian, *Adv. Marcionem* I, 13 and 14. Cf. Harnack, Marcion, p. 144f.

[2] Cf. the *Manichæan Psalm-book* 116.13f.; the *Gospel of Philip* 126.20ff.

[3] Resch, *Agrapha*,[2] p. 68; Jeremias, Unbekannte Jesusworte, p. 19; *Letter of Ptolemæus to Flora* (Epiphanius, *Panar.haer.* XXXIII, 5, 8).

[4] Cerfaux, op. cit., p. 321.

[5] Cf. E. Lohmeyer, Der Brief an die Kolosser (1953), p. 122; E. Percy, Die Probleme der Kolosser-und Epheserbriefe (1946), p. 138ff.

Another expression of this general negativism over against the created world is to be found in Logion 78.

> Jesus said:
> Why did you go out into the desert?
> To see a reed which moves in the wind?
> Or to see a man dressed in soft garments?
> [See, your] kings and great men are those who wear soft [garments]
> And they [shall] not be able to know the truth.

The logion shows considerable resemblance to Lk. 7.24b—25 and Matt. 11.7b—8, but parts company from these texts because on the one hand it lacks situation, and on the other has been given an additional line towards the end, which gives the logion a new meaning. Luke and Matthew include the saying in a longer passage on John the Baptist, where Jesus asks questions, and teaches on John the Baptist as a prophet. It is built up—in its first part—around the question, "Why did you go out?" repeated three times, and is both logical and clear. This construction has been shattered in Logion 78; only a fragment has been used, and made into an independent logion without the least reference to John the Baptist. As on many other occasions in the *Gospel of Thomas*, the saying has been torn out of its context; one result is that the logion has become illogical—it was not a man in soft garments who was out in the desert![1] This interference with the text has also given the logion a new meaning. It has become a pronouncement on how the "great men" of this world are hindered, by their dependence upon the world, from attaining to the truth and being saved. By choosing from the New Testament text just those clauses dealing with wealth and clothes, there has been created a logion which accords with

[1] The Coptic word can also mean "country," a nuance which somewhat moderates the logion's mode of expression.

the negative attitude to the world. The additional line, " And they [shall] not be able to know the truth," sums up the tendentious reinterpretation in a nutshell.

This interpretation of " soft garments " by contempt for the world recurs in the *Acts of Thomas*, where it once more appears independent of the New Testament context—Jesus' evaluation of John the Baptist. In the passage which tells about the dragon and the young man, the Apostle Thomas says that a distinction must be drawn between things which are seen, and which belong to this transitory world, and the things of heaven. The enlightened man has no need of the riches of this world. " If we speak of apparel of raiment wherewith they that are luxurious in this life are clad, it is named and it hath been said: They that wear soft raiment are in the houses of kings. And if of costly banquets, concerning these we have received a commandment to beware of them, not to be weighed down with revelling and drunkenness and cares of this life—speaking of things that are—and it hath been said: Take no thought for your life, what ye shall eat or what ye shall drink; neither for your body, what ye shall put on; for the soul is more than the meat and the body than raiment. . . . But we speak of the world which is above, of God and angels, of watchers and holy ones, of the ambrosial food and the drink of the true vine, of raiment that endureth and groweth not old, of things which eye hath not seen nor ear heard, neither have they entered into the heart of sinful man, the things which God hath prepared for them that love him." Ch. 36. The saying on " soft garments " was evidently used, in such circles as were responsible for Logion 78 and the *Acts of Thomas*, with a meaning quite different from that of the New Testament; the question is whether or not the logion has been taken out of some homiletical context, or doctrinal exposition, and made into an independent saying.

The exposition given in the *Acts of Thomas* also contains a combination of the saying on " soft garments " and a number of expressions drawn from Jesus' saying on anxiety for food, drink and clothes. Matt. 6.25ff. and Lk. 12.22ff., with the addition of the words quoted by Paul in I Cor. 2.9; those things which " no eye has seen."[1] Both these sayings occur in the *Gospel of Thomas* as independent logia: the latter as Logion 17 and the former as Logion 36. Both appear, however, with tendencies in their details which may very well be taken to mean that they have become more " Gnostic " than they were in the *Acts of Thomas*.

The negative attitude to this earthly life, which we have in the *Gospel of Thomas*, may also lie behind one of the shortest logia.

> Jesus said:
> Become, by passing away, *παράγειν*.
>
> Logion 42

Irrespective of whether this saying be interpreted in such a way that earthly life is described as a pilgrimage (it can also be translated as " Become passers-by ")[2] and that the Gnostic is not to find peace here on earth, or whether it purely and simply refers to the extinction of everything belonging to the material world, it clearly expresses scorn for the world. Any attempt to describe in more detail what lies in this logion must first get to grips with the translation of the verb *παράγειν*. If we interpret this as " pass by," the emphasis of the logion is then laid on this verb, and " become " is not stressed. It is not easy to find other texts to serve as illustration of the meaning of this expression.[3] But if the emphasis is laid on the first verb, " become," the following verb is best translated as " pass away," and thus becomes an explanation of the expression to " become."[4] In the New Testament the verb *παράγειν* has two main meanings: one

[1] Lk. 21. 34 and Matt. 19. 33 are also included here.
[2] So the English edition.
[3] Cf. Jeremias, Unbekannte Jesusworte, p. 92f.
[4] Giversen, Thomasevangeliet, p. 84.

concrete, that Jesus " passed by," and the other, in the transferred meaning, " to pass away," as in I Cor. 7.31, ". . . and those who deal with the world as though they had no dealings with it. For the form of this world is passing away."[1] The first meaning does not fit at all well into the context; the second makes good sense. It seems to me most reasonable to settle for this meaning —" to pass away "—in Logion 42; this is supported by the fact that the same verb in Logion 11 (the only other occurrence in the *Gospel of Thomas*) also has this meaning.

Behind this expression " pass away " there may lie a concept related to the Johannine idea that death leads to life, as expressed in the saying of the grain of wheat which falls to the earth and dies. We may also call to mind a similar expression in the *Pseudo-Clementines*, where the Apostle Peter refutes Simon Magus's contention that the world is evil, and created by an inferior God. Peter claims that the world was not created as an end in itself, but only to provide the basis of a new world. " So also, therefore, it is necessary that the condition of this world pass away, that the sublimer condition of the heavenly kingdom may shine forth." Rec. III, 28. But although both these texts speak about a " passing away " which has to do with physical death, there is another concept which makes " passing away " a part of what happens during the course of earthly life. This may be illustrated from the *Acts of John*, and the story of Drusiana. As Callimachus was on the point of committing an atrocious crime against the dead body of Drusiana, he was met in a vision by an angel of God, who said, " Callimachus, die that thou mayest live, ἀπόθανε ἵνα ζήσῃς." Through this vision, Callimachus was hindered from fulfilling his terrible intentions, and was instead brought to his senses, and to faith. He recognised the fatally evil influence which dwelt in his body, and said, " I would become one of them that

[1] Cf. John 2. 8 ". . . because the darkness is passing away and the true light is already shining " and 2. 17, " And the world passes away, and the lust of it; but he who does God's will abides for ever."

hope in Christ, that the voice may prove true which said to me, 'Die that thou mayest live': and that voice hath also fulfilled its effect, for he is dead, that faithless, disorderly, godless one, and I have been raised by thee. I who will be faithful, God-fearing, knowing the truth, which I entreat thee may be shown me by thee." Ch. 76. When the lusts of the flesh and seductive forces are killed, and ignorance concerning the truth is conquered, the soul is brought to life, that soul which possesses eternal life. As this word to Callimachus stands, it is expressive of the same concept as in Logion 42, except that the elements are reversed, so that instead of an exhortation to die and thereby to win life, we have the call to become, and die in the process.

The concept which we encountered in Logion 42 and the *Acts of John* is further supported in the writings of Valentinus. In a fragment of one of his sermons we read, "You are immortal from the beginning, and you are children of an eternal life, and you wish to distribute death among you in order to annihilate and devour it, so that death may die in you and through you. For when you break down the world, but are yourselves not broken down, then you are lords over all creation and mortality." Fragment 4 (Clement of Alexandria, *Strom.* IV, 89, 1ff.). Those men who possess eternal life, through their particles of light, are the ones who fight death and the world, and become lords over mortality. In other words: "Become, by passing away."

There are other logia which express a generally negative attitude to this world. Logion 81 reads:

> Jesus said:
> He who became rich may become king
> And he who has power may deny it.

The saying may be understood as an exhortation to those who are great and rich in the things of this world to resign all power and possessions—all that has to do with the world—if they would be saved. Or the terms " become rich," " become king," " have power " may refer to the " elect " who, because of their share in the heavenly world, are and possess the highest. The exhortation to " deny " would then imply the consequence of the Gnostic life: to withdraw from this world.

We meet with a variation on the same theme in Logion 110, where the term " rich " may refer either to a share in the heavenly world or to the kingdom of this world.

> Jesus said:
> He who found the world and became rich,
> May he reject the world.

A less transparent expression of this scorn for the world or mastery of the world on the part of the enlightened man is found in Logion 106.

> Jesus said:
> When you make the two into one,
> You shall be the children of man.
> And when you say, " Mountain, be moved,"
> It shall be moved.

We have already observed the important role played by the concept of " unity " in the theological thought-world of the *Gospel of Thomas*, as expressive of the state of salvation. Thus to " make the two into one " implies to bring division to an end and to unite the individual soul-spark with the heavenly world, by means of saving knowledge. According to the logion, this salvation also means to become " children of man," an expression in which " man " most probably refers to " the first immortal man," the Saviour.[1] When this " state of salvation " comes to pass, man will be able to say, " Mountain, be moved," and it will happen. This image, of moving a mountain, is found several

[1] Cf. Schmidt-Till, Koptisch-gnostische Schriften, p. 364; *Pistis Sophia* 96.

times in the New Testament, and always as a strong expression for the victorious power of the Christian faith. " For truly, I say to you, if you have faith as a grain of mustard seed, you will say to this mountain, ' Move hence to yonder place,' and it will move; and nothing will be impossible to you." Matt. 17.20; "... and if I have all faith, so as to remove mountains, but have not love, I am nothing." I Cor. 13.2. Cf. Matt. 21.21, Mk. 11.23, Lk. 17.6. But there is no word about faith in Logion 106; instead it is the Gnostic's state of salvation which is discussed, and that does not come about by faith, but by knowledge, gnosis.

Since the pre-suppositions for the saying about the mountain in Logion 106 are different from those of the New Testament, it is not surprising that the meaning of the saying has also changed. I consider that it would be most reasonable, and would accord with what is said elsewhere in the *Gospel of Thomas*, if these words were to be interpreted as they are e.g. in the *Pseudo-Clementines*. There we in fact twice encounter traditions of interpretation in which the saying on the " mountain " has been given a special meaning. In one text it is said that the man who is enlightened by knowledge is able to break free from the sufferings forced upon man by the evil spirits and his own flesh. " He is the true worshipper of God, who not only is himself free from sufferings (*liber a passionibus*), but also sets others free from them; though they be so heavy that they are like mountains, he removes them by means of the faith with which he believes in God." *Rec.* V, 34. He who is pure in his faith and knowledge overcomes the suffering which the demons and the evil impulses impose upon man. The " mountain " which man is capable of moving is the power of these evil influences.[1] Furthermore, this suffering is given an important place among the Gnostics;[2] this

[1] Cf. *Rec.* V,2 and *Hom.* XI, 16.

[2] A comparison might possibly be made here with Logion 58, "Jesus said : Blessed is that man who has suffered. He has found lfe." Cf. Quispel, the Gospel of Thomas and the New Testament, Vig. Christ 11 (1957), p. 204

can be supported by reference to Valentinus's own words. "And through him (the Father) alone can the heart be pure, in that every evil spirit is driven out of the heart. For many spirits who dwell in it do not allow it to be pure, but every one of them fulfils its deeds, by making it impure in many ways by unseemly desires."[1] It seems to me that the sayings concerning the "mountain" in Logia 106 and 48—the latter a variant of the former—should be understood on the basis of some such expository tradition. It is also said here that unity in man, "in the body," is the pre-supposition for overcoming the suffering with which the powers of this world seek to corrupt man.

> Jesus said:
> If two make peace with each other in this single house,
> They shall say to the mountain:
> "Be moved," and it shall be moved.
>
> Logion 48

The question is whether we ought not to take into consideration at this point two logia which contain the term διώκειν, "persecute," "attack," which in Gnostic scriptures refers to the attempt made by the material powers to attack "men of light" and thereby prevent their salvation.

> Jesus said:
> Blessed are they who were persecuted διώκειν, in their hearts,
> These who truly knew the Father.
>
> Logion 69a

The alteration which has been made in the New Testament text is—from a Gnostic point of view—typical. "Blessed are those who are persecuted for righteousness' sake, for theirs is the kingdom of heaven." Matt. 5.10. There is no longer any

[1] Clement Alex., *Strom.* II, 11,43f.

question of persecution having to do with participation in the kingdom of heaven; it is now something which follows upon knowledge. Further, it has nothing to do with an outer suffering, but instead the persecution is of the " heart," exactly the place which Valentinus quoted as the centre of the struggle. The situation in Logion 68 seems to me to be similar.

> Jesus said:
> Blessed are you when they hate you and persecute you,
> And find no place, τόπος, there where you have been persecuted.

The measure of disagreement with the New Testament texts which appear to lie behind this logion, Lk. 5.22 and Matt. 5.11, is not negligible. What is meant by these words is that hate and persecution belong to the conditions of the enlightened man. What is, however, essential is that the material powers are to find no " place," no control point, where persecution has taken place; this would appear to refer to man's innermost heart, where there is suffering and where the Father is in control.

Against Marriage and the Sexual Life

The negative attitude to the world often focuses in Gnostic circles—as well as in many others—on marriage and the sexual life. For instance, Marcion considered them to be degrading and undesirable, and forbade the faithful to enter the state of matrimony. He considered it essential to use all possible means to limit the Creator-God's sphere of influence, and thus to avoid bringing children into the world. In this way it was possible to demonstrate that one did not owe allegiance to the Demiurge, by protesting against flesh and matter.[1] The same point of view, negative in principle, holds good for the *Gospel of Thomas*, where

[1] Harnack, Marcion, p. 97 and 186f.

we have a number of logia expressing this theme, though none in such uncompromising terms as Marcion used. One of the clearest is:

> His disciples said:
> " When will you reveal yourself to us,
> And when shall we see you?"
> Jesus said:
> " When you take off your clothes without being ashamed
> And take your clothes and lay them under your feet
> Like little children, and tread upon them,
> Then [you shall become] children of the Living One
> And you shall not be afraid."
>
> Logion 37

Here we have a further example of the way in which an eschatological question is pushed into the background. The disciples' question can be interpreted as having to do with Jesus' *parousia*, but the answer, immanent in its emphasis, turns to the victory of the " inner " man over physical impulses. When enlightened man can neutralise the sex-life to such an extent that he is as innocent as a little child, and not ashamed of his nakedness —then salvation has become a reality. Expressions similar to the one we have here in Logion 37 recur in other texts, witnessing to the diligence with which the theme was utilised. The *Gospel of the Egyptians* in particular seems to have contained more than one saying connecting up with this logion. " When you have trampled on the garment of shame, and when the two become one and the male with the female (is) neither male nor female.' And again, " The Saviour himself said: 'I came to destroy the works of the female.' "[1] In addition, we may refer to a couple of phrases from the *Manichæan Psalm-book* as evidence that

[1] Clement Alex., *Strom.* III, 13, 92 and 9, 63. Cf. Schneemelcher in Neutest Apokryphen, p. 109ff.

apocryphal sayings of Jesus about taking off and trampling upon clothes were used to support a basically ascetic view. " The word of Jesus the Saviour came to . . . fitting: the vain garment of this flesh I put off, safe and pure; I caused the clean feet of my soul to trample confidently upon it . . ." 99.26f.[1]

The way in which these concepts can also be reflected in narrative passages of the apocryphal acts may be exemplified through a passage of the *Acts of Thomas.* There Jesus appears in the bridal chamber and tells the king's only daughter, who has just been married, to avoid sexual intercourse, which will only bind them both to what is mortal. If they would preserve the purity of their souls before God they must live in a " white " marriage, and thus " receive that incorruptible and true marriage, and ye shall be therein groomsmen entering into that bride-chamber which is full of immortality and light." Ch. 12. On the following morning the young couple prove to have followed his advice, and have attained insight into the saving mysteries; the daughter says, " I will no more veil myself, because the mirror of shame is removed from me; and (therefore) am I no more ashamed or abashed, because the deed of shame and confusion is departed far from me." Ch. 14. We encounter the same basic point of view in the *Acts of John*, where the Apostle John stands by his own grave, which he has had dug, takes off his clothes and, in a long hymn of praise, thanks God that he has been kept from marriage. God, " who when I saw clearly didst ordain that it should be grievous to me to look upon a woman: who didst save me from the temporal fantasy and lead me unto that which endureth always: who didst rid me of the foul madness that is in the flesh . . ." Ch. 113.[2] Here it is purity which stands at the centre, that purity which is considered necessary in order to be

[1] Cf. The *Dialogue of the Saviour* (Puech in Neutest. Apokryphen, p. 174), and the *Book of Thomas the Athlete* (Puech, op. cit., p. 223).

[2] Cf. the *Acts of Peter* (The *Vercelli Acts*) XXXIII; the *Acts of Andrew* 4 (James, p. 351); the *Acts of John* 107.

able to see God or, as we read in Logion 37, " Then [you shall become] children of the Living One."

This negativism against marriage and the procreation of children appears once more in a logion which is made up of two Lukan texts.

> A woman in the crowd said to him:
> " Blessed be the womb which bore you
> And the breast which nourished you."
> He said to [her]:
> " Blessed are they who have heard the word of the Father
> (And) kept it in truth.
> For days will come when you shall say:
> Blessed is that womb which has not conceived
> And the breast which has not given suck."
>
> Logion 79

The first text which has been used here is Lk. 11.27f., the words spoken by the woman in the crowd, which are reproduced correctly, with the exception of two important divergences: " the word of God " has given place to " the word of the Father," and the words " in truth " have been added—" And kept it in truth." The alterations are in line with an overall gnosticising, since both " the Father " and " truth " are vital for Gnostic terminology. The other text is Lk. 23, 29, which corresponds closely to the logion. The combination here has brought together two sayings which in Luke have nothing whatever to do with each other. Jesus' answer to the woman's blessing of his mother has been given an exposition taken from his apocalyptic teaching on the agony of the last days. This combination, as we now have it, with the conjunction " for," makes sense only if we remove the apocalyptic aspect and make the latter half of the logion into a blessing on the " non-sexual " life. It is the ascetic element on which the logion focuses. The combination is thus not merely determined by the key-word principle, but is the result of conscious theological reflection. It is not only an ethical principle of purity which lies behind these statements of an Encratite attitude; in the Gnostic systems the man-woman relationship is motivated basically by the structure of the heavenly world, the male and female powers which are striving after unity. It is probably such an aspect which appears in the final logion in the *Gospel of Thomas*.

> Simon Peter said to them:
> " Let Mary depart from us,
> For women are not worthy of life."
> Jesus said:
> " See, I shall lead her,
> So that I make her a man,
> That she too may become a living spirit,
> Who is like you men.
> For every woman who makes herself a man
> Shall enter the kingdom of heaven."
>
> Logion 114

The conflict here reflected between Peter and Mary occurs in several other passages in Gnostic literature. Thus in the *Gospel of Mary*, Peter bursts out, after Mary had mentioned that the Saviour had revealed high mysteries to her, " Does he then speak with a woman, hidden from us and not openly? Shall we be converted and all listen to her? Has he preferred her to us?" 17.18ff. The tension between the two is also noticeable in *Pistis Sophia*, where Peter says, " My Lord, we shall not be able to endure this woman, for she takes our opportunity, and has not let any of us speak, but talks all the time herself." Ch. 36.[1] This conflict is, however, not the main theme of the logion, but only a compositional device in order to allow Jesus to say what are

[1] Cf. *Pistis Sophia* 146.

the principal and essential factors determining the man-woman relationship. Jesus states that a woman cannot enter the kingdom of heaven unless she is first " made a man." Nothing is said about how this is to come about, and no explanatory text is given, but some illuminating material is forthcoming from other Gnostic texts. There exists, however, such a mass of textual material illustrative of the man-woman relationship that it is only possible to quote a few which deal directly with these remarkable words about woman becoming man.[1]

In the *Pseudo-Clementines* we see how the basic Gnostic view of the construction of the world makes its presence felt when we read that " the female " is identical with the cosmos, the created world. " For, since the present world is female, as a mother bringing forth the souls of her children, but the world to come is male, as a father receiving his children." *Hom.* II, 15,3. There is also talk of two kinds of prophet, of which one is the female, whose word accords entirely with the created world, and which has proceeded from the female superintendent of this present world, III, 23,2. The male is the one who speaks from the coming, higher world. This orientation with reference to the two ages—the present as female, the future as male—gives *one* explanation of the words of Logion 114, that a woman must become a man in order to enter the kingdom of heaven.

The Valentinian gnosis reflected in *Excerpta ex Theodoto* offers us further possibilities for the explanation of this logion. There is taught about two elements, of which the first proceeds from the Saviour, ὁ Ἄρρην, " the male seed," and is carried on by the angels, as " male "; the " male element " is mediated by them to Adam. The second proceeds from " the woman on high," Sophia, whose unfortunate giving of birth was the cause of the useless created world, and is carried through Eve to man as " the

[1] See the references in Strecker, Das Judenchristentum in den Pseudoklementinen, p. 155ff.; Puech in Neutest. Apokryphen, p. 219; Doresse, L'Evangile selon Thomas, p. 160f.

female seed." "So also in the case of Adam, the male remained in him but all the female seed was taken from him and became Eve, from whom the females are derived, as the males are from him." 21.2.[1] Thus the male element belongs to the Saviour, the angels and the higher world. The female element is that in man which can be saved, and those who are of the enlightenment—who are "pneumatics"[2]—are called "women," "female." Only if the female is "led" to union with the male (with the angels) in the higher world, so that they become "one," can salvation be brought about. "Therefore the males are drawn together with the Logos, but the females, becoming men, are united to the angels and pass into the Pleroma. Therefore the woman is said to be changed into a man, and the church here on earth into angels." 21.3.[3] If we follow these Valentinian trains of thought the words about man and woman in Logion 114 should apply not so much to the distinction between the two sexes as metaphorically to the cosmological aspect. Be that as it may, it is evident that it is on the basis of such a world of ideas that we have to judge the logion. We may also add that this attitude to man and woman implies a negative view of this world and marriage.

In Logion 22, which we expounded above on the basis of the Gnostic expression "unity," standing for salvation, there was a passage which also dealt with "unity" in connection with male and female.

> ... And when you make male and female into a single one,
> So that the male shall not be male
> And the female (shall not) be female,
> When you make eyes instead of an eye,
> And a hand instead of a hand

[1] Cf. the *Gospel of Philip* 116.22ff. "When Eve was [in] Adam, death did not exist When she became separate from him, death came into being. When <she> en[ters] again and he receives <her>, death shall exist no more." Cf. Schenke, col. 15.

[2] Cf. Sagnard, Extraits de Théodote, p. 98ff.

[3] Cf. 67.2-4 and 68.

And a foot instead of a foot
An image instead of an image,
Then shall you enter [the kingdom].

The fact that " unity" can be brought about means that man belongs to the circle of the " elect " who are to be saved. However, the final unity does not come about until man's heavenly soul is united with his " angel " in heaven, when it can enter the Pleroma. But when man has become enlightened on earth, through gnosis, and thus already belongs to the company of the saved, the resulting state of unity is manifested, *inter alia*, in the " neutralisation " of the sexual life, so that the person in question becomes practically sexless, and pure—a sign that " male and female have been made into a single one."[1] The peculiar words which follow, on the eye, the hand, the foot and the image, show that we are within our rights in treating these statements in this aspect. The first three of these subsequent clauses are easily associated with Mk. 9.43-47, where it is said that if a hand, a foot or an eye are the cause of sin, then it shall be " cut off" or " plucked out." This text links these words with the leading astray of "one of these little ones who believe" in Jesus, precisely as in Logion 22. Furthermore, the words are linked in Matt. 5.27-30 with Jesus' teaching on adultery: a further indication of the way in which " leading astray " may be interpreted. In the logion, though, these words have been brought together with the saying on the man and the woman who are to cease being man and woman, showing that it is to be interpreted with reference to marriage and the sexual life. It does not say that drastic methods are to be used to prevent the limbs from leading the way to sin, as does the New Testament; what is said is that there must be a " substitution," so that the parts of the human body are not dominated by physical desire but by the man of light. In the

[1] Cf. *Pistis Sophia* 143; the *Acts of Thomas* 129.

Manichæan Psalm-book, as well as in Mandæan texts we find a similar idea of substitution, so that the human senses and parts of the body are exchanged for such as are pure, detached from earthly things.[1] Then as far as the strange phraseology—" eyes instead of an eye, and a hand instead of a hand "—is concerned: this most probably stems from the doctrinal of retribution in Deut. 19.21, " a life for a life, an eye for an eye, a tooth for a tooth, a hand for a hand, a foot for a foot."

[1] T. Säve-Söderbergh, Studies in the Coptic *Manichæan Psalm-book* (1949), p. 98ff.

VIII

SEEKING AND REST

He who Seeks, Finds

When Origen wrote his commentary on St. John's Gospel he quoted here and there passages from a commentary on the same Gospel by the Valentinian Heracleon. In one of these fragments the exposition has to do with the woman of Samaria in John 4, and particularly Jesus' words, ". . . for such the Father seeks to worship him," (in spirit and in truth) v. 23. According to Heracleon, this refers to "pneumatic" men, who are "predestined" for salvation. The Saviour has come to seek them, for even these have gone astray in "the deep *hylē* of error," in spite of having belonged to the Father. Ignorance is named as the cause of this, Fragment 19. This seeking on the part of the Saviour is also a central theme in other Gnostic theology, and we have already come across it in the *Gospel of Thomas*, in Logion 107, the parable of the lost sheep, a text especially esteemed by the Gnostics. It is, however, not the Saviour's search which stands at the focus of special interest in the *Gospel of Thomas*, but man's answer to the Saviour's call and search, man's own search for knowledge of the heavenly element imprisoned in him. This seeking recurs several times in the logia, and comprises one of the many important terms in this gospel's doctrinal system.

Logion 24 accords very well with the passage we have quoted from Heracleon, which said that it is those who have a particle of light who are to be saved. The logion begins with these words:

His disciples said to him:
" Teach us about the place where you are,
For it is necessary that we seek it . . ."

Here the disciples are represented as ignorant, but sufficiently aroused to seek. The " place " where Jesus is, is the heavenly world and it is this world from which the disciples once came, and to which they must find their way back in order to be reunited with the Father. The continuation of the logion also makes it clear that it is precisely this relationship between " men of light " and the Father which conditions the search. Substantially the same thought is expressed in another logion.

The disciples said to Jesus:
" Tell us how our end will be."
Jesus said:
" You have indeed discovered the beginning.
In order to seek for the end,
For where the beginning is, there shall the end be.
Blessed is he who shall stand (upright) in the beginning,
And he shall know the end
And he shall not taste death.

Logion 18

The disciples inquire after "the end," by which they principally mean the final salvation, the consummation. It is clear from Jesus' answer that behind the question there lies a mistaken conception of what " the end " is: something altogether new, remote from present experience, belonging only to the future. Instead, what is most important is " the beginning," that which is now to be won, for in this way the end will be good. His answer aims at showing that the beginning and the end belong together, and that they express the same divine reality. The disciples have discovered the beginning, i.e. they have won the first part of gnosis; this implies that they have been brought into a new reality which embraces all things between the beginning and the end, " for where the beginning is, there shall the end be." A continuation of the search will fortify them. We may here make a comparison with what is said about God in the *Pseudo-Clementines*, " Himself being the rest, and having the infinite age to come as his image, being the beginning and the end." *Hom.* XVII, 9,3. Since the coming æon is the image of God, it also is described as the beginning and the end. A similar concept is expressed by Jesus' first words in *Pistis Sophia*, " I have proceeded from the first mystery, which is the last mystery, the twenty-fourth." Ch. 1. Once more the entire light-world is described by reference to the beginning and the end; farther on in the same document, Jesus promises his faithful that he will speak with them " from the beginning to the consummation and from the inner to the outer and from the outer to the inner." Ch. 6.[1]

In the logion's continuation, the same thing is repeated, but this time in the form of a " beatitude ": " Blessed is he who shall stand in the beginning, and he shall know the end." We must pay special attention here to an important term, to " stand," which in Gnostic literature is frequently used in connection with the one who has obtained insight, who has been raised up through conversion and baptism.[2] Therefore, that man is happy who " stands " in the beginning, for he is thereby initiated into that perfection which extends over both beginning and end, and shall not die, but shall be set free from matter into the liberty of life with the Father. The search is thus conditioned by the Gnostic concept of the world and of man which we found earlier in the *Gospel of Thomas.*

This seeking process has different stages, which may be characterised by various terms. Thus in Logion 2 we encounter

[1] Cf. *Pistis Sophia* 60; the *Gospel of Truth* 33.6.
[2] E. Segelberg, Masbuta. Studies in the Ritual of the Mandæan Baptism (1958), p. 171.

a series of five lines, each of which denotes a step on the way to salvation.

> Jesus said:
> He who seeks shall not cease seeking
> Until he finds.
> And when he finds, he is dismayed,
> And when he has been dismayed, he is filled with wonder,
> And he shall become king over the All.

The logion is clearly derived from a saying of Jesus which was greatly valued in Gnostic circles, Matt. 7.7f., Lk. 11.9f., "... seek, and you will find ... and he who seeks finds," but which is here expanded by the addition of several clauses having no New Testament equivalents. Good parallels to Logion 2 are, however, to be found in other texts, e.g. the words from the *Gospel according to the Hebrews* quoted by Clement of Alexandria, *Strom.* V, 14,96, " He shall not cease from seeking until he find, and having found, he will be amazed, and having been amazed will reign, and having reigned will rest." These words are practically identical with *Ox. Pap.* 654, lines 5-9, and thus offer a form somewhat different from that of Logion 2.[1] Since the text forms part of the Oxyrhynchus collection, it has already been discussed; the conclusion has been drawn that it seems to belong in a world of Gnostic mysticism.[2] It describes stages on the way to salvation, a description characteristic of Hermetic Gnosticism in particular,[3] which also speaks of " amazement " as one stage on this way, and " rest " as the final salvation. We may also add that " amazement " as one of the first steps toward spiritual perception is found in ancient philosophy, as well as in other texts of religious character.[4]

[1] Cf. Puech in Neutest. Apokryphen, p. 216.
[2] Vielhauer in Neutest. Apokryphen, p. 106.
[3] M. Dibelius, Die Formgeschichte des Evangeliums (1933), p. 285.
[4] Puech in Neutest. Apokryphen, p. 225.

Logion 2 might thus be interpreted in this way: that man's task is to seek knowledge, gnosis, and when he has found it he becomes dismayed, for the insight into the light-world frightens him—a reaction which in Gnostic texts almost always accompanies man's first contact with heavenly power and light. But fear gives way to amazement at the riches within man. If he has discovered the right relationship between matter and the light-world, he has also attained salvation—expressed in the words, " become king over the All " (or in the Greek tradition, " rest "). This latter expression occurs on a number of occasions in *Pistis Sophia* to indicate the condition of the Gnostic who has received " the mystery of the unutterable." Ch. 99.

The first sentence of Logion 2 gives an expanded version of the New Testament saying of Jesus, " He who seeks *shall not cease seeking until he* finds." (The Greek version puts the sentence into a form with the imperative meaning, " Let him who seeks not cease until he has found.") The same development has also taken place in the other textual traditions, in Clement of Alexandria and Ox. Pap. From the point of view of content, this longer version expresses an increased intensity compared to the New Testament, which may be explained on the basis of the demand for work, striving and intensity on the part of the one who would find gnosis. The exhortation not to give up the search recurs in *Pistis Sophia* in an exposition of the New Testament saying on seeking and finding, Matt. 7.7. " Therefore proclaim to all mankind: Cease not to seek by day or by night until you find the purifying mysteries; and say to mankind: Deny the whole world and all the matter which is found in it." Ch. 100.[1] This development of the saying occurs only in a Gnostic context, from which we may draw the conclusion that the addition has been made purely in order to interpret the saying in a Gnostic way. It throws into relief the necessity for not giving

[1] Cf. *Pistis Sophia* 102 and 111.

up the search, which *may* be based on the idea that the "elect" are predestined to find, and should therefore not stop seeking. In *Pistis Sophia* the longer version was an exposition of the New Testament saying of Jesus, which is reproduced correctly, with the introduction, "I once said to you." The expansion is characteristic of the "pneumatic" exposition of the saying, and for this reason Logion 2 should be understood as being an indication of the way in which the existence of alterations and developments is due to the needs of interpretation, and does not imply the existence of independent traditions.

According to the *Acts of Andrew*, 10f., the Apostle once preached for a man called Stratocles, who was inspired by his words. The Apostle joyfully sees this as a sign that his soul has been touched, and that the same God who dwells within him, Andrew, has a counterpart within Stratocles. "Do I find myself in thee? Is there in thee one that speaketh whom I see to be mine own? . . . Doth he wish to be made one with him? . . . Doth he find in him any rest? Hath he where to lay his head?" In this way the heavenly nature is awakened from its slumbers in man, and he receives salvation through the discovery of self-knowledge. We have earlier in the *Gospel of Thomas* encountered this connection between introspection and seeking, e.g. in Logion 3, "When you know yourselves, then shall you be known, and you shall know that you are children of the living Father . . ." We may at this point mention another logion which has the same basic view.

> Jesus said:
> To him who holds in his hand shall be given,
> And from him who has nothing
> Shall be taken even the little he has.
>
> Logion 41

This saying is found in various contexts in the New Testament.

Logion 41 has, however, small alterations such as " in his hand " and " the little," which have been added. The latter addition probably serves as an attempt to moderate the paradox provided by the saying in the New Testament.[1] Behind the logion in the *Gospel of Thomas* would seem to be the idea that the one who preserves his share in the kingdom of heaven within himself will reach its union with the heavenly world. Or, as the saying is expounded in the *Gospel of Philip*, " It is not fitting that all should learn to know themselves. Some, if they do not learn to know themselves, will not put what they have to good use; others, however, who have learned to know themselves, will make use of that (which they have)." 124.18ff. To seek within and find what is there, is the way of salvation. The same idea lies behind a further logion.

> Jesus said:
> When you bring forth that within you,
> That which you have shall save you.
> If you have not that within you,
> That which you do not have shall kill you.
>
> Logion 70

It is difficult to decide what is meant by " that "—the heavenly particle of light or the Saviour. Whichever interpretation we choose, it is nevertheless clear that it is normal Gnostic doctrine which is being presented: salvation cannot take place without the divine in man, for the divine is the saving quality. But some day the material will be annihilated by the divine light; therefore if man has no part in that light it will kill him. The only way is to discover oneself and bid farewell to the world, as in Logion 111b:

[1] We notice also in Lk. 8. 18 how the paradox is moderated through the addition of " what he thinks that he has."

Jesus says:
He who finds himself,
Of him is the world not worthy.

He who Finds, obtains Rest

There are many expressions in the *Gospel of Thomas* for the state of salvation, and we have already come across several of them. Thus he who has won true knowledge " shall not taste death " (18), " shall be filled with light " (61b), " shall enter the kingdom " (22), and " shall see the Father " (27). Nevertheless, the most important term is " rest," *ἀνάπαυσις*, for this is a special term in Gnostic literature, denoting salvation. It occurs in the New Testament, with the meaning of refreshment for the spirit, Matt. 11.28f., I Cor. 16.18, Philemon 7 and 20, or of rest in the world to come, Rev. 14.13.[1] The point of departure for the use of this word, " rest,"[2] has to some extent been the Lord's rest from the work of creation on the seventh day. But in the New Testament the word is not a technical term directly connected with the state of salvation, as it is in Scriptures Gnostic in origin or influenced by Gnosticism. A typical illustration of this latter category is provided by the use of the term in the *Gospel of Thomas*. At the close of the above-quoted logion of the Samaritan who carried a lamb into Judæa we read,

He said to them:
You yourselves seek a place of rest
Lest you become a corpse
And be eaten.

Logion 60

" Rest " here serves to describe that condition in which man,

[1] O. Bauernfeind, art. ἀνάπαυσις Theol. Wörterb. I, p. 352f.
[2] O. Michel, Der Brief an die Hebräer (1949), p. 102ff.

having allowed himself to be illuminated by gnosis, is no longer in the power of, and can no longer be corrupted by, the material world. " Rest " is, however, not connected merely with the condition of enlightenment here upon earth, but belongs most of all to descriptions of perfect rest with the Father. Occasionally one may detect a duality in expression, when the term may refer to both these aspects, since salvation here and now is a condition which " continues " beyond death. Indeed, the Gnostic is said not to " see death," which means that he has already reached the " quality " which governs the heavenly world. It is just this aspect of " rest " which we encountered in Logion 51, where the disciples asked the Saviour, " On which day shall the rest of the dead come and on which day shall the new world come ? " This question was in fact directed towards a future day of the Lord, an orientation which the Gnostic could not accept. Therefore, Jesus is made to answer.

> He said to them:
> That which you expect has come,
> But you do not recognise it.

A similar shift in thought, from the heavenly rest to the earthly, can also be seen in the *Gospel of Truth*, which sometimes speaks of paradise as the place of rest, 36.38, sometimes of the rest of the æons in the Father, 24.20, and sometimes of rest as the state of the saved here. " Then he has gnosis, he does the will of him who called upon him, and he wishes to please him; and he obtains rest." 22.9f. But in general the term " rest " seems to stand with a view to the final reunion of the man of light with the Father. This heavenly reunion between the scattered light-elements from the material world and the permanent inhabitants of the light-world is often described metaphorically in Gnostic literature as a wedding. " Then comes the marriage feast, common to all who are saved, until all are equal and know each other." *Excerpta ex Theodoto* 63.2. This wedding can also be described as "the intellectual and eternal marriage of the Syzygy," characterised by "joy and repose," 65.2. The meaning of Jesus' self-revelation to man was that all who were predestined to be saved—because of their inner quality of light—should attain to the sphere from which they were once removed, and to which they still belong, thanks to their nature. When the goal of salvation is eventually reached, the wedding takes place in heaven, and joy and rest prevail. The true Gnostic can then unite his voice with that of the prince in the *Acts of Thomas* 5, in thanking the Saviour "who hast shown me how to seek myself and know who I was and who and in what manner I now am, that I may again become that which I was: whom I knew not, but thyself didst seek me out: of whom I was not aware, but thyself hast taken me to thee . . ."

Date and Place of Origin

DATE AND PLACE OF ORIGIN

THE DIFFICULTIES which we encounter when trying to determine the date at which the *Gospel of Thomas* came into being, and the place where this happened, are at present insurmountable. We can make observations of important principles determining the gospel's construction, and we can recognise them as recurring in other Christian and Gnostic literature, but the source material at our disposal does not permit of greater precision as regards time and place. The same applies when we look at the meaning of the logia, and the alterations, evidence of the "Compiler's" theological pre-suppositions, which have been made to the texts of New Testament sayings of Jesus. The result of our investigations may tell us to which currents of thought the *Gospel of Thomas* can be referred, but there exist no absolute criteria for determining the definite milieu which produced the gospel.

Earlier published works on the *Gospel of Thomas* have aired the following theses. The manuscript, Codex III, containing the Coptic text, has been given various dates.[1] There has been talk of the Gnostic congregation or group which used this codex having been active during the 3rd, 4th or 5th centuries A.D. W. Till considers that the text dates from about A.D. 400; Puech mentions the 4th-5th centuries.[2] But if the manuscript is thus to be dated relatively late, this tells us nothing about the date when the gospel originated. Hitherto there has been a fair measure of agreement over the date A.D. 140-150, and no one has shown any desire to refer it to any earlier period. As an answer to the

[1] Puech's division. Cf. Doresse, L'Evangile selon Thomas, p. 23, who calls it number X.

[2] W. Till, New Sayings of Jesus in the Recently Discovered Coptic "Gospel of Thomas," Bull. of J. Rylands Libr. 41 (1959), p. 451; Puech in Neutest. Apokryphen, p. 202.

question of where the group was active have been advanced two alternatives: Egypt or Syria.[1]

I have no objections to raise against such theses, the very vagueness of which is eloquent testimony to the difficulty one has in being precise about the date and place of this gospel. As we have already pointed out in the introductory sections, it is possible to locate the *Gospel of Thomas* in the Gnostic currents flowing from such men as Valentinus and Marcion. Valentinus, who was educated in Alexandria, was active in Rome *circa* A.D. 150, as was Marcion and the Syrian Gnostic Cerdo. Thus, at that time when the *Gospel of Thomas* is supposed to have originated, there existed connections between Alexandria, Rome and Syria, all influenced by Gnostic ideas; it is in these currents that I consider that the *Gospel of Thomas* should be placed. The link between Rome and Syria can also be supported by textual traditions which may occasionally be traced in the gospel, and this is a further indication of the direction in which we must look for its place of origin. The theological content of the gospel also seems to indicate that its concepts belong in the same context as those of Marcion, Valentinus and Cerdo. If the *Gospel of Truth* is reckoned as coming from Valentinian circles, the same ought to apply to the *Gospel of Thomas* since the resemblance between the two is so great. Many of the individual logia naturally have their own history in tradition, since they are taken from different scriptures and traditions; but the overall theological picture of the *Gospel of Thomas*, as we now have it, speaks of a Gnostic world of ideas and connects it with the theological currents which we have described.

[1] E.g. Cerfaux, Les Paraboles, Le Muséon 70 (1957), p. 319; Guillaumont, Sémitismes dans les logia de Jésus, Journal Asiatique 246 (1958), p. 117. Puech in Neutest. Apokryphen p. 207, considers that the *Acts of Thomas* is dependent upon the *Gospel of Thomas*, and that both can be traced to a common place of origin in Syria. Doresse, L'Evangile selon Thomas, p. 73f. is of a similar opinion.

Index of Logia and General Index

INDEX OF LOGIA

GENERAL INDEX